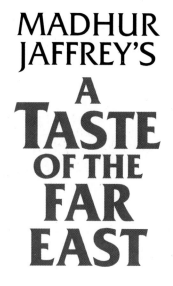

MADHUR
JAFFREY'S
A
TASTE
OF THE
FAR
EAST

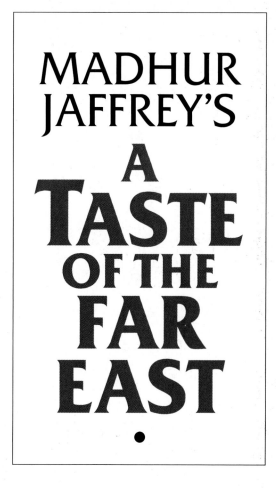

MADHUR JAFFREY'S

A TASTE OF THE FAR EAST

Deirdre [?]
w/love of
cooking

CAROL SOUTHERN BOOKS

NEW YORK

To my husband, Sanford Allen

Published by Carol Southern Books, an imprint of Crown Publishers,
Inc. 201 East 50th Street, New York, New York 10022.
Member of the Crown Publishing Group.

Random House, Inc. New York, Toronto,
London, Sydney, Auckland

Carol Southern Books and colophon are trademarks of Crown Publishers, Inc.

Manufactured in Italy
Design by Bernard Higton
Library of Congress Cataloging-in-Publication Data

Jaffrey, Madhur
[Taste of the Far East]
Madhur Jaffrey's A Taste of the Far East.
recipes from Thailand, Malaysia, Hong Kong, Philippines, Japan, Vietnam,
Korea, and Indonesia / by Madhur Jaffrey;
photographs by James Murphy and Michael Freeman.
p. cm.
Includes index.
ISBN 0-517-59548-6: $35.00

1. Cookery, Oriental. 2. East Asia—Social life and customs.
I. Title

TX725.A1J328   1993   93–19283
641.595—dc20   CIP
ISBN 0-517-59548-6
10 9 8 7 6 5 4 3 2 1
First Edition

CONTENTS

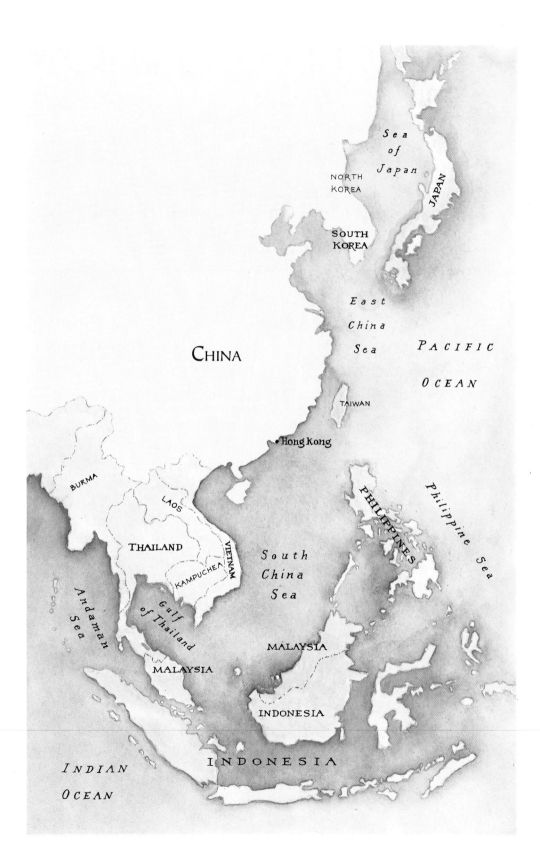

INTRODUCTION

Fish poached with tomatoes, coconut milk and Swiss chard from the Philippines; grilled fish smothered with a dressing of crushed sesame seeds, soy sauce and vinegar from Korea; and raw oysters served with a chilli-radish dip from Japan – these are some of the recipes that await you in the following pages.

Why do people eat what they eat? Why do nations eat what they eat? There must be a hidden logic in there somewhere, some convoluted mathematical formula. Perhaps if one fed into one's computer all the known facts about a country – its history, geography, trade relations, intermarriages, royal divorces, national products, invasions, even the size of its teacups, one might be able to get a print-out of its culinary practices. But there are just so many unknowns. Perhaps a careless – or greedy – customs inspector let in some forbidden fruit, or some forbidden seeds. So far, it still takes a human being to tramp around and get the information.

Foods travel. Sometimes more easily than people. No country's cuisine is writ in stone. As foods move, they are changed, adapted and remodelled in other images. Take *sushi*, the little canapés of raw fish and rice that we think of as quintessentially Japanese. They originated elsewhere, in the little villages tucked inside the much warmer regions of South-East Asia. Cooked rice, when put together with raw fish, preserves it for some magical reason.

The ancient Thais knew this. I found myself, somewhat by chance, in a tiny village in north-eastern Thailand. Here, as they have done for centuries, they were putting fish to 'pickle' in layers of cooked rice. The rice would be thrown away and only the preserved fish eaten. It was this dish that first travelled to Kyoto and was adopted there. Then, it began changing. The first step was to eat both the pickled fish and the preserved rice. They still do that in Kyoto today. In Tokyo, it was discovered that, with refrigeration, fresh fish could be put on top of freshly cooked rice and served immediately. Only, it was decided to add a little vinegar and sugar to the rice to give a faint pickled taste in memory of what it had once been. Hence was born the *sushi* we all know and love today. So, while foods travel, at some point they get stamped with a national image.

The best part of food is, without doubt, the eating of it. In that sense, the best part of poetry is the reading of it. But surely, as one reads a poem, it conjures up earlier references and other images. Those references and images make the experience richer. When a food is on my tongue, the taste is of course paramount. But while my tongue savours it, my mind relishes all the little details I know about it, where it originated, when it is eaten, what version of the same dish is eaten in another country and whether it is meant to have any medicinal value.

The purpose of this book, then, is not only to give you some of the best recipes from Thailand, Malaysia, Indonesia, Vietnam, the Philippines, Hong Kong, Korea and Japan – some quite unknown in the West, others somewhat different versions of old classics – but to put the foods in their settings, to take you into the homes and restaurants where I have been and to give you a little bit of the culinary history of all these eight nations as you cook and eat.

I shall say no more. I will let the following eight chapters, on eight Far Eastern countries with rich culinary heritages, speak for themselves.

Note: Because the recipes in this book have been written for readers in America, England and on the Continent, you will find three sets of measurements. My hope is that, as you use the book, your eye will automatically light on your measurements and the others will not distract you. Americans should take care not to use the English pint as it is 20 fluid ounces rather than 16.

As the exact ingredients used in the Far East are not always easily available in the West, I have suggested substitutes, where necessary, in brackets after the ingredient of first choice.

THAILAND

Thai food starts with certain assumptions – not rigid demands for minimalist perfection as in Japan nor ancient rules and recipes geared to keeping the body at a harmonious balance as in China, but simple, gentle and unselfconscious assumptions that foods be seasonal and the seasonings impassioned.

Freshness and seasonality are common to the cuisines of all of East Asia. It is the use of highly aromatic, fresh flavourings – citrus leaves that ooze an intense, sweet, sun-drenched liminess, basils by the bunch, green coriander roots that most people throw away, jasmine flowers that perfume desserts and rice bowls, lemon grass stalks that appear stiff and dry but then, like harmless grenades, release a sublime, lemony attar – combined with the seemingly uninhibited but actually perfectly balanced use of all the tantalising tastes nature has to offer – sweetness, sourness, saltiness, hotness, nuttiness and, at times, even bitterness – that make Thai cuisine like no other in Asia.

Witness the approach of summer. A humble group in the small village of Sawatee in the north-east sit on low, wooden, platforms set under the shade of a leafy mango tree, mending fishing nets. This is the main occupation here – mending the flaws in factory-made fishing nets. The men mark the flaws with bright blue ties, the women mend them. Roosters and hens cluck their way around vats filled with rain-water. A baby in a tiny hammock is given a tiny push when a hand is free. All the time there is a pounding sound – thump, thump, thump.

The snack *tam muang*, perhaps more goody than snack, is being prepared by an elderly lady. It will be popped into

Opposite: Fishermen haul in their catch – the bounty of the Gulf of Thailand.

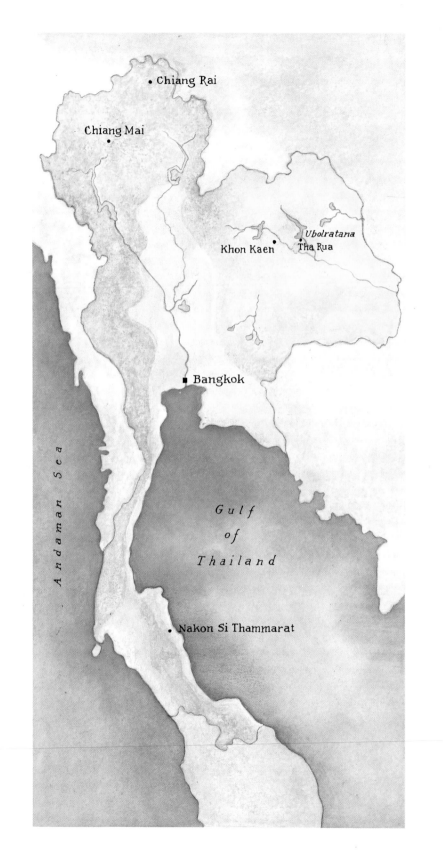

mouths at regular intervals, just as we might eat chocolate or toffee. Green, unripe mangoes, freshly off the tree and still sour, have been peeled and cut into julienne strips. These are put into a clay mortar. A stone mortar would pulverise them while a clay one, used with a wooden pestle, just opens their pores to receive the seasonings. In go sugar, powdered red chillies and a clear, salty fish sauce (*nam pla*) which is used here as soy sauce is in China. Then thump, thump, thump with the pestle . . . All is lightly pounded and mixed and is ready to be devoured – a celebration of contrasting tastes using the cheapest of everyday ingredients.

About 400 kilometres south-west, in the city of Bangkok, a group of prosperous women – bankers, lawyers and publicists – are meeting for a Friday lunch in the home of Mrs Trishnananda. They are all smartly dressed in Western clothes right down to their fashionable pumps. All shoes, even the fashionable pumps, are left at the door as they enter. Propriety and tradition are ingrained. The new house is swathed in the finest, landscaped greenery: exotic apple-mango trees from Hawaii, jackfruit, papaya and bread fruit trees, coconut palms, even a small pond, prettily hedged on one side with bamboo. The endless noise of city traffic is kept firmly at bay.

Inside, in the cool dining-room, the table is laid for rice noodles with a coconutty prawn sauce (*khanom chin nam prik*). It sounds simple, and it can be – but not the way it is done here. Hands have been busy in the kitchen, grating coconut and squeezing out its milk, pounding and frying chilli paste, slicing shallots, peeling galangal (a variety of ginger) and pounding garlic.

The centre-piece at the dining-table, rather like a magnificent epergne, is a two-tiered arrangement of baskets, all cleverly masked with braided, woven and rolled banana leaves. The lower and larger tier holds the vegetables that are eaten with the noodles – some blanched, such as the long beans, carrots, and mange tout (snow peas), others

A Thai fishing boat. Fish is combined with spices and herbs to make aromatic dishes that are among the glories of Thailand's cuisine.

stir-fried, such as the highly nutritious swamp morning glory (*pak bung*). The upper tier holds the raw vegetables, mainly a julienne of crisp, banana flowers. Nearby, in pretty containers, are the prawn sauce and assorted garnishes-cum-flavourings such as crisply fried shallots and chillies and wedges of lime. In yet another basket are the fresh noodles, all folded into demure swirls.

These noodles (*khanom chin*), soft, slithery and utterly delicious, are twice cooked before they reach the market: a ball of rice flour dough is first poached in water and then squeezed through a showerhead with tiny holes. Fine strands fall like rain into boiling water. These are scooped up, bathed in cold water and very deftly folded into small swirls and laid in banana-leaf-lined baskets. They last but a day or so. Our lady guests take two swirls of these noodles each and douse them with the very hot, sweet, sour prawn sauce, all creamy with coconut milk and aromatic with the rind of kaffir lime. Fried red chillies and crisp shallots get sprinkled over the top. The vegetables are nibbled on the side, partly to mellow the heat of the sauce and partly for the crunch they provide.

It is very Thai, this mixture of fiery foods with crisp vegetables. Fiercely hot salads – and they make salads here of everything from squid to rose petals – are served with a forest of raw vegetables. Thais seem to thrive on the big bang of opposing tastes and textures coming at each other like express locomotives from different directions, only to meet headlong in one mighty, glorious explosion.

One of the simplest meals in a village might consist of rice served with a *nam prik*, a sauce or relish that always has some sort of fermented fish paste or fish sauce as well as chillies in it. Raw vegetables or a simple salad of cucumbers or green papaya would be served on the side. This would be eaten with the hands. (The use of fork and spoon, now the current practice among the Westernised, came in with other European customs in the nineteenth century. I once asked Chalie Amatyakul, the great Thai chef at the Oriental Hotel, when exactly this change occurred. He scratched his head for a bit and then answered cheekily, 'Around Yul Brynner's time!'). To this simple meal may be added a piece of fried fish and a soupy stew, rich with local vegetables. All the foods are placed in the centre of the table at the same time. Well-seasoned soups and soup-stews, both called *kaeng*, are eaten with the meal, not before it. A spoon is used for the liquid.

If it is the seasonings that give Thai meals their effervescence, it is rice, the primary starch here, that keeps it grounded. It is generally cooked plain, without salt, and acts as the most perfect foil to the incendiary curries, salads and soups. Rice, anthropologists believe, may well have originated in this region, perhaps in the north where some of the oldest grains have been found. Today, it is the well-watered central plains around Bangkok that have turned into the nation's rice basket.

What kind of rice and what specific meals a Thai family might eat would depend very largely on where it lives, and on the season. Thailand, the country shaped like an elephant's head, is almost the size of France with as much regional variety in its food as its Mediterranean counterpart. The north-west was once influenced, and ruled, by Burma. The population of the north-east is made up of Lao peoples and the south is almost Malay. And everywhere, the Chinese and the Indian influence can be felt.

It is early summer when I visit Chiang Mai, almost 700 kilometres north-west of Bangkok. The brick walls and moat which once enclosed this ancient city have mostly gone but mountains nearby provide psychological protection and cooling breezes. Trees with sprightly orange flowers – peacock's crest, they call them here – and purple jacarandas line the roads. The climate here is so hospitable that garlic, onions, strawberries, cherry tomatoes, melons, cauliflowers, baby corn and luscious, luscious litchis grow with ease. The annual litchi festival is just days away.

In the evening, I sit with a young local friend, 'Ting' Woodtikarn, in the patio of the Aroon (Rai) restaurant. She is an English professor at the university. We drink Thai Singha beer and nibble on northern seasonal delicacies – fried crickets and fried wasps. These are no ordinary wasps. They lay their eggs deep in the earth and rise up from there, buzzing phoenixes headed straight for the wok. There is only one way to eat them: you pick them up by their wings and then bite off their bodies. They are as addictive as peanuts. (No, you do not eat the wings.) The crickets are particularly good, tasting very like fried okra.

While many of us still hunt in the West, the 'gathering' half of our primeval form of subsistence has mostly been forgotten. A few may still seek the truffle and the wild mushroom, even the occasional wild berry or plover's egg, but mostly we rely on farmed produce. Here, in northern Thailand, the link chain with gatherers of yesteryear remains unbroken. Each month brings its pleasures. If it is May, then these include wasps and crickets.

For our main courses that day, Ting orders *naem pad*, a dish of salami-like, preserved, slightly sour pork, sliced and stir-fried with eggs, spring onions (scallions), pickled garlic, cherry tomatoes and red chilli, quite exquisite in its flavour and *kaeng kae*, a curry of chicken (it could be made with pork) using, among other things, Thai aromatics like lemon grass

and a Burmese-style curry powder as well as local vegetables such as heart of palm. With the two dishes come the mainstays of north-eastern food: glutinous rice served from individual, palm leaf baskets and *nam prik num*, a relish.

A word about the last two. Glutinous rice is eaten all over northern Thailand. It is harder and richer in protein than plain long-grain rice and is normally soaked overnight and then steamed. Once cooked, it is packed into baskets which keep it warm. To eat the rice, small portions are removed from the basket and put on one's plate. A tiny amount is broken off, formed into a ball with the finger tips, flattened slightly and eaten with a

---

A young man sells sausages from a stall in one of Thailand's many markets.

---

bit of meat, vegetable or relish. Rice is eaten at most meals though noodle dishes such as *khao soy* – egg noodles with a coconut-milk-based chicken curry – are often substituted at lunch.

Nam prik num is only a relish but when Bangkok residents come here to breathe the cool air, this is what they return with – bagfuls of it. Roasted ingredients – green chillies, garlic, shallots and shrimp paste – are pounded in a mortar. Then local cherry tomatoes, fish sauce and lime juice are added and lightly pounded as well. Now the relish may be eaten with rice and a curry or else used as a dip with raw or blanched vegetables.

Pork is the favoured meat here, going into curries, a host of sausages and into relishes as well. In Muing Kung, a village of potters, about 10 kilometres outside Chiang Mai, I am

treated to another *nam prik*, called *nam prik ong*, but this one is more like a spaghetti sauce than a relish. An old woman, puffing on a hand-rolled cheroot and chewing on fermented tea leaves, comes down from the upper floor of her hut-on-stilts to borrow some coals from the common kiln and light a small, outdoor stove. The kiln glows at the back as pots, gleaming water vessels, are fired. She skewers 10 red chillies and casually roasts them in a few seconds by waving them near the mouth of the kiln. These are dropped into a stone mortar and pounded. Roasted cakes of a hard, fermented soy bean paste are also pounded, as is roasted shrimp paste. Then in go garlic, shallots, hand-minced (ground) pork, some cherry tomatoes, a little sugar, and fish sauce. Once these are pounded, they are quickly cooked in garlic-flavoured oil to be eaten for lunch that day with glutinous rice and blanched greens. 'This is a Burmese-style dish,' the old lady informs me as she departs, puffing away, to tend her bees.

On my last night in Chiang Mai, I am treated to a *khan tok* dinner by a friend of Ting's, an art professor. A *khan tok* is a raised teak tray-table, round in shape and coated with layers of fine, burnt-orange lacquer. Four to six people can sit around it on the floor to eat. Traditionally, the feasts served on the trays had religious connotations but this is no longer the case today.

With drinks, we are served poppadam-like rice wafers encrusted with sesame seeds, and another seasonal, foraged delicacy: black, forest mushrooms. 'I want you to taste them in their purest form,' my host says. 'They have just been blanched in salted water.' Oh the mushrooms! Charcoal black and almost fully round, they are hard and crisp on the outside and very soft and creamy inside. They may also be stir-fried with pork or put into curries. Here, in their plain form, they start the meal on a high, earthy, note.

The feast that follows has us eating home-made, spicy pork sausage, a superb soup of cabbage greens cooked in a gingery pork broth (*jhaw pak*), a Burmese-style pork curry (*kaeng hunglay*), the spaghetti-sauce-like *nam prik om* cooked with the addition of young tamarind leaves, pork brain baked in a banana leaf, baby river prawns steamed in salted water, pork cracklings, the relish *nam prik num* and, for good measure, a bowlful of fried wasps. Litchis follow, bunches and bunches of them, to be eaten outdoors under the stars, the juice dripping all over the rich earth and over us as well.

The north-east of Thailand is another story. Dry, dusty and poorer, the land is peopled mainly with proud Lao men and women. The earth seems cracked, droughts abound. In the countryside, brilliantly hued lotus flowers rise out of drying ponds, bright sparks against a muddy background. In May, rockets are fired into the sky imploring the gods to make rain for the forthcoming rice-planting season. If the rockets misfire, doom is predicted. The men tend to leave in droves for Bangkok where they steer taxis or work on construction sites, returning just in time to harvest the all-important winter rice crop. This is glutinous rice again, the same as in the north-west. The food, referred to as Issan food, is in some ways similar to that found in the north-west but without its Burmese-style curries, or its gracious *khan tok* dinners. It does, however, have a gutsy character of its own.

I take a walk through the markets of Khon Kaen, a good-sized city that reminds me, strangely, of the American Wild West. I smell roasting meat. Charcoal grills are set up along the sidewalk, loaded with whole marinated chickens split open along the back (*kai yang*), beef sausages made with the addition of a little liver, rice and garlic (*mam*) and similar chicken and pork sausages as well as assorted udders, livers and other meat parts. Meat is enjoyed in hunks, generally accompanied by a relish such as the one called *jaew* (see p. 32) which is made with roasted chillies and shallots and tomatoes, some glutinous rice and *som tam*, a mouthwatering salad of julienned green papaya.

The process of julienning is an interesting one: I watch as a lady with a large knife holds a whole, peeled green papaya in front of her. She hits it repeatedly with the knife, making vertical cuts very close to each other. These are then peeled off and perfectly even, long strips fall magically into a bowl. They are pounded lightly with a coarse paste of red chillies and garlic. Fish sauces of different sorts, sugar, cherry tomatoes and peanuts are added and the salad (*som tam*) is emptied into a plastic bag. A quick tie with a rubber band and one salad is ready to go.

Perhaps the best-known north-eastern dishes are the salads of raw or rare beef. No one knows quite where they originated. Perhaps they came with the Mongols who moved into China in the Middle Ages. Perhaps they are even older and native to the land. Certainly the origins of the raw fish eaten in Japan, *sushi*, lie somewhere in this general region. Here, as I witnessed in the village of Tha Rua on the Ubolratana lake, raw fish was, and still is, preserved in cooked rice. It is called *pla som* (sour fish).

Laab is one of the beef salads. I am invited to an Issan restaurant where this is a speciality. The cook works with the speed of a manic magician. For an order of *laab neua suk*, he puts some minced (ground) beef into a pot, adds a little broth, cooks it for a second – it is still rare – and then adds lime juice, some powder made with roasted glutinous rice, roasted red chilli powder, sugar, fish sauce, some spring onions (scallions) and some mint. A quick toss and it is ready to be served. A similar dish can be made with liver (*laab tapwan suk*, see p. 85) or with raw beef, either minced (ground) or in slices.

The use of roasted and ground rice is confined to the north-east of Thailand. It adds an unusual, nutty taste and, in the local soups and stews where it is used, a little flavoured thickening as well. With our *laab*, we order just such a soup, *tom kreung nai*, made with innards including tripe. It is uncommonly good. I had seen what might be called starter packs for this slow-stewed soup in the vegetable market – lemon grass, galangal, lime leaves and chillies, all tied up together in a neat bundle. Now here was the soup itself, further dressed up before serving with chillies and shallots, fish sauce and lime juice. We are also served glutinous rice in small baskets and a whole plate of raw green vegetables to munch on the side.

Glutinous rice can be seen cooking outdoors not only here but at every corner in the marketplace. Huge tubs of soaking rice sit on the sidewalks. Near them are small braziers topped with rounded pots of water. Stuck into the mouth of the pots are conical baskets. The soaked rice is removed with a plastic strainer and emptied into a basket. Here it steams for about 15 minutes after which it is flipped over expertly so the top gets a chance to feel the hot steam, and cooked another 15 minutes. It is then emptied on to a shallow leaf-lined basket and loosely covered with plastic. When a buyer approaches, the sales lady grabs a handful of rice through a plastic bag, inverts the bag so the rice is now inside, ties it with a rubber band and hands it to the customer. Most people buy their daily rice from the market.

I am invited to dinner at a private home one night and my host, Chainarong Thongnoi, does the same. He buys cooked rice from the market. He explains that glutinous rice keeps very well. At home, it will be transferred to a closed bamboo basket where it will stay warm and moist. Farmers, he says, carry rice baskets to the fields and eat it simply with *som tam* or with *nam prik pla ra*, a spicy relish made with the addition of a local, greyish fish sauce.

Our own meal is exquisitely elaborate. We enter the Chainarong home through a gate. In the front garden are two spirit houses. Bananas sit in them as offerings. The guests are offered the best of a newer world, Cokes in bottles. We sip them, seated on a wooden platform outdoors, and then slip out of our shoes for the meal inside. 'Nok' – which means 'bird' – Chainarong's wife, has

prepared stir-fried pork with pumpkin, a stew of *pak wan*, a green vegetable, a local *nam prik* accented with lemon grass and fermented fish, a dish of noodles served with a topping of an aromatic fish purée and, the dish I will never forget, *kaeng om*, a light, delicate stew of fish and greens, laden with dill (see p. 18). One taste of it and I know that it is headed for this book!

To go south, you have to go down the elephant's trunk, as it were. A very narrow

Chillies (above) with their fiery flavour are essential ingredients in many Thai relishes and dishes. Chillies, tamarind, garlic and shallots (opposite) form the basis of many Thai sauces.

strip of land connects the bulk of Thailand to Malaysia. The aridness of the north-east is replaced by a green lushness. There are not one but two rice harvests here. Dozens of rivers can be seen meandering past rubber and pineapple plantations and cashew groves, making their way to the Gulf of Thailand. The mouth of each such waterway is a haven for sweet prawns and oysters. These are fried

in a rice batter or put into soups or eaten with noodles in restaurants that overhang the water. Half the people here are Muslim, so much more fish is eaten and much less pork.

The small town of Nakhon Si Thammarat is almost 800 kilometres south of Bangkok. I am staying at the airy, colonial home of Dr Jongdee Mitrakul and breakfast has been sent for. 'Very few people make breakfast,' Dr Mitrakul explains. 'It is so much easier to send for it. All we do is open banana leaf packets and just eat.' It is raining gently, making a patter on the tin roof. I can smell the wet earth outside. On the dining-table are jugs of steaming, freshly roasted coffee, to be had with condensed or evaporated milk (fresh milk is hardly ever used), as well as bowls of bananas and oranges. Beside them, each placed on a plate of its own, are opened packets of three rice dishes: rice cooked with coconut cream and topped with curried prawns; glutinous rice cooked with lime leaves and powdered dried prawns; and a glorious fried rice flavoured with garlic, shallots, red chillies and turmeric (*khao yam kluk*, see p. 30). If there is one ingredient very special to southern Thailand, it is fresh turmeric. Many dishes have a yellow hue from this rhizome.

Fresh turmeric also goes into a superb, sweet and sour, soupy stew of a whole fish (*kaeng pla tom som*) and even into some of the relishes. Rice is eaten but rice noodles (*khanom chin*) are often the choice for lunch and dinner. At their best, they are served with *nam kaeng*, an absolutely grand, aromatic and fiery curry sauce thickened with puréed fish.

But it is Bangkok that is the centre of Thailand and it is this noisy, crowded, frustrating and yet eternally exciting city that remains the heart of Thai cuisine. Most people seem to revel in eating out. Even those who say that they mostly eat at home, go out at least six or seven times a month. And why not? Food is exquisitely fresh, and reasonable in price. A neighbourhood market will provide such irresistible offerings as stir-

fried noodles with prawns, aubergines (eggplants) sautéd with minced (ground) pork, spicy stuffed omelettes, curried beef and grilled *satays* of skewered pork.

To lure the diners further, there are numerous gimmicks. Do you wish to pick out live seafood from large tanks and have it cooked according to the restaurant's recipes? Crabs, prawns, lobsters await your demands. Perhaps you would like to take your children for a picnic, rent fishing rods and fish for your supper? Lakes have been created just for your pleasure and stocked with fish. You pull them out and hand them to the kitchen staff. Then you relax on a picnic bench under a tree. When the fish is cooked, a young man on a bicycle will bring it to you. This picnic is trouble-free.

Are you looking for speedy service? Would waiters on skates be the thing? One of the largest restaurants in Bangkok provides just such a service.

Thai cuisine 'palace style': a cucumber is carved to form an ornate and perfect 'leaf'.

You want none of the above? Instead, you would rather pick your own seafood and vegetables and then have them cooked according to your own recipe? No, you are not carrying things too far. The newest trend is the supermarket-restaurant. You take a trolley, choose from hundreds of types of fish and seafood, move on to the vegetables, pick mushrooms or greens and then hand them all to a waiter with precise instructions: 'I would like the river prawns and straw mushrooms made into a soup with lemon grass. The squid should be stir-fried quickly with the baby corn. And the crabs, could you please curry them with coconut milk?'

Some of the more delicate, refined and ornate dishes, such as a soup of stuffed baby squid, belong to what many refer to as the 'palace' style of cooking and presentation. This is Thailand's *haute cuisine*, created in the royal palaces by women who had the leisure to make highly detailed, almost baroque, lidded boxes out of taro roots, lifelike roses out of beetroots, ears of corn out of carrots and flowering artichokes out of pomelos. The

tradition continues, with the plebeians trying hard to learn from the royals.

I once happened to visit a member of the Thai nobility just when she was preparing to send a tray of food to a royal princess. The start of summer is celebrated in the palace with iced rice. Ice cubes are not just dunked into a bowl of rice. No. First, old rice must be soaked in alum water and then washed well to remove all the starch. Then the grains must be polished with cloth to make them shine. Then the rice is parboiled for 5 minutes and rinsed in cold water. It is par-boiled again and rinsed another couple of times. Then the rice needs to be steamed briefly. After which it is mixed with crushed ice and jasmine-scented water. A rose petal or two is floated on the top.

That is not all. With the rice must be served stuffed peppers enclosed in the finest netting made out of eggs, dried shreds of sweetened beef, salted fish dipped in batter and fried, a julienne of preserved radish, stuffed shallots, little balls of shrimp paste in batter and a plate of assorted vegetables, all carved to perfection. I do not often long to be a princess but the time I watched that tray go by was certainly one of them.

Perhaps the one summer dish that unites all Thais in ecstasy is a plate of fully ripe mangoes served with sweetened rice. When mango fever hits, only the best rice will do – glutinous rice from Chiang Rai, just north of Chiang Mai. Long queues form at the shops. This rice is cooked with coconut milk, sugar and salt. It is then topped with coconut cream and with a sprinkling of roasted mung beans. It is heavenly.

The safe lines between savoury and sweet, so clear in the West, are just not taken seriously here: a sweet, custard-filled pastry shell could be garnished with crisply fried shallots; slices of orange could be topped with sweet and salty minced (ground) pork and garnished with fiery red chillies. It is brilliantly engineered and it is all geared to keeping you eating. That is what Thai food is all about.

RECIPES FROM THAILAND

An illuminated sign for a noodle restaurant.

Central Thailand

GALLOPING HORSES
MA HAW

One bite of this snack and you will instantly get a sense of Thai culinary passions. Here, as in many foods from central Thailand, hot, sweet, sour, nutty and salty flavours are all combined in a feverish pitch of intensity. Fruit slices serve as a base, almost as if they formed the bottom of an open sandwich. (I have used orange slices cut from a Western-type orange but pineapple sections are equally popular.) On top of each slice goes a dollop of pork, cooked only as the inspired Thais know how. If you do not eat pork, use dark chicken meat instead.

I serve this as an appetiser.

Note: The garnishes here are essential to the final taste of the dish.

SERVES 4

2 oranges
1 tablespoon vegetable oil
4 tablespoons peeled and finely sliced shallots
115 g / 4 oz minced (ground) pork
4 tablespoons Roasted Peanuts, see p. 201, lightly crushed
2 tablespoons palm sugar or light brown sugar
1 tablespoon fish sauce, *nam pla* (or salt to taste plus 1 tablespoon water)

Garnish:

1–2 fresh, hot red chillies (green will do), cut crossways into thin slices
About 10 fresh green coriander leaves

Peel the oranges with a paring knife, making sure to cut all the white pith away. Cut crossways into about 5 good slices each. The small end slices should not be used. Lay the slices in a single layer in a serving dish.

Heat the oil in a non-stick frying-pan over medium heat. When hot, put in the shallots. Stir and cook until they just start to brown. Put in the pork. Stir and cook it, breaking up lumps, until it is no longer pink in the slightest. Turn the heat to low. Add the peanuts, sugar and fish sauce. Stir and cook until the sugar has melted. Turn off the heat. Put a good dollop, about 1 tablespoon or more of the pork on the centre of each piece of orange. Stick a slice of chilli and a green coriander leaf on the top of each piece and serve at room temperature.

Bangkok, Thailand

STUFFED CUCUMBER SOUP
KAENG JUED TAENG KWA SOT SAI

One of the very delicate Thai soups that definitely belongs to the more refined 'palace' style of cooking, this is not in the least bit chilli-hot. It does not, however, lack in character as it contains that charming triumvirate of Thai seasonings, coriander root, garlic and white pepper, a combination, I suspect, that dates back to ancient times, long before the arrival of the chilli pepper from the Western hemisphere.

Cucumbers come in such a variety of sizes that I have given the amount needed in length. Get a little extra so you can afford to discard the tapered end pieces.

SERVES 4

6 green coriander roots, coarsely chopped
1 clove garlic, peeled and coarsely chopped
½ teaspoon white peppercorns
85 g / 3 oz minced (ground) pork
115 g / 4 oz unpeeled prawns (shrimp), peeled and deveined and very finely chopped, or 85 g / 3 oz peeled and deveined prawns (shrimp), very finely chopped
1 tablespoon fish sauce, *nam pla* (or salt to taste)
30 cm / 12 inches usable cucumber (see above)

For the seasoned stock:

1.2 litres / 2 pints / 5 cups Chicken Stock, see p. 197
3 whole green coriander plants
5 fresh or dried kaffir lime leaves (or 5 slivers of lemon rind)
2 teaspoons fish sauce, *nam pla* (or extra soy sauce or salt to taste)
¼ teaspoon Chinese dark soy sauce
¼ teaspoon sugar

Garnish:

About 2 tablespoons fresh green coriander leaves

Combine the coriander roots, garlic and the peppercorns in the small container of an electric blender. Blend. Alternatively, you could pound all three in a mortar.

Put 1 teaspoon of this mixture in a bowl. Add the pork, prawns and fish sauce and mix well.

Peel the cucumber and cut it crossways into eight 4 cm / 1½ inch sections. Hollow out these sections by removing all the seeds. I use a grapefruit spoon to do this but any small spoon will do. Stuff these sections with the seasoned pork and prawn (shrimp) mixture.

Combine all of the ingredients for the seasoned stock. Add the remaining coriander root mixture and bring to a boil. Cover, turn the heat to low and simmer very gently for

30 minutes. Strain. Taste for saltiness, adding more fish sauce or salt, if needed. Put the stock in a wide pan.

Stand the stuffed cucumber pieces inside in a single layer and bring to a simmer. Cover and poach on low heat for about 5 minutes or until the cucumbers are just cooked through. Divide the soup among 4 soup bowls, giving each person 2 pieces of cucumber. Float a few green coriander leaves over the top and serve.

Central Thailand
HOT AND SOUR CHICKEN SOUP
TOM YAM KAI

Soups in Thailand are really treated like light stews and are eaten along with the meal. They can be very mild or fiery hot. Even when filled with chillies, their heat is somewhat ameliorated as they are invariably eaten with soothing spoonfuls of plain rice. I tend to serve this dish all by itself as a soup course and therefore keep its heat a little in check.

For this soup, I make the stock as I go but you may choose to simplify your life and use ready-made stock with chicken meat that has been skinned and boned by unseen hands at the supermarket. My preference is always for dark chicken meat. If, however, you wish to use boned and skinned breast, get about 195–225 g / 7–8 oz meat, dice it and poach it in the soup very gently at barely a simmer, just until it turns white all the way through.

SERVES 4

4 green coriander roots, coarsely chopped
1 clove garlic, peeled and coarsely chopped
¼ teaspoon white peppercorns
1–2 fresh, hot green chillies, coarsely chopped
340–370 g / 12–13 oz chicken legs, boned, skinned (see p. 207) and cut into 2.5 cm / 1 inch dice (save the bones for stock), or see above
1 stick of fresh lemon grass, lightly mashed at the bulbous end or 1 tablespoon dried, sliced lemon grass (or a generous strip of lemon rind)
6–8 green coriander stems
2 slices of fresh or dried galangal (or fresh ginger)
One 425 g / 15 oz can of straw mushrooms, drained
2 tablespoons fish sauce, *nam pla* (or salt to taste)
2 teaspoons lime or lemon juice
2 teaspoons tamarind paste, see p. 218 (or more lime or lemon juice to taste)
1 teaspoon sugar

Garnish:

Green coriander leaves
Red and green 'bird's eye' chillies, *prik-khi-nu* if available, whole or sliced into rounds. (If the soup is already too hot for you, cut up a few slivers of red and green pepper)

Combine the coriander roots, garlic, white peppercorns and green chillies in the small container of an electric blender and make a coarse paste. Alternatively, you could mash all the same ingredients very finely in a mortar.

Put the chicken bones in a pan with 1.2 litres / 2 pints / 5 cups water and bring to a boil. Remove the scum as it forms at the top and then put in the coriander root paste, the stick of lemon grass, coriander stems and galangal. Bring to a simmer again. Cover, turn the heat to low and simmer gently for 30 minutes. Strain the soup and add the diced chicken. Bring to a simmer again, cover, turn the heat to low and simmer gently for 10 minutes. Now put in the drained straw mushrooms, fish sauce, lime juice, tamarind paste and sugar. Bring to a simmer again and simmer gently for another 2–3 minutes.

This soup may be made ahead of time. Just before eating, re-heat it and sprinkle the garnishes over the top. Serve immediately.

Northern Thailand
FISH STEW WITH DILL
KAENG OM

If you are looking for a light but flavourful dish, consider this northern speciality which I had in the home of Chainarong Thongnoi and his wife, Nok. It is a fish stew where the broth is perked up with tamarind, fish sauce, red chillies, basil and dill. It is thickened just very slightly with roasted and ground rice and has floating in it not just choice pieces of fish but green vegetables as well.

When I want a light meal, I often serve this stew with some jasmine rice (in the north, glutinous rice would be served) or crusty French bread. This way, the entire meal is fat- and cholesterol-free.

The fish sauce used in the north is *pla ra*. Almost a fish paste, it is greyish and opaque, consisting of both the liquid and the small, flat, fermented fish from which it is made. It is strained before being used in such stews. Every household seems to have a vat of it. Ordinary fish sauce (*nam pla*) is the best alternative.

If you do not have any fish sauce at all, my only suggestion is to use fish stock instead of water and then salt it to taste. The green leafy vegetable used in the stew I ate was the Chinese *choy sum*, of the cabbage family. It is sold by most Chinese grocers. You may use broccoli instead, as I have done.

SERVES 4

1½ tablespoons long-grain or glutinous rice
285 g / 10 oz broccoli
1–2 dried, hot red chillies, de-seeded and coarsely crumbled
3 tablespoons fish sauce, *nam pla* (or see above)
1 tablespoon tamarind paste, see p. 218 (or lemon juice to taste)
675 g / 1½ lb thick fillets of fish, such as haddock, cod, snapper, salmon or tile (or fish steaks), cut into 5 cm / 2 inch squares
180 g / 1 oz / 6 tablespoons chopped fresh dill
A handful of fresh basil leaves (*bai menglak* if available)

Set a small cast-iron frying-pan over medium-high heat. When hot, put in the rice and stir it for 2–3 minutes or until it turns golden.

Fish stew with Dill (this page).

Some grains might even pop. Remove the rice from the pan, cool slightly and then grind to a powder in a clean coffee-grinder or other spice-grinder.

Peel the broccoli stems and cut them crossways into 5 mm / ¼ inch thick slices. Cut the rest of the head into delicate spears.

Put 950 ml / 32 fl oz / 4 cups water in a wide pan. Add the rice powder, red chillies, fish sauce and tamarind paste. Bring to a boil. Stir and turn the heat to low. Simmer gently for 10 minutes. Put in the fish and broccoli stems. Bring to a simmer and cook very gently for 2 minutes. Now put in the broccoli spears, dill and basil. Cook for another 2 minutes or until the fish is just done.

Central Thailand

FISH SAUTÉD WITH AROMATIC HERBS
TOM YAM HAENG

This dish cooks fast and easily. It is best to have fresh herbs and seasonings but if you cannot get them, here is what I can suggest for substitutions: if you cannot get fresh lemon grass, add 1 teaspoon powdered lemon grass or 2 teaspoons of freshly grated lemon rind to the sauce; if you cannot get fresh kaffir lime leaves, try for another aroma altogether – that of 2 spring onions (scallions), cut into 5 cm / 2 inch lengths; if you cannot get fresh galangal, use fresh ginger instead. The three seasonings mentioned above are not meant to be eaten as they are quite chunky. They are generally just pushed to the side, like bones.

Thai chilli paste (*nam prik pow*) is sold in bottles by Thai grocers (see p. 211). There is also a recipe for it on p. 200. If it is unavailable and you do not feel up to making it, use about ¼ teaspoon chilli powder (cayenne pepper) in its place.

Fish are arranged in perfect symmetry on a market stall. Thai food is as appealing to the eye as it is to the palate.

Serve this with plain rice and a Thai vegetable. You may also serve it, Western style, with rice and a salad.

For the sauce:

2½ tablespoons fresh lime
or lemon juice

2½ tablespoons fish sauce, *nam pla* (or Chinese light soy sauce)

1½ teaspoons sugar

3 fresh, hot green or red chillies, cut into fine rounds. (The Thais would use 'bird's eye' chillies, *prik-khi-nu* – any hot chillies, in any amount, may be used here)

You also need:

3 tablespoons vegetable oil

2 sticks of fresh lemon grass, their bulbous ends lightly mashed and the bottom 15 cm / 6 inches of the stick cut into 2.5 cm / 1 inch lengths (or see above)

3–4 fresh kaffir lime leaves, central veins removed (or see left)

6 slices of fresh galangal (or see left)

1 tablespoon Thai chilli paste, *nam prik pow*, see p. 200 (or see left)

900 g / 2 lb of 2 cm / ¾ inch thick fillets of white-fleshed fish, such as haddock, cod, halibut or tile (or fish steaks of the same weight and thickness, cut into 4 cm / 1½ inch squares)

Combine all the ingredients for the sauce. Mix and set aside.

Just before eating, heat the oil in a large non-stick frying-pan over medium-high heat. When hot, put in the lemon grass, lime leaves and galingal. Stir for 10 seconds. Add the chilli paste and stir for another minute. Put the fish pieces into the pan in a single layer and turn the heat to medium low. Add about 1½ tablespoons of the sauce and 1 tablespoon water. Cook for 1 minute. Then carefully turn the pieces over and add another tablespoon of water, if necessary. As soon as the fish has cooked through, remove it carefully and put it in a serving dish.

Spoon the remaining sauce over the top of the fish and serve.

Central and southern Thailand

PRAWN/SHRIMP CURRY
KAENG PHET KUNG

As with many Thai curries, this one uses not only the highly aromatic local seasonings such as lemon grass and kaffir lime leaves, but Indian curry powder as well. It is a heady blend. This curry should be served with rice, plain or jasmine.

Note: The cumin and coriander seeds needed here may be roasted and ground together. The curry paste can be made ahead of time and frozen. If you like, you can make double the amount of curry paste, use half and freeze the rest for later use. You will need only about half a stick of lemon grass for this recipe. Save the rest in the freezer.

SERVES 6

For the curry paste:

5 dried, hot red chillies, soaked in
4 tablespoons hot water until soft (a microwave oven will do this very quickly)

1 teaspoon roasted and ground cumin seeds, see p. 213

1 teaspoon roasted and ground coriander seeds, see p. 212

1 clove garlic, peeled and coarsely chopped

2 medium-sized shallots or half a small onion (20 g / ¾ oz), peeled and coarsely chopped

1 tablespoon fresh lemon grass that has been finely sliced crossways from the bulbous end (or 1 teaspoon powdered lemon grass)

2 teaspoons curry powder. (Use a good 'Madras' type)

1 teaspoon bright red paprika

You also need:

4 tablespoons vegetable oil

About 3 shallots or 1 small onion (30 g / 1 oz), peeled and finely sliced

One 400 ml / 14 fl oz can of coconut milk mixed with 250 ml / 8 fl oz / 1 cup water, or 650 ml / 22 fl oz / 2¾ cups fresh coconut milk, see p. 212

2 medium-sized potatoes (130 g / 4½ oz), boiled, peeled and quartered

2 teaspoons salt

2 teaspoons tamarind paste, see p. 218 (or lemon or lime juice)

6 fresh kaffir lime leaves, central veins removed (or 6 dried kaffir lime leaves or six 2.5 cm / 1 inch strips of lemon rind)

450 g / 1 lb unpeeled, medium-sized prawns (shrimp), peeled and deveined, or 340 g / 12 oz peeled and deveined prawns (shrimp)

Garnish (optional):

A few extra fresh kaffir lime leaves, if available, and some small whole, red and green, 'bird's eye' chillies, *prik-khi-nu* (or ordinary green and red chillies, cut into smaller segments if necessary)

Combine the dried red chillies and their soaking liquid as well as all the other ingredients for the curry paste in the small container of an electric blender. Blend until you have a fine paste.

Put the oil in a wok or wide pan over medium-high heat. When hot, put in the shallots. Stir and fry until they start to brown. Put in the curry paste. Stir and fry it for 3–4 minutes, sprinkling lightly with water if it seems to stick. Now put in the coconut milk mixture, potatoes, salt, tamarind paste and kaffir lime leaves. Stir well and bring to a simmer. Turn the heat to low and simmer gently for 5 minutes, stirring now and then. Put in the prawns (shrimp). Stir them about until they turn opaque. Turn off the heat. Put the curry in a serving dish, scatter the garnishes over the top and serve.

North-eastern Thailand

GRILLED CHICKEN, ISSAN-STYLE
KAI YANG ISSAN

Stands of freshly grilled meats, prepared in the semi-outdoors so that their sweet, smoky smells can entice the unwary passer-by, are a common sight all over north-eastern Thailand. It is mostly chicken that is cooked, held firmly in place by what look like long bamboo clothes pegs. Why the bamboo does not burn up, I'll never understand. Perhaps the marinade wets it sufficiently to prevent it from flaring up. A variety of sausages are also grilled and are immensely well liked. Unlike the finicky Southerners and Bangkok residents who nibble on delicate *satays*, the Northerners seem to like their grilled meat in hunks. Sometimes a whole chicken is opened up, cut down the back so it can be flattened out. At other times just chicken parts are grilled. Sometimes the marinade is as simple as garlic and salt, at other times, such as in this recipe, a few more seasonings are added. Grilled meats are eaten with Steamed Glutinous Rice (see p. 29) and *som tam*, a spicy salad of shredded green papaya (see my variation, Kohlrabi and Carrot Salad, on p. 26).

SERVES 4

3 cloves garlic, peeled and coarsely chopped
5 green coriander roots, coarsely chopped
1 teaspoon white peppercorns
1 tablespoon Chinese dark soy sauce
1 tablespoon fish sauce, *nam pla* (or salt to taste)
2 teaspoons sugar
1 kg / 2¼ lb chicken pieces

Combine all the ingredients except the chicken in the small container of an electric blender and blend until you have a paste. Alternatively, you could pound the first 3 ingredients in a mortar and then slowly add the others. Put the paste in a bowl. Add the chicken and rub it well with the mixture. Marinate for at least 2 hours or overnight.

Heat your outdoor or indoor grill (broiler). If you can control the fire, do not make it too hot or the chicken will char as there is sugar in the marinade. Cook the chicken until browned and cooked through, about 10 minutes on each side. If you cannot control the heat outdoors, move the chicken to one side after it has browned, away from a direct flame, allowing it to cook more slowly. Indoors, once the chicken has browned sufficiently on both sides, it is a good idea to turn off the heat and allow the chicken to sit for a few minutes under the still-warm grill (broiler) to cook through.

Central Thailand

CHICKEN STIR-FRIED WITH TOMATOES AND BASIL
KAI PAD MAKAUTED

A somewhat modern Thai creation, this is my adaptation of a dish prepared by Chalie Amatyakul of the Oriental Hotel. Serve it with rice – Thai Jasmine Rice (see p. 29) would be perfect – and a vegetable or salad of your choice.

SERVES 4

3 tablespoons vegetable oil
3 dried, hot red chillies
2 cloves garlic, peeled and finely chopped
1 tablespoon shrimp paste, *kapi* (or anchovy paste)
450 g / 1 lb boned and skinned chicken meat (preferably from the leg), cut into 2.5 cm / 1 inch squares
1 teaspoon bright red paprika
2 medium-sized tomatoes (about 180 g / 6 oz), dropped into boiling water for 10 seconds, peeled, seeded and chopped
100 g / 3½ oz / ½ cup drained, canned straw mushrooms
2 tablespoons fish sauce, *nam pla* (or salt to taste)
15 g / ½ oz / ½ packed cup fresh basil leaves (*bai kaprow* if available)

Heat the oil in a wok or large frying-pan over highish heat. When hot, put in the red chillies and garlic. Stir once or twice and put in the shrimp paste. Stir that for about 10 seconds, breaking it up, and put in the chicken. Stir and fry the chicken until it is lightly browned. Put in the paprika and give a good stir.

Now put in the tomatoes, mushrooms and fish sauce and basil. Stir for 1 minute. Now turn the heat to low and simmer gently for 10 minutes, stirring every now and then.

This dish may be made ahead of time and re-heated.

Central Thailand

BEEF CURRY WITH GREEN SAUCE
KAENG KHIAO WAN NUA

In Thai markets, basinsful of curry pastes, piled high like green, red and yellow hillocks, sit waiting for customers. Some people do indeed make their curry pastes at home, but most find it more convenient just to go out and buy what they need. After all, these curry pastes are made every day and have no additives. They are, indeed, the best kind of convenience foods. Coconuts, too, are grated by huge machines which, rather like snow-making contraptions in the West, spew out the stuff in the hundreds of kilos (pounds). The housewife can buy what she needs then go home and make her curry with ease and speed. This is certainly the case in a big city like Bangkok, where many women need to work.

In the West, we have electric blenders that can speed things up. I do think that it is a good idea to make double the quantity of curry paste. The unneeded half can be frozen and retrieved on another day when one is perhaps more tired. It is just like money in the bank.

This dish is traditionally garnished with kaffir lime leaves and tiny, raw pea aubergines (eggplants), sold only by Thai grocers. Green chillies may be used instead.

SERVES 4–6

Green curry paste:
4 fresh, hot green chillies, coarsely chopped
2.5 cm / 1 inch cube of fresh galangal (or fresh ginger), peeled and coarsely chopped
Two 2.5 x 5 mm / 1¼ inch (approx.) strips of fresh (or dried) kaffir lime rind (if dried, soak in water first – do not use the soaking water as it is bitter)
1½ tablespoons finely sliced fresh lemon grass that has been cut crossways from the bulbous end (or 1 teaspoon powdered lemon grass)
3 green coriander roots, coarsely chopped
3 cloves garlic, peeled and coarsely chopped
3 shallots or half a small onion (20 g / ¾ oz), peeled and coarsely chopped

1 teaspoon shrimp paste, *kapi* (or anchovy paste)

1 teaspoon roasted coriander seeds, see p. 212

½ teaspoon roasted cumin seeds, see p. 213

¼ teaspoon ground mace

¼ teaspoon ground nutmeg

30 g / 1 oz / 1 packed cup fresh green coriander leaves

You also need:
450 g / 1 lb beef skirt

7 tablespoons vegetable oil

1½ tablespoons fish sauce, *nam pla*, or a bit more (or salt to taste)

175 ml / 6 fl oz / ¾ cup canned coconut milk mixed with 120 ml / 4 fl oz / ½ cup water, or 300 ml / 10 fl oz / 1¼ cups fresh coconut milk, see p. 212

A small handful of fresh basil leaves (*bai horappa* if available)

Garnish (optional):
Kaffir lime leaves and pea aubergines (eggplants) or green chillies (see left)

Combine all the ingredients for the curry paste in an electric blender. Add about 3–4 tablespoons water and blend, pushing down when necessary, until you have a smooth paste. Cut the beef against the grain into pieces that are 5–7.5 cm / 2–3 inches long, 2.5 cm / 1 inch wide and 1–3 mm / 1/16–1/8 inch thick. If you have bought your meat in one continuous piece, cut it into 7.5 cm / 3 inch segments first and then cut each segment against the grain, holding the knife at a 135° angle to your work surface. This will give you the required width.

Heat the oil in a large, non-stick frying-pan over medium-high heat. When hot, put in the curry paste. Stir and fry until the oil separates and the paste is lightly browned, about 6–7 minutes. Add the meat and the fish sauce. Stir and cook for 2 minutes. Add the coconut milk and bring to a simmer. The meat should be tender. If not, cook just a little bit longer. Check for salt, adding more fish sauce or salt if you need it. Throw in the basil leaves and stir them in.

Southern Thailand
STIR-FRIED 'DRUNKARD'S' BEEF
NEUA PAD KEEMAO

The Nakorn Inn restaurant is set in a pretty, airy pavilion in the southern town of Nakhon Si Thammarat. A sign here proclaims that *no monosodium glutamate* is used in the kitchen. As we settle down with a cooling, thirst-quenching Singha beer, this dish arrives, apparently a choice accompaniment for those who like to imbibe. It consists of stir-fried, delicately spiced minced (ground) beef, eaten with scoops made out of crisp lettuce leaves.

It is so good that it warrants a trip to the

A young girl in her school uniform looks at a street vendor selling plump, grilled bananas. Open-air, movable stalls with their freshly made 'convenience foods' are the Thai equivalents of Western take-aways.

kitchen to watch its preparation. The beef here, as in many parts of South-East Asia, is minced (ground) by hand – rather, two hands, each wielding a sharp cleaver and both going chop, chop, chop alternately in rapid succession until the meat acquires the desired fineness.

Having learnt the trick, I sometimes practise it myself, especially when small quantities of meat are required.

Note: Lao whisky was swished into the wok at one stage of the cooking. Unable to get that, I have used Chinese rice wine. Dry sherry would also do.

In spite of the many ingredients, this is a quick and easy dish to prepare. The cooking time is about 4–5 minutes. You may serve it with lettuce leaves, or with rice or, if you do not mind being a bit unorthodox, stuff the meat into the hollow of a pitta bread along with shredded lettuce, cucumber slices and chopped tomatoes.

SERVES 4 AS A MAIN COURSE, 6 AS AN APPETISER

340 g / ¾ lb good quality minced (ground) beef

8 green coriander roots, very finely chopped

5 tablespoons minutely diced green coriander stems. Cut them crossways

2 tablespoons peeled and finely chopped shallots or onion

1 tablespoon fresh lemon grass that has been finely sliced from the bulbous end and then finely chopped (or 1 teaspoon powdered lemon grass or 1 teaspoon grated lemon rind)

4 tablespoons finely shredded fresh basil leaves (in Thailand *bai kaprow* would be used) or fresh mint

1–2 fresh, hot green chillies, finely sliced in rounds

3 tablespoons vegetable oil

1 clove garlic, peeled and finely chopped

150 ml / 5 fl oz / ⅓ cup Beef Stock, see p. 197, or Chicken Stock, see p. 197

1 tablespoon oyster sauce

1½ teaspoons sugar

2 teaspoons Chinese dark soy sauce

2 tablespoons Chinese rice wine

Leaves of crisp lettuce, such as cos (Romaine)

Combine the beef, coriander roots, coriander stems, shallots, lemon grass, basil leaves and chillies in a bowl. Mix lightly.

Heat the oil in a wok or large frying-pan over high heat. When hot, put in the garlic. Stir a few times and put in the seasoned meat. Stir and fry, breaking up all lumps. Dribble in the stock from the sides and stir. Add the oyster sauce, sugar, dark soy sauce and rice wine. Stir vigorously for a few minutes, until the meat is cooked through. Put the meat on a serving plate and arrange the lettuce leaves on one side. To eat, scoop up some meat with a leaf – or with a section of a leaf.

Central and southern Thailand

CURRIED KEBABS
SATAY

These skewered kebabs are what the Thais often nibble on during a break in a dance performance or football game, or during an evening stroll through a park. It is fast food but of high quality, sometimes made at home, but more often bought from a vendor in the street or at a restaurant.

Here is a brilliant version of *satay*, from a recipe provided for me by Patcharee Amsamang. She used pork so I have done the same. Chicken or beef may be substituted. Whatever you use, you will need rectangles of meat that are about 5 mm / ¼ inch thick, about 4–5 cm / 1½–2 inches long and about 2.5 cm / 1 inch wide. For pork, it is best to cut slices that are 5 mm / ¼ thick off a boneless roll of loin meat meant for roasting, and then cut these slices further into rectangles.

For a *satay*, about three such meat pieces are threaded on to a small bamboo skewer and then grilled outdoors over charcoal. People eat *satays* by the stick. You may do so too if you wish. Bamboo skewers are sold by oriental grocers. They need to be soaked first in water for about 30 minutes to discourage their burning. Even then, you have to grill carefully, keeping the meat but not the skewers over the fire. In Thailand, long, narrow braziers are designed for the purpose.

I have worked out a more convenient method: I pan-fry. After that, I can stick toothpicks into the meat pieces and serve them with drinks, or serve the *satays* as a main course, which I love to do, dispensing with toothpicks and skewers altogether, making a neat pile of the meat pieces in a serving dish, and garnishing it with sprigs of fresh mint. This *satay* may be served, Western style, with boiled potatoes and vegetables, or Thai style, with perhaps a noodle dish, a soup and a stir-fry.

Note: I used canned coconut milk here. If you do the same, stir the contents well before measuring out what is required. (Freshly made

coconut milk does not need to be diluted.) Patcheree used 1½ tablespoons de-seeded, dried red chillies in the dipping sauce. I have used three chillies. You have a choice.

SERVES 4 AS A MAIN COURSE,
6–8 AS AN APPETISER WITH DRINKS

For marinating the meat:

2 cloves garlic, peeled and coarsely chopped
8 green coriander roots, coarsely chopped
1 teaspoon white peppercorns
2 teaspoons sugar
4 teaspoons Chinese dark soy sauce
½ teaspoon curry powder. (A good 'Madras' type is best)
2 tablespoons canned coconut milk
900 g / 1 lb boneless loin of pork, cut as suggested left

For the dipping sauce:

3 dried, hot red chillies, de-seeded
⅛ teaspoon roasted cumin seeds, see p. 213
¾ teaspoon roasted coriander seeds, p. 212
3 cloves garlic, peeled and coarsely chopped
3 medium-sized shallots or half a small onion (30 g / 1 oz), peeled and coarsely chopped
1 tablespoon paprika
1½ tablespoons vegetable oil
175 ml / 6 fl oz / ¾ cup canned coconut milk combined with 120 ml / 4 fl oz / ½ cup water, or 300 ml / 10 fl oz / 1¼ cups fresh coconut milk, see p. 212
4 tablespoons Roasted Peanuts, see p. 201, finely crushed
2 teaspoons palm sugar or light brown sugar
½ teaspoon salt, or to taste

For basting the satay and the final cooking:

250 ml / 8 fl oz / 1 cup canned coconut milk
2 teaspoons curry powder (the same type as used in the marinade)
A pinch of salt
A little vegetable oil

Put the garlic, coriander roots and white peppercorns into the small container of an electric blender and blend until you have a coarse paste. Alternatively, you could use a mortar and pestle. Put the paste in a bowl. Add all the other ingredients for the

marinade except the pork and mix well. Add the pork and mix again. Cover and marinate for 2 hours or even overnight, refrigerating if necessary

Soak the chilli skins in 1½ tablespoons hot water until slightly softened (a microwave oven does this in a minute). Put the chillies, their soaking liquid, cumin, coriander, garlic, shallots and paprika into the container of an electric blender and blend until smooth. Add a tiny bit more water only if you need it.

Heat the oil in a small pan over medium heat. When hot, put in the paste. Stir and fry for 3–4 minutes or until it starts to brown. Add the coconut milk, peanuts, palm sugar and salt. Stir and bring to a simmer. Stir and cook for a few minutes or until thick.

Just before eating, combine the coconut milk for basting with the curry powder and salt. This is the basting sauce. Brush a well-seasoned cast-iron or non-stick frying-pan with oil and set it to heat over medium-high heat. Dip some meat pieces in the basting sauce and lay them down in the hot pan, only as many pieces as will fit in a single layer. Cook them for about a minute or until lightly browned. Turn the pieces over and brown the second side the same way. Remove and put on a warm plate. Do all the meat pieces this way and serve immediately.

Khon Kaen, North-eastern Thailand

CALVES' LIVER SALAD
LAAB TAPWAN SUK

Khon Kaen is dry and dusty, and seems almost like a frontier town of the old American Mid-West. The food in the region can be quite hearty. It is here that they make salads of raw and rare beef. In fact, beef is very well liked and appears in many forms. This liver salad is one of them. It is liver and onions the northern Thai way. Raw liver is cut into thin slices and put in a bowl. Boiling stock is poured into and out of the bowl several times and then the liver is dressed. Very spicily, of course. Sometimes, instead of the boiling stock treatment, the liver is grilled lightly. It is always cooked thoroughly on the outside and it always stays pink on the inside, just as good liver should. With the salad comes a forest of raw vegetables and herbs for nibbling – some sweet, some bitter, some earthy – of which I recognised only long beans, Chinese cabbage and basil (*bai borappa*) – and a covered basket of glutinous rice.

Two seasonings in northern dressings are unusual. One, which is now becoming a bit more familiar in the West, is roasted and ground rice. The other is roasted and crushed red chillies. The rice that is roasted and ground in the north is the rice they eat: glutinous rice. If you do not happen to have it, just use plain long-grain rice. It hardly makes any difference. As for the chillies, when they are roasted before being crushed, they do have a different flavour. But I do not recommend roasting them in a closed kitchen. The fumes are powerful. Use ordinary chilli powder (cayenne pepper).

SERVES 3–4

For the salad:

2 tablespoons long-grain or glutinous rice

1 tablespoon vegetable oil

225 g / 8 oz calves' liver, cut into about two 5 mm / ¼ inch thick slices

3 spring onions (scallions), cut into 5 cm / 2 inch lengths all the way up their green sections, then cut lengthways into fine slivers

2 tablespoons lime or lemon juice

2 tablespoons fish sauce, *nam pla* (or salt to taste)

1½ teaspoons sugar

¼ teaspoon chilli powder (cayenne pepper), or to taste

A good handful of fresh mint leaves

Possible vegetables to serve on the side:

Crisp lettuce leaves

Crisp, tender green beans, or long beans cut into smaller sections

Fresh basil

Tender inner cabbage leaves

Set a small cast-iron frying-pan over medium-high heat. When hot, put in the rice and stir

it for 2–3 minutes or until it turns golden. Some grains might even pop. Remove the rice from the pan, cool slightly and then grind to a powder in a clean coffee-grinder or other spice-grinder.

Put the oil in a frying-pan and set over high heat. When hot, put in the slices of liver. Cook for about 1½ minutes on each side, or until the outside is browned and the inside is still a bit pink. Remove from the heat and cut into 2.5 cm / 1 inch squares. Put in a bowl. Add the ground rice and all the other ingredients for the salad. Toss well and empty on to a serving plate. Serve raw vegetables on the side.

Most of Thailand

AUBERGINES (EGGPLANTS), STIR-FRIED WITH PORK
MAKUA PAD MOOH

Following a longstanding Far Eastern tradition of cooking vegetables with small amounts of meat or fish or the stock thereof, here are meltingly tender aubergines (eggplants) cooked with minced (ground) pork. They are best served with Thai Jasmine Rice (see p. 29), though I happen to love them with Southern Fried Rice (see p. 30) as well. If you do not eat pork, use chicken or turkey.

Long, slim aubergines (eggplants) would be the ideal variety to use here. They are halved or quartered lengthways, and then cut into 5 cm / 2 inch long fingers. If only fat, chunky purple aubergines (eggplants) are available, cut them into fingers that are 5 cm / 2 inches long and about 2.5 cm / 1 inch thick and wide.

SERVES 4–6

450 g / 1 lb aubergines (eggplants), cut as suggested above

3 tablespoons vegetable oil

1–2 cloves garlic, peeled and cut into fine, long slivers

6–8 shallots or 1 small onion (45 g / 1½ oz), peeled and cut into fine slivers

2 fresh, hot green chillies, cut crossways into rings

225 g / 8 oz minced (ground) pork

2 tablespoons fish sauce, *nam pla* (or Chinese light soy sauce)

2 teaspoons sugar

30 g / 1 oz / 1 cup fresh basil leaves, *bai borappa* (or fresh mint)

Put the aubergines (eggplants) in a steaming utensil, cover and steam for about 10 minutes. (If steaming instructions are needed, see p. 208.) Or poach them, covered, in about 1 cm / ½ inch water for about 6 minutes.

Heat the oil in a wok or large frying-pan over medium-high heat. When hot, put in the garlic and shallots. Stir and fry until they start to brown. Put in the chillies. Stir once or twice. Put in the pork. Stir and fry, breaking up all lumps, until all the meat turns whitish. Add the fish sauce and sugar. Stir to mix. Turn the heat down to medium-low. Put in the aubergines (eggplants) and add 120 ml / 4 fl oz / ½ cup water. Stir gently and bring to a simmer. Cover and cook on low heat for 7–10 minutes. Uncover, put in the basil and gently fold it in. Cook for another minute.

This dish may be made ahead of time and re-heated gently.

North-eastern Thailand

KOHLRABI AND CARROT SALAD
SOM TAM

Som tam, a spicy, nutty salad, is made with a julienne of green (unripe) papaya. This humble fruit-when-ripe-but-vegetable-when-green grows in practically every South-East Asian garden and, in its green form, has the texture and colour of kohlrabi – or broccoli stem for that matter – but its taste is much more delicate.

It can be used as a tenderiser (it contains papain, the main ingredient in meat tenderisers) and, because it retains its crisp texture, excellent pickles can be made with it.

Calves' Liver Salad (page 25).

It is almost impossible to get green papaya in the West. The solution, according to many Thais, is to use peeled kohlrabi, or, failing that, peeled broccoli stems.

All the ingredients in this salad are lightly crushed in a wooden or ceramic mortar. Thais use two sorts of mortars: hefty stone ones to pulverise (our electric blenders can do that) and lighter wood or ceramic ones to crush very lightly – just enough to retain original textures but force all the flavours to meld. We have no gadget that quite does this. For some of the ingredients I use an electric blender. Then I put the remaining ingredients in a heavy bowl and mash them lightly with a potato masher. I have an old, wooden Swedish potato masher. Look around your house and see what you have. Just use your imagination. *Som tam* is served with grilled meats in the north-east.

SERVES 4

| 6 dried shrimp (or 1 teaspoon anchovy pastè) |
| 1 clove garlic, peeled and crushed to a pulp |
| 1 fresh, hot green chilli, finely chopped |
| 2 small carrots (4 oz / 115 g), peeled and cut into 5 cm / 2 inch long, fine matchsticks |
| Kohlrabi or broccoli stems, peeled and cut into 5 cm / 2 inch long matchsticks (enough for 85 g / 3 oz / ⅔ cup) |
| 3 tablespoons Roasted Peanuts, see p. 201, lightly crushed |
| 2 teaspoons tamarind paste, see p. 218 (or lemon juice) |
| About 4–5 cherry tomatoes (85 g / 3 oz), cut into quarters |
| 2 teaspoons sugar |
| 1 tablespoon fish sauce, *nam pla* (or salt to taste) |

If you are using dried shrimp, you will need to grind them to a powder in the container of a clean coffee-grinder or other small spice-grinder. Empty into a bowl. Add the garlic, chilli, carrots and kohlrabi. Start crushing with a heavy object. Add the peanuts and crush some more. Put in the tamarind paste, anchovy paste if using, tomatoes, sugar and fish sauce, crushing and mixing as you go. Serve at room temperature.

Fresh baby corn, fresh straw mushrooms and mange tout (snow peas) are everyday ingredients that go into fiery soups and curries.

Chiang Mai, North-western Thailand

STIR-FRIED WATERCRESS (OR SPINACH) WITH CHILLIES
PAK BUNG FAI DANG

This dish is normally made with *pak bung*, sometimes sold as *kang kung* by South-East Asian grocers. In English, this leafy vine is often referred to as 'swamp cabbage' or 'swamp morning glory' (to which it bears a distinct resemblance, both in leaf and flower). It grows in swampy areas all over north-western Thailand and is as delicious as it is nutritious. Its cold climate cousin is watercress, though the two have very different flavours. Spinach makes as good a substitute as watercress.

I witnessed what is perhaps *pak bung's* most dramatic cookery in the north-western town of Chiang Mai where the dish is called 'flying swamp morning glory'. Once you place an order, a young man collects all the ingredients for the dish – greens, garlic, bean sauce, oyster sauce and sugar – on a plate. Then he puts a wok over a gas fire which is so intense that flames engulf it on all sides. A little oil is thrown in, then all the ingredients in the plate as well. They are stirred vigorously a few times and the contents of the wok are then emptied on to a serving plate. The dish is cooked. Then the fun starts. The greens are tossed up, seemingly to mix them again, and caught on the same plate. They are tossed higher and higher, eventually going up about 6 metres (20 feet). Then, in a final fit of bravado, the greens are tossed across the road where an assistant runs to catch them on another serving plate. Then the assistant runs back to place the plate of greens in front of you. It is hard to know whether to clap or to eat. It is quite a show.

SERVES 2–3

560 g / 1¼ lb watercress or spinach
3 tablespoons vegetable oil
2 cloves garlic, peeled and finely chopped
1–2 fresh, hot green chillies, finely sliced
1 teaspoon yellow bean sauce, finely crushed if necessary
3 tablespoons chicken stock mixed with
1 tablespoon oyster sauce.
½ teaspoon sugar

If using watercress, chop it coarsely. Spinach leaves may be left whole. Bring a large pan of water to a rolling boil. Put in the greens. Cook rapidly for about a minute or until thoroughly wilted. Drain and refresh under cold water. Drain.

Heat the oil in a wok or a large frying-pan over highish heat. When hot put in the garlic. Stir once or twice. Put in the chillies and yellow bean sauce and give another few stirs. Put in the greens. Stir once and pour in the stock-oyster sauce mixture and sugar. Stir briskly a few times and serve.

Most of Thailand
THAI JASMINE RICE
KHAO HOMMALI

Thai jasmine rice, sold by virtually every oriental grocer, is ideal for most South-East Asian meals. It does, indeed, smell of jasmine flowers and, when cooked, is shiny with just a pleasing hint of stickiness. In our family, we love the rice so much that we buy it in 11.25 kg / 25 lb bags and store it in large crocks. I do not use it for Indian food, which requires a very dry rice, but I do find it to be

the ideal accompaniment for all Chinese, Vietnamese, Thai, Malaysian, Filipino and Indonesian meals.

What with all the new cleaning methods and packaging, Thai jasmine rice does not need to be washed. I find that the results are almost better this way.

SERVES 4

Thai jasmine rice, measured to the 350 ml / 12 fl oz / 1½ cup level in a measuring jug

Combine the rice with 525 ml / 18 fl oz / 2¼ cups water in a heavy-bottomed pan. Bring to a boil. Cover tightly, turn the heat to very, very low and cook without uncovering for 25 minutes.

Rice being winnowed in a Thai village. The perfect foil to incendiary curries, salads and soups, it is eaten at most meals. In northern Thailand 'sweet' or glutinous rice is a staple food.

All over Thailand
STEAMED GLUTINOUS RICE
KHAO NIAW

Glutinous rice, sometimes labelled 'sweet rice', is used throughout the nation for making snacks and desserts, but in the north it is a staple that is eaten at all major meals. It has much more protein than ordinary rice and, as cooked in cities like Chiang Mai in the north-west and Khon Kaen in the north-east, tends to be harder in texture. Just as marathon runners in the West are told to eat pasta before a race to give them sustained energy over a long period, Thai farmworkers in the north are told to eat enough glutinous rice to carry them through a heavy work-day.

In Khon Kaen, large conical baskets filled with glutinous rice steam away in the markets. It seems that most people, rather than making it at home, just go and buy a bagful from the bazaar, the way a Frenchman would buy his *baguette* from the local baker. The accompaniments – fish stews, salads,

grilled meats and soups – are then cooked by the housewife. Glutinous rice also lasts well, better than ordinary rice. It retains its texture for 24 hours or longer without refrigeration. In Chiang Mai, it is stored in lacquered baskets where it retains some heat for long periods. It is served in small portions and formed into little balls then eaten with other foods.

Glutinous rice may be cooked in a double boiler but it is generally steamed. You may soak it overnight, or soak it in boiling water for a couple of hours.

SERVES 4

Glutinous rice, measured to the 350 ml / 12 fl oz / 1½ cup level in a measuring jug

Cover the rice well with boiling water and soak for 2 hours. Drain. Get your steaming equipment ready. (If you need directions, see p. 208.) Spread a piece of muslin, cheesecloth or a man's handkerchief over a perforated tray (or colander) and empty the rice on to the tray, spreading it out as much as possible. Put the tray in the steaming utensil, cover, and steam over high heat for 25 minutes. (If using a colander, turn over the rice once during this period.) Keep extra boiling water handy as you must not let the steaming utensil dry out.

When the rice is cooked, store it, covered, in a bowl. Do not refrigerate. It should last a good 24 hours. The only way to re-heat it easily is to steam it again for a few minutes.

Southern Thailand
SOUTHERN FRIED RICE
KHAO YAM KLUK

For lovers of both spice and rice, there could be no better dish. This is everyday breakfast food for many southern Thais, bought from the market all neatly wrapped in a banana leaf package, and eaten at home with hot coffee, sweetened – and diluted – with condensed milk, with oranges and bananas to follow.

You may use any inexpensive, freshly cooked, long-grain rice here but I do think that Thai jasmine rice, sold now by virtually every oriental grocer, is ideal. The recipe on p. 29 gives just the amount that you will need for this dish. The rice should be freshly made. It could be warm or it could be hot, it does not matter. It should *not* be cold or have been refrigerated.

SERVES 4

About half a red pepper (85 g / 3 oz), de-seeded and coarsely chopped

¼ teaspoon chilli powder (cayenne pepper)

4–5 medium-sized shallots or 1 small onion (30 g / 1 oz), peeled and coarsely chopped

2 cloves garlic, peeled and coarsely chopped

4–5 green coriander roots

¼ teaspoon ground turmeric

1 teaspoon shrimp paste, *kapi* (or anchovy paste)

4 tablespoons vegetable oil

Thai Jasmine Rice, see p. 29

1¼ teaspoons salt

20 g / ¾ oz / 4 tablespoons tender green beans, cut crossways into fine rounds

2 fresh kaffir lime leaves, central veins removed, cut into hair-thin shreds – use a pair of kitchen scissors for this (or 1 teaspoon very finely shredded lemon rind)

2–3 tablespoons chopped, fresh green coriander leaves

Put the red pepper, chilli powder (cayenne pepper), shallots, garlic, coriander roots, turmeric and shrimp paste into the container of an electric blender. Blend until you have a paste.

Heat the oil in a large, non-stick frying-pan or wok over highish heat. When hot, put in the spice paste. Stir and cook it for 3–4 minutes or until it is well fried. Now put in the cooked rice and the salt. Turn off the heat and mix the rice with the spice paste as thoroughly as possible. Add all the remaining ingredients, mix and serve. The Thais nearly always eat this at room temperature – but then their rooms tend to be quite warm.

Central Thailand
STIR-FRIED RICE NOODLES WITH PRAWNS (SHRIMP)
KUAY TIAO PAD THAI

Noodle shops, noodle stalls, noodle vendors and noodle hawkers all abound in Bangkok. Noodles, almost always fresh, make for much-loved snacks and light meals. Usually, a salesman offers several types of fresh noodles: thin and thick egg noodles and slithery rice noodles that go from threads to broad ribbons. You make a selection, such as, 'I want egg noodles in soup with long beans and chicken,' or 'I want stir-fried medium-thin rice noodles with pork and squid'. Fresh noodles cook in seconds and most other ingredients are either pre-prepared, or need just a quick blanching or re-heating. The wait is never very long. Once at your table, you can season your noodles further with crushed peanuts, fish sauce, sugar, vinegar or lime juice and crushed red chillies. These are the traditional seasonings that are there, unfailingly, in every noodle shop, sitting on the tables with as much steadfastness as salt and pepper in the West.

Having little access to fresh rice noodles, most of us will have to make do with dried ones. These flat noodles are sold by every oriental grocer, but often under their Vietnamese name, *banh pho*, even if they are manufactured in Thailand! As a substitute, you could use ordinary egg noodles. Cook them until they are slightly underdone, rinse them out in cold water and then proceed with the recipe.

This recipe also calls for preserved radish (see p. 216 for more on the subject). It is sold only by Chinese and other oriental grocers. If you cannot find it, just leave it out.

SERVES 4

115 g / 4 oz dried, flat rice noodles, *banh pho* (or see above)

5 tablespoons vegetable oil

2 cloves garlic, peeled and very finely chopped

12 medium-sized prawns (shrimp), peeled and deveined and cut into thirds

A floating noodle stall. Noodles, made from wheat or rice flour, are popular snacks and light meals.

45 g / 1½ oz / ⅓ cup finely diced preserved radish (see left)

2 tablespoons fish sauce, *nam pla* (or more oyster sauce)

2 tablespoons oyster sauce

1 tablespoon sugar

¼–½ teaspoon chilli powder (cayenne pepper)

2 tablespoons cider vinegar or lemon juice

225 g / 8 oz / 3 cups fresh bean sprouts

2 tablespoons Roasted Peanuts, see p. 201, coarsely crushed

3 spring onions (scallions), cut into 4 cm / 1½ inch lengths all the way up their green sections, then cut into fine, long strips

Garnish:

2 tablespoons Roasted Peanuts, see p. 201, coarsely crushed

For extra seasonings on the table, see opposite

Soak the noodles in cold water for 2 hours or until soft. Drain.

Heat the oil in a large non-stick pan over medium-high heat. When hot, put in the garlic. Stir a few times and then put in the noodles.

Turn the heat to medium and put in about 120 ml / 4 fl oz / ½ cup water. Also put in the prawns (shrimp), the preserved radish, fish sauce, oyster sauce, sugar, chilli powder and vinegar, mixing and stirring as you go. Add the bean sprouts and stir them in. Next, put in the crushed peanuts and spring onions (scallions). Stir them in as well.

Empty the noodles into a serving dish, garnish with more crushed Roasted Peanuts and serve.

Most of Thailand
SEASONED FISH SAUCE
NAM PLA PRIK

Here is one of the many variations of this everyday sauce. You could easily double or triple the ingredients in the recipe, if needed.

A morning market in the Chiang Mai region. Piles of vegetables are offered for sale, many of which, like the tomatoes, are grown locally.

SERVES 2

1 tablespoon fish sauce, *nam pla*

1 tablespoon lime juice
or lemon juice

1 fresh, hot red or green chilli, cut into fine rounds. (Thais would use a 'bird's eye' chilli, *prik-khi-nu*)

Mix the fish sauce, lime or lemon juice and chilli rounds together and put them in a tiny bowl to serve.

North-eastern Thailand
GRILLED CHILLI AND TOMATO RELISH
JAEW

This is a Lao relish served commonly through much of north-eastern Thailand. It has an exquisite, roasted flavour and may be served with all Thai meals from any region. The chillies and shallots are wrapped – these days foil is used – and then roasted in hot ashes until they get just a bit charred. They are

then combined with grilled tomatoes and coarsely crushed. As chillies vary so much in size, you might need to adjust the amount of saltiness and sourness.

It is a fiery condiment so it should be eaten in small quantities.

SERVES 4–6

2 fresh, hot green chillies, coarsely sliced

2 fresh, hot red chillies, coarsely sliced (or 2 more green chillies if red ones are unavailable)

5 medium-sized shallots or 1 small onion (45 g / 1½ oz), peeled and coarsely sliced

3 cherry tomatoes (60 g / 2 oz) or a small tomato

2 teaspoons lime or lemon juice

1 tablespoon fish sauce, *nam pla* (or salt to taste)

Put the chillies and shallots on a piece of foil large enough to enclose them and make a flat packet. Put the packet right on top of a low flame. Move the packet around so that all parts of it get equally exposed to the flame, and cook for about 7 minutes. Remove the chillies and shallots and either pound coarsely in a mortar or crush coarsely in a blender. Remove the paste and put in a bowl. Hold the tomatoes over a lowish flame, one at a time, and grill until lightly charred. Chop coarsely and add to the chilli mixture. Add the lemon juice and fish sauce and mix well.

All over Thailand

BANANAS IN BATTER
KLUAY KHAEK

There are banana varieties by the dozen in Thailand, and they are enjoyed in different ways. Green ones are eaten as a vegetable, riper ones may be grilled and doused with syrup or boiled in coconut milk with salt and sugar. Those designated for frying (*kluay nahm wab*) hold their shape exceedingly well. We can manage to get ours to do the same if we start off with ripe, but very firm, bananas, cut them into smaller pieces and then fry them quickly in very hot oil. They should be served as soon as they are made. They may be offered with afternoon tea – they are

really like small, melt-in-the-mouth cakes – or served as a dessert.

SERVES 4

For the batter:

4 tablespoons canned coconut milk, well stirred and mixed with 6 tablespoons water, or

10 tablespoons fresh coconut milk, see p. 212

Yolk of a large egg

115 g / 4 oz / 1 cup rice flour

½ teaspoon baking powder

¼ teaspoon salt

You also need:

2–3 ripe but very firm bananas

Oil for deep-frying

Icing sugar (confectioners sugar) for dusting over the top

Combine all the ingredients for the batter in an electric blender. The batter should be thick enough to coat the banana pieces well – but it should still be pourable. Cover and set aside.

Just before eating, heat the oil in a wok or deep-fryer over high heat. While it heats, peel the bananas and cut them crossways into 2.5–3 cm / 1–1¼ inch segments. When the oil is hot, dip the bananas into the batter to coat them thoroughly and then put them into the oil. Fry, turning around, for 3–4 minutes or until they are crisp and golden. Remove with a slotted spoon, drain well on paper towels and put on a serving dish. Dust with the sugar and serve hot.

Most of Thailand

GLUTINOUS RICE CAKES WITH SESAME SEEDS
KHOW NIAW DEANG

Here is a traditional sweetmeat, encrusted with sesame seeds, that is very easy to make. The ingredients are only found at oriental grocers but that should not stop you. If you like glutinous rice as much as I do, you will enjoy eating this enormously. Sometimes I serve a square or two of this sweetmeat with a plate of tropical fruit.

SERVES 8

Glutinous rice measured to the 250 ml / 8 fl oz / 1 cup level in a measuring jug

120 ml / 4 fl oz / ½ cup canned coconut milk, well stirred, or the same quantity of the thick creamy portion that collects at the top of fresh coconut milk, see p. 212

140 g / 5 oz / ½ cup palm sugar (or light brown sugar)

2 tablespoons freshly roasted sesame seeds, see p. 217

About ½ teaspoon vegetable oil

Cover the rice well with boiling water and soak for 2 hours. Drain. Get your steaming equipment ready. (If you need directions, see p. 208.) Spread a piece of muslin, cheesecloth or a man's handkerchief over a perforated tray (or colander) and empty the rice on to the tray, spreading it out as much as possible. Put the tray in the steaming utensil, cover and steam over high heat for 25 minutes. (If using a colander, turn over the rice once.) Keep extra boiling water handy as you must not let your steaming utensil dry out. Empty the rice out on to a plate, spread it out well and let it cool and dry out for 2 hours or a bit longer.

Put the coconut milk and palm sugar into a large, non-stick frying-pan and cook, stirring, on medium heat, until the mixture is very thick and viscous and somewhat caramelised. Turn the heat to low and put in the rice. Stir until the rice and the sugar mixture are thoroughly blended. Turn off the heat.

Rub a medium-sized plate or a 18–20 cm / 7–8 inch cake tin with just a little oil and spread out the rice evenly. Scatter the sesame seeds over the top, making a solid crust. Let the cake cool completely, then cut it into small 2.5–4 cm / 1–1½ inch squares or diamonds. You could serve the cakes on a banana or canna leaf. *Do not refrigerate.* The cakes will keep beautifully, just the way they are, for a good 24 hours.

After that, cover with cling film (plastic wrap) and leave in a coolish spot. They will keep for a few days.

This Hanoi restaurant is no more than a hole in the wall. A young woman in synthetic silk pants and with two long braids squats on the sidewalk outside it and slices shallots with speed and precision. The minuscule kitchen, half outdoors to lure passers-by and half indoors to feed the regulars, is masterminded by an old lady with no teeth and antiquated equipment. And yet, this old woman and the young one together produce the most magnificent *banh cuon*, stuffed, rice flour pancake-rolls, I have ever eaten. Soft as butter, slithery as silk, they can only be made this way when the rice is ground fresh on a stone and the watery batter steamed on a piece of muslin stretched taut over a boiling pan.

I did not know what to expect when I set out for Vietnam to examine its culinary heritage. I had been there once before, for a very short trip during the Vietnam War. It rained in sheets that time, obscuring all views and making travel impossible. On this trip, as I arrived in Hanoi in a Vietnamese aircraft, my views were obscured again, this time by fogged-up windows. I had tried cleaning them off earlier with a tissue but the fogging, by design or age, was permanent. It is strange to land in a country where you cannot see a speck of earth or sky as you hit the ground. On that, and subsequent trips, I became convinced that while Communism had managed to spread some of the world's most banal food through much of the Soviet Union, it had not done so here.

There is deprivation for sure. There is hardly any cooking oil so all the cooking is done in lard. But, in spite of the deprivation, the cooking techniques have not been lost – crisp,

Opposite: A traditional fishing net in a Vietnamese harbour.

35

batter-fried frogs' legs, encrusted with sesame seeds, are turned out with perfection – nor has the determination to eat well. The Vietnamese spirit, much like that of its erstwhile rulers, the French, during the two World Wars, would just not allow it.

The *banh cuon* restaurant is a good example. The old toothless lady stirs her thin rice batter and pours a little over the muslin, spreading it out with the back of her ladle to form the most delicate pancake. She covers it and lets it steam for a minute. Then, she scrapes it off with a chopstick, somewhat doubled up on itself, and lands it on a tray rubbed well with warm lard so it does not stick. Very fast, she stuffs it with a cooked mixture of minced (ground) pork and mushrooms, and rolls it shut. Some crisply fried shallots and green coriander leaves go on top, a few slices of sausage go on the side. This is where I come in.

I am seated at a rough, low table on a stool. My cutlery is a pair of chopsticks and a dented, tin Chinese-style spoon. The pancake-rolls come with a bowl of dipping sauce – pork stock seasoned with fish sauce (*nuoc mam*, which is used as soy sauce is in China), vinegar, sugar and chillies. Then a waiter, if one can call him that, comes with a tiny vial. He pushes a tiny swizzle stick into the vial and then into the sauce. All at once there is an intense, jasmine-like smell in the air. Was it jasmine attar? No, it was the expensive and rare extract from a water beetle, *Lecotherus indicus* to be exact. I will never forget the first bite: the satin texture of the pancake, the meaty-mushroomy stuffing, the hot, sour and sweet sauce, the crisp, savoury shallots, the garden fresh coriander and, added to that, the perfumed extract from the beetle. It was an exhilarating moment.

Eating a morsel of Vietnamese food is often like strolling through a tropical garden and then, when the moment is right, taking a bite from it. It can be intensely perfumed, with something green in it and something crisp as well. The Vietnamese even tend to form their morsels differently from anyone

else in the world. Take the pork kebabs (*bun cha*), marinated and grilled on bamboo skewers, that are sold all over Hanoi. To eat one of them, you first douse it in a dipping sauce, then you put it on a soft lettuce leaf. On top go thin rice noodles, sprigs of fresh mint, green coriander and oriental basils, plus some crushed peanuts. Then you close up the lettuce leaf package, dip it in sauce again and eat. It is all so leisurely, with no self-absorbed sense of cut and thrust, and with all diners reaching out casually with chopsticks, again and again, towards the common serving plates. Grilled meat and fish are eaten this way and so are prawn (shrimp) pancakes (*Banh Tom*, p. 42) and crisp spring rolls. The ever-present 'garden platter' not only holds lettuce leaves and herbs but could have cucumber, green banana and pineapple slices, bean sprouts, star fruit slices and lime wedges. Each mouthful can be varied slightly.

I remember once being taken to a restaurant just outside Ho Chi Minh City, right on the Saigon River. It was a resort restaurant, set up with ponds and palms in the middle of a tropical garden. The officials who were with us loved to eat and ordered up all the delicacies they felt we – and they – would enjoy. There was a shrimp salad with lotus roots, a whole chicken braised and then quickly fried until crisp, grilled and partially peeled lobster to be eaten with just salt, pepper and lime juice, minced (ground) prawns (shrimp) wrapped around sugar-cane and grilled, and a whole fish roasted over charcoal. To eat the fish, one first spread out a round of rice paper (*banh trang*). These paper-thin sheets, dried on mats until they are brittle, are softened in water until pliable before being eaten. On top of the rice paper went the lettuce leaf, then some fish, then one or more of the herbs – there was a whole basket of various mints, basils and more – *rau que, rau tia to, rau hung cay, rau hung lui, rau ram* and *rau vap ca* – then a piece of pineapple or star fruit. One wrapped it all in the rice paper, dipped it in watery sauce and ate. It really was like eating the garden we were in

and taking a dip in the pond, besides.

It is exactly this use of raw greenery that makes Vietnamese food so entirely different from that of its powerful neighbour, China, who ruled and dominated the northern Red River delta area for over 1000 years from the second century BC. I remember once being in the kitchen of a Cantonese friend in Hong Kong. He was preparing a dish of pork and

long beans. As he cooked, I idly picked on the lovely green beans, munching on them with great delight. The Chinese around me seemed horrified. 'How can you eat raw vegetables?' one asked. I had never thought about it before. There are no raw greens in Chinese cuisine. Lightly cooked, yes. Raw, absolutely not. It was anathema to me. I consulted an anthropologist, Eugene Anderson of the University of Southern California and author of *The Food of China* to find out why. He suggested that because the Chinese have used night soil to fertilise their fields since ancient times the genuine fear of bacteria could well be the reason. But why were the countries south of China unaffected by this? At any rate, there is a clear line between the large, influential country that looks at raw vegetables and seems to say, 'We are not amused' and the countries south of it that seem to breathe them in. The line is drawn at Vietnam.

From the Chinese, the Vietnamese acquired the use of chopsticks and soup bowls. They learned how to drink tea, in little handle-less cups, from teapots kept 'cosied' in padded baskets, and how to eat egg noodles, bean curd and bean sprouts, use soy sauce (though not too frequently) and live with Confucian values.

From the French, who had virtually taken over the country by the late sixteenth century, they learned how to make sausages out of meat and fish, to make variations of pâté, to make crab and asparagus (canned, alas) soup and enjoy French breads, croissants and butter. (A Hanoi friend told me that his mother, who happens to be a staunch member of the Communist Party, insists, to this day, on having her rice with fish sauce *and* butter.) They also learned to enjoy cognac – flambéd bananas (see p. 56) are a great favourite – speak French and wear jaunty berets.

On one cyclo (tricycle-rickshaw) trip to Madame Dai's, a restaurant in Ho Chi Minh City which came highly recommended and where we shed our official escorts and

Steamers like this one are used to cook foods from fresh rice noodles, a staple of the Vietnamese diet, to the cassava being prepared here.

sneaked off on our own, we found ourselves tucking into *bifteck* (*saignant, mais naturellement*) and *pomme frites*!

The Indians began setting up trading posts *en route* to China well before the start of the Christian era, and their influence is ever-present but harder to define. Curry pastes and curry powders certainly go into dishes in the south – we were once fed an outstanding chicken stir-fried with lemon grass, shallots, red chillies and a touch of curry powder. There is also the all-pervasive influence of Buddhism with vegetarian days at least twice a month.

Then, there is the matter of pancakes and rice noodles. The Vietnamese eat a large variety of pancakes, many of which require mung beans and/or rice in some form. Mung beans originated in India and pancakes are mentioned in ancient Indian texts going back 4000 years. No one is quite sure where rice originated. Ancient grains have been found both in the Indus valley of what is now Pakistan and in northern Thailand. What I do know for sure is that if one travels to South India today, one will find freshly steamed rice noodles and steamed rice cakes – all prepared from ground rice batter – being made in every single home, using much the same techniques as the lady making *banh cuon* in the hole in the wall in Hanoi. There *is* a connection. I am convinced of it. Though who influenced whom is harder to sort out.

Transporting a boat – Vietnamese-style. Fish sauce is an ingredient in *nuoc cham*, the country's national condiment.

Anthropologists will, no doubt, track it down for us some day. Rice noodles probably did not originate in China. Once, much of China, especially the north, did not have rice at all. It was the planting of hardy Champa rice from Vietnam that made large areas of China change from eating millet, barley and, later, wheat to eating rice.

In spite of all the foreign influences, Vietnamese food is charmingly itself, garden fresh, irresistible, and like no other in East Asia.

It is rice, fresh rice noodles and fish sauce that may be considered the staples of Vietnamese cuisine. To these, the poorest people in the north might add some *rau muong* (swamp morning glory) stir-fried with garlic

and chillies. We certainly saw large quantities of this nutritious water vine being carried home on the backs of bicycles. There are fish – a lot of them from the many rivers and lakes – as well as crabs and prawns (shrimp), frogs and lobsters in the diet. Pork is the most common meat. As with the rest of South-East Asia and China, almost every part of the pig is consumed, including its skin which is particularly good in cold, jellied dishes. Pork is marinated and grilled, made into meatballs and sausages and stewed with dried bamboo shoots. Pork is also minced (ground) and combined with crab to go on top of toast. It is used as a filling for snails and, when vegetables are stir-fried, little bits are added for extra flavour. Beef, which came into China and Korea with marching Mongols, entered Vietnam the same way. Hanoi's most famous noodle soup, *pho*, is traditionally made with rare beef, though today most people seem to make do with chicken *pho*. For thousands in the northern capital, *that* is the perfect breakfast.

I am in need of breakfast. The charming but crumbling Thong Nhat hotel where I am staying has nothing good to eat. I head for Cam Chi Street where there is plenty. That is where the citizens eat.

The stock for *pho* bubbles away in a cauldron at the crack of dawn. The steam, bearing the characteristic smell of roasted ginger and onions, rises up at first and then hangs low on this bitter-cold morning. Offices open early here. The flimsy plastic rainwear of summer has been replaced by heavy khaki, grey and blue jackets and coarse sweaters. On many heads there is some sort of hat or beret. Some cyclists, and there are thousands of them, speed by with masks over their mouths. Children on the backs of bicycles are shielded from the biting wind with large plastic bags. The trees that line the wide avenues look cold and dusty. Grand colonial mansions, their paint crumbling, have closed up their long green shutters. On this chilly December day, it is clear that Hanoi is not quite the tropics.

What better way to warm up than with a bowl of *pho* from one of the many food stalls on Cam Chi Street. As soon as the order is placed, fresh rice noodles are dipped in hot water to heat them. They go into a bowl. These can be topped with cooked chicken, fully cooked beef, medium-rare beef or raw beef, the price ascending with each choice. Mints, coriander, spring onions (scallions) follow. Then hot stock gets ladled over the top, wilting the greens and perfuming the air still further. As a change from *pho*, there is *bun thang*, another noodle soup with a prawn- (shrimp-)flavoured broth containing pork balls and mushrooms. There are other choices. How about glutinous rice with cane sugar embedded in it, or duck eggs, hard-boiled and fried? Men who have breakfasted squat in a circle around a black-toothed lady wearing black pants and a black scarf. She offers tea, sweet mung bean cakes and, to conclude, toothpicks. They cover their mouths with one hand and pick away.

Lunch offers other choices. The largest crowd seems to be outside the open-fronted shop where hundreds of smallish French *baguettes* are stacked up against a wall. Buyers swoop in on bicycles and form a line. Two young women work with speed. One splits open a loaf and butters it – it is Russian butter. Another fills it with cheese – it is Russian cheese – or with Vietnamese sausage (see p. 48) or with slices of pâté (called *baté* here). She also salts and peppers it, rolls it in paper (which may well contain a print-out of a political speech or be an old page from the BBC's now defunct *Listener*), and then twists a rubber band around the roll. The enclosed sandwich speeds away on a bicycle.

Those with a little more money may choose the Railway Restaurant, known for its fried pigeons, and feast on crab egg-drop soup, marinated and fried pigeon, rice and salad. The salads are usually excellent. They may be made with bean sprouts or with kohlrabi and carrots or with mung bean threads and chicken. The dressings are usually made without oil, with only vinegar,

Open-air food stalls are a feature of Vietnamese life. Some, like this village one, are comparatively simple. Others, in cities, are more sophisticated and the food they sell is a reminder of the many influences that have merged to form Vietnamese cuisine: baguettes from the French, pancakes from India and egg noodles from the Chinese.

salt and sugar as basic flavourings and herbs, chillies and peanuts added for intensity.

Most workers tend to take their own lunches to work from home – perhaps some vegetables stir-fried with pork or beef stir-fried with bamboo shoots. Both are eaten with rice. Tea is ever-present in thermos flasks. There is always a flask of strong tea and a flask of hot water to dilute it with. Dinners are rather like lunches, with soup, rice, a vegetable, and a meat, chicken or fish for those who can afford it. Sometimes people opt for snacks from the market: shrimp-filled pancakes (see p. 52), or simply a fertilised duck egg, boiled and eaten with salt, chilli, shredded ginger and herbs.

If Hanoi has the feel of hard Spartan existence that, with better markets and supplies, is improving by the day, Ho Chi Minh City, formerly Saigon, has the feel of a sweet life turned sour. Teenage Amerasians wearing 'I love New York' T-shirts were selling pathetic packets of peanuts near our hotel and our local guide was in tears over her change of circumstances. Restaurants like Madame Dai's – she was once a very successful lawyer, her husband was a doctor – exist precariously under the watchful gaze of the government. Hulking ships moored on the Saigon River, that were once vast, floating restaurants and dance halls, appear almost skeletal. And yet, this city has so much more than its northern counterpart. We saw artichokes in the market – 'they should be boiled with a pork bone, salt, sugar and monosodium glutamate,' I was advised, wonderful bean curd marinated with lemon grass and chillies, vats of pickles, enormous rice wafers encrusted with black sesame seeds (beyond compare, I yearn for one now) and roasted meats, ready to go. Our official escorts from Hanoi vied with each other to accompany us here. For them, this was the big fun city, throbbing with restaurants, bars and music. There is indeed, among the younger set here, a sense of fun and hope. The young men zoom around on motor cycles and the young women get their hair done at salons and wear lipstick.

Ho Chi Minh City is warmer than Hanoi and definitely tropical. Southern food is often spiked with lemon grass, chillies and curry powders, the sharper flavours sometimes mellowed and sweetened with fresh pineapple, which is used almost like a vegetable, or coconut milk. But, with better transport and communication between north, south and the centre, many regional differences have blurred.

Of the many restaurants we ate in – and

Dried noodles are in the foreground on this market stall – as they are in the Vietnamese diet.

the food was superb in all – there was one devoted mainly to hotpots. Freshwater fish, prepared with pineapple, tomato and okra and garnished with herbs and crisply fried shallots, seemed the hot favourite there. Another restaurant, slightly out of town, which looked like a zoo complete with caged snakes and fruit bats, was devoted entirely to exotica. Each animal, or reptile, is meant to have certain properties and you come here when your body needs fine-tuning – or when you can afford it as it is very expensive. In assigning medicinal properties to foods, the Vietnamese are very like the Chinese. Indeed, the snake soup we ate there was made with Chinese medicinal herbs. It was dark in colour and tasted somewhat like, but far better than, the best *pot-au-feu* I have ever eaten. I am sure it was good for me.

On our last day in Vietnam, we are invited to lunch by an old couple. Both husband and wife are veterans of wars with the French, the Japanese and the Americans. They share their home with their children and grandchildren. The government is obviously proud of them.

Medals and citations, as well as pictures of Ho Chi Minh, decorate the blue walls of the living-room. A ceiling fan whirs overhead cooling off the ancient warrior with bushy white brows and gentle smiling face, who swings in a hammock, his wits and humour still with him. He was once the treasurer for the Viet Cong and saw to it that money was transported wherever it was needed.

A small hall connects the living-room to the next room, which is used for dining. It is really a multi-purpose room as it not only houses the round dining-table with its brightly flowered plastic tablecloth, but a new motor cycle and an ironing board. The younger women of the house, granddaughters and daughters-in-law, are all clustered in the farthest room, the kitchen, their hair held back with determined head-bands.

Rice has already been set to steam in an electric rice cooker. Families such as this one receive subsidised foods – noodles, rice,

cakes, flour – through a food service. The midday meal is simple. There is a pork soup with carrots, beets and spring onions (scallions) in it; egg noodles stir-fried with pork strips and green beans; rice; and fried

Women at work in a paddy field. Steamed rice is an essential part of most Vietnamese meals and is also ground to make the flour used in pancakes, noodles and rice cakes.

fish. All the cooking is done on two paraffin stoves and a hotplate. As we sit and eat around the table, reaching out with chopsticks towards the foods in the centre, dipping our fish into the seasoned fish sauce and pouring soup into our rice bowls, a young granddaughter advises me. 'Take some more chillies,' she says. She also tells me about her Russian language homework and I tell her about the outside world. She is only 10 years old and full of curiosity.

RECIPES FROM VIETNAM

Urns in front of a Vietnamese temple.

Hanoi, Vietnam

AROMATIC FISH SOUP WITH DILL
CANH CÁ THIÁ LÁ

We were served this soup out of a small office in Hanoi. Desks were cleared of dusty files and a small stove set up in their stead. This is done with some frequency for parties: people hardly ever entertain at home. At such functions, everyone pitches in and cooks.

As with many soups in South-East Asia, this is really a soup-stew. It is traditionally served with the meal and eaten with plain rice, vegetables, salads and condiments. I tend to serve it separately, Western-style, as just a soup. It is sour, aromatic and hot and stands well on its own. You could even serve some crusty French bread with it.

River fish steaks are used in Hanoi but any firm, white-fleshed fish would do: fillet of sole or flounder, cut into neat squares, or chunks of cod, halibut or grey mullet. I have also tried the soup with prawns (shrimp) and it was superb.

SERVES 4–5

6 dried Chinese mushrooms

340 g / 12 oz boned, firm, white-fleshed fish (see above)

Salt

2 medium-sized tomatoes (340 g / 12 oz), dropped into boiling water for 15 seconds then peeled

1.2 litres / 2 pints / 5 cups Chicken Stock, see p. 197, lightly salted

2 tablespoons tamarind paste, see p. 218 (or lemon juice to taste)

1 tablespoon fish sauce, *nuoc mam* (or salt to taste)

2 spring onions (scallions), cut into very fine rings all the way up their green sections

4–5 tablespoons finely chopped fresh dill

1–2 fresh, hot red (or green) chillies, cut into fine rounds

Soak the mushrooms in hot water for 30 minutes or until soft. Cut off and discard the hard stems. Cut the caps into quarters.

Cut the fish into 2–2.5 cm / ¾–1 inch pieces. Sprinkle about ¼ teaspoon salt on all sides of the fish and set aside for 20 minutes.

Cut the tomatoes in half crossways. Hold one half at a time in your hand and gently squeeze out as many seeds as possible. Cut the shell into 5 mm / ¼ inch dice. Set aside.

Combine the stock, tamarind paste and fish sauce in a pan. Bring to a simmer. Taste and adjust seasonings, if needed. Drop in the fish and mushrooms and simmer very gently until the fish is cooked through. This will happen quite quickly. Now put in the spring onions (scallions), dill, chillies and tomatoes. Cook for another 30 seconds. Serve hot.

Hanoi, Vietnam

POTATO PANCAKES WITH PRAWNS (SHRIMP)
BÁNH TÔM

Matchstick potatoes with whole prawns (shrimp) embedded in them, held together with a light batter and then fried – that is what these crunchy, crusty and quite wonderful pancakes are all about. They are cut into wedges and eaten with a salad, mainly lettuce and fresh herbs.

Vietnamese friends reminisce about going to eat these pancakes near Hanoi's West Lake when they were students. The pancakes were abundant but their funds were not. So they would order up very few pancakes (which had to be paid for) and a mound of salad (which was free), much to the annoyance of the vendor.

This dish makes an ideal appetiser though you may also serve it as a snack. You may prepare it, partially, ahead of time. Do all the steps except the last frying. The pancakes will hold for a good few hours. The last frying should be done just before you eat so that the pancakes remain crisp.

You may substitute sweet potatoes for the potatoes.

MAKES ABOUT 12 PANCAKES

About 20 medium-sized prawns (shrimp), peeled and deveined. (You may leave tails attached, if you wish)

75 g / 2½ oz / ½ cup strong (all purpose) white flour

75 g / 2½ oz / ½ cup rice flour

About 275 ml / 9 fl oz / 1 cup hot, skimmed milk

½ teaspoon ground turmeric or a few drops of yellow food colouring

¾ teaspoon baking powder

½ teaspoon salt

Lots of freshly ground black pepper

340–370 g / 12–13 oz potatoes, peeled and cut into matchsticks. (Keep in water until needed, then drain and pat dry)

About 4–5 tablespoons vegetable oil plus more for shallow-frying

For the salad:

A head of soft lettuce, the leaves separated and washed

Lots of sprigs of fresh mint

Lots of sprigs of fresh green coriander

Fish Sauce with Lime Juice and Chilli, see p. 56, divided among individual bowls. (Make an extra batch, if needed)

About 4 tablespoons Chilli Oil, see p. 199

A floating village on one of Vietnam's many waterways. Lakes and rivers are a prolific source of freshwater fish.

Cut each prawn (shrimp) in half lengthways. Set aside. Put the 2 flours in a bowl. Slowly add the hot milk, mixing well with a whisk. This batter should be just a little thicker than crêpe batter. Adjust the amount of milk to achieve this. Allow the mixture to cool and then add the turmeric, baking powder, salt and black pepper. Mix. Add the potatoes and mix again.

Heat 2 tablespoons vegetable oil in a frying-pan (preferably non-stick) over medium heat. Remove about 2 heaping tablespoons of the batter-potato mixture and put it in the pan. Spread it out quickly with

the back of a spoon so that it is not too thick. Quickly embed 3 prawn (shrimp) halves in it, pressing them in well. Pour out 1 or 2 pancakes more, just as many as your pan will hold easily and press in prawn (shrimp) halves as before. Cook for about a minute, just until the bottom is set. (You are not cooking the pancakes through at this point.) Turn over the pancakes and cook the prawn (shrimp) side for another 30 seconds or until it, too, is set. Remove. Prepare all the pancakes this way, adding only a little more oil to the pan as needed.

Just before eating, arrange the lettuce

River fishermen at work in their traditional, flat-bottomed boats.

leaves and herbs on a large serving plate and set on the table. Also put out the bowls of Fish Sauce with Lime Juice and Chilli and the Chilli Oil. Heat about 5 mm / ¼ inch oil in a large frying-pan over medium-low heat. When properly heated, put in as many pancakes as will fit in easily. They should sizzle immediately. Fry slowly for about 4–5 minutes on each side. Remove with a slotted spoon and drain on paper towels. As the first few pancakes get made, keep them warm or eat immediately. Make all the pancakes this way.

To eat, cut each pancake into 3–4 wedges. Diners can do this on their own plates. Put one wedge inside a lettuce leaf, put a sprig of mint and another of coriander on top and dribble a drop of Chilli Oil on top of that. Fold the lettuce over to make a bundle, dip the bundle in the Fish Sauce with Lime Juice and Chilli and eat.

Ho Chi Minh City, Vietnam

PRAWN (SHRIMP) SALAD
GỎI NGÓ SEN

From the Khu Du Lich Binh Quoi Thanh 'Da restaurant near Ho Chi Minh City

This salad consists of basil-flavoured, stir-fried (or grilled/broiled) prawns (shrimp) arranged around a salad of boiled and slivered lotus root, slivered carrots and Chinese celery. Since it is hard for many of us to find lotus roots and Chinese celery, I have left them out and substituted ordinary celery in the place of both. If you can get lotus roots, peel or scrape one 'link' and cut into julienne strips about the same size as the carrots. Keep them in water until cooking time. Then steam or boil them until they are tender. This can take from 20 minutes to over an hour, depending upon the maturity of the roots. Drain and use.

SERVES 4

For the salad:

2 tablespoons vegetable oil

3 cloves garlic, peeled and cut into fine slivers

2 spring onions (scallions), cut into fine rounds all the way up their green sections and put in a bowl

1 celery stick (about 40 g / 1½ oz) from the middle of the bunch, cut into fine, 5 cm / 2 inch long julienne strips

2 medium-sized carrots (about 150 g / 5 oz), peeled and cut into fine, 5 cm / 2 inch long julienne strips

1 large onion (120 g / 4½ oz) peeled, halved lengthways and cut into fine half-rings

½ teaspoon sugar

¼ teaspoon salt

1 tablespoon fish sauce, *nuoc mam* (or salt to taste)

2 teaspoons lime juice (or lemon juice)

Freshly ground black pepper

2 tablespoons Roasted Peanuts, see p. 201

For the prawns (shrimp):

2 tablespoons vegetable oil

3 cloves garlic, peeled and finely chopped

275 g / 10 oz unpeeled medium-sized prawns (shrimp), peeled and deveined, or 215 g / 7½ oz peeled and deveined prawns (shrimp)

1 tablespoon fish sauce, *nuoc mam* (or salt to taste)

1 tablespoon lime juice (or lemon juice)

8–10 fresh basil leaves

8–10 fresh mint leaves

Garnish:

A few sprigs of fresh green coriander

Fresh, hot red (or green) chillies, cut into slices, slivers or flowers, see p. 211

Make the salad: Heat the 2 tablespoons oil in a small frying-pan over medium-low heat. When hot, put in the garlic. Stir and fry until they are golden and crisp. Remove with a slotted spoon and spread out on paper towels. Take the hot oil in the frying-pan and pour it over the spring onions (scallions). This will wilt them.

Combine the celery, carrots and onion in a

Fisherman in a coracle.

bowl. Combine the sugar, salt, fish sauce, lime juice and black pepper in a small cup. This is the salad dressing. Coarsely chop the peanuts and set them aside.

Just before serving, pour the salad dressing over the celery, carrots and onions. Add the fried garlic, the spring onions (scallions) and the oil they are in, as well as the peanuts. Toss well.

Heat the oil for the prawns (shrimp) in a frying-pan over high heat. When hot, put in the garlic. Stir and fry for 30 seconds or until the garlic is golden. Put in the prawns (shrimp). Stir and fry for 2–3 minutes or until the prawns (shrimp) are opaque. Add the fish sauce and lime juice. Stir. Tear up the basil and mint leaves and throw them in. Stir once or twice.

Arrange the salad in the centre of a serving plate. Garnish with the green coriander sprigs and chillies. Surround it with the cooked prawns (shrimp) and serve.

Ho Chi Minh City, Vietnam

WHOLE FISH WITH SWEET AND SOUR SAUCE
CÁ BÔNG LAU SAUCE CHUA NGOT

If you do not wish to cook a whole fish, you may salt and flour fish steaks and then cook them in exactly the same way. In Vietnam, as in China, whole fish are auspicious and heads are offered to honoured guests. (When a Western friend was offered an eel's head she politely, but firmly, returned it!)

Instead of the *bong lau*, a freshwater fish, you may use rainbow or plain trout, grey mullet, sea bass, catfish, carp or red snapper. Even whole sole and flounder may be used. If steaks are preferred, try cod, haddock or halibut. I have used a whole sea bass.

SERVES 3–4

For seasoning the fish:

Whole 800 g / 1¾ lb fish (see above), cleaned and scaled

1 teaspoon salt

1 teaspoon sugar

Freshly ground black pepper

For the sauce:

3 tablespoons vegetable oil

1 large onion (115 g / 4 oz), peeled and cut crossways into thin half-rings

2 small carrots (115 g / 4 oz), peeled and cut into 5 cm / 2 inch julienne strips

175 ml / 6 fl oz / ¾ cup Chicken Stock, see p. 197, or Pork and Chicken Stock, see p. 197

1 teaspoon cornflour (cornstarch) dissolved in about 1 tablespoon stock or water

¾ teaspoon salt, or to taste

1 tablespoon tamarind paste, see p. 218 (or lemon juice)

2 teaspoons sugar

Freshly ground black pepper

75 g / 2½ oz / ½ cup fresh pineapple slices, each cut into 8 wedges (or, at a pinch, unsweetened, canned pineapple in its own juice)

1 small tomato, cut into wedges

1–3 fresh, hot red or green chillies, cut crossways into thin slices

You also need:

About 1.5 litres / 2½ pints / 6 cups oil for deep-frying

Cornflour (cornstarch) for dredging the fish

Season the fish: Wash the fish well and pat dry. Cut deep, diagonal cuts across it on both sides, about 5 cm / 2 inches apart, going all the way down to the bone. Rub inside and out with the salt, sugar and black pepper. Set aside for 20–30 minutes.

Make the sauce: Heat the oil in a medium-sized pan over medium-high heat. When hot, put in the onion and carrot. Stir and fry until they wilt. Put in the stock, cornflour (cornstarch) mixture, salt, tamarind paste, sugar and black pepper. Stir and bring to a boil. Turn the heat down to a simmer. Taste for balance of sweet and sour, making adjustments if necessary. Add the pineapple, tomatoes and chillies. Stir once and turn off the heat. Leave the sauce in the pan.

Heat the oil for deep-frying in a large wok over medium-high heat. While it is heating –

and it will take time to heat up – dredge the fish well in the cornflour (cornstarch). Shake extra flour off it. When the oil is really hot – a piece of bread should foam instantly – slip the fish into it carefully, head first. Baste the top with oil, using a large kitchen spoon, and fry for 5–6 minutes. Using 2 spatulas, carefully turn the fish over and fry them for another 5–6 minutes. Keep basting the top with the hot oil. When the fish is firm and crisp, turn off the heat. Now remove the fish very carefully from the oil with 2 spatulas. Pause briefly over the wok to let the extra oil drain off, then transfer the fish to a large serving dish.

Heat the sauce again and pour over the length of the fish. Serve immediately.

Ho Chi Minh City, Vietnam

GRILLED CHICKEN WITH LIME JUICE AND LEMON GRASS
GÀ NUÒNG

This exquisitely seasoned dish may be cooked over charcoal or under the kitchen grill (broiler). Rather like *tandoori* chicken, it requires an overnight marinading period but is otherwise quite straightforward in its preparation. It is slightly hot, sweet, sour and aromatic – in other words, utterly delicious. You will want to make it again and again.

Traditionally, this chicken is served with Glutinous Rice (see p. 199) and an array of fresh herbs and lettuce leaves. I serve it both hot (with Asian salads, vegetables and rice) and cold (at picnics).

Use four dried red chillies if you want it mild, eight if you want it hot. If lemon grass is unavailable, double the ginger.

SERVES 6

2.35 kg / 4¾ lb chicken pieces (legs and breasts)

7 tablespoons lime juice (or lemon juice)

Salt

3 spring onions (scallions), cut into very fine slices all the way up their green sections

1 tablespoon dried, sliced lemon grass or 1 stick of fresh lemon grass, if available (or see above)

8–10 slices dried galangal

4–8 dried, hot red chillies

Half a large red pepper (about 125 g / 4 oz), de-seeded and coarsely chopped

2.5 cm / 1 inch cube of fresh ginger, peeled and coarsely chopped

Half a medium-sized onion (40 g / 1½ oz), peeled and coarsely chopped

2 cloves garlic, peeled and finely chopped

2–3 tablespoons sugar

2 tablespoons vegetable oil

2 tablespoons fish sauce, *nuoc mam* (or an extra ½ teaspoon salt)

Freshly ground black pepper

Separate the whole chicken pieces into drumsticks and thighs. Cut 2–3 deep, diagonal slits on each side of each drumstick and into the fleshy part of each thigh. Halve each breast lengthways and then cut each section in half crossways. Cut 2 deep slits into the fleshy part of each breast section, staying away from the edges.

Spread the chicken out on 1 or 2 large serving plates in a single layer. Sprinkle ¾ teaspoon salt over one side and then dribble 3 tablespoons of the lime juice over the same side. Rub the spices in, going well into the slits. Turn the pieces over and do the same on the other side with another ¾ teaspoon salt and 3 tablespoons lime juice. Sprinkle spring onion (scallion) slices over both sides of the chicken and rub these in as well. Set aside for 30–60 minutes.

In a small bowl, combine the dried lemon grass, the dried galangal and 4 tablespoons water. Crumble the dried red chillies and put them to soak in the same bowl. Soak the dried spices for about 30 minutes. (If using fresh lemon grass, cut crossways into very fine slices, from the bottom and going up about 15 cm / 6 inches. Set aside.)

In the container of an electric blender, combine the red pepper, ginger, onion and

Grilled Chicken with Lime Juice and Lemon Grass (this page).

Ho Chi Minh City, Vietnam

STIR-FRIED BEEF WITH LEMON GRASS
BŌ XAŌ XĀ ÍỔŤ

This simple and wonderful recipe comes from the Nha Hang Noi Nha Be, a floating restaurant on the wide Saigon River. It must have been a rocking, throbbing place once, when the Americans were here. We climb a gangplank to get to the ship and find the place mostly deserted. A massive hall and a stage for an orchestra are ghostly shells, gathering rust and dust. The only sounds are of busy boats, determinedly plying the waters. We sit at the tables set up on the deck and enjoy the breeze. Besides us, there are only five or six other takers. Our guide recalls the good times and sings us a plaintive song.

This dish is very simple to prepare. All the chopping and cutting can be done ahead of time. The last-minute cooking takes all of 5 minutes. Serve it with plain rice and any vegetables or salads of your choice.

SERVES 4

For the marinade:

450 g / 1 lb lean beef steak, cut crossways against the grain with the knife held at a slight diagonal, to get thin slices. (It helps if the meat is slightly frozen first.)

1 stick of fresh lemon grass, first cut into very fine rings starting from the bulbous bottom and going up about 15 cm / 6 inches then very finely chopped (or 1 teaspoon powdered lemon grass)

1 fresh, hot red (or green) chilli (more, as desired), very finely chopped

1 small onion (30 g / 1 oz), peeled and very finely chopped

¾ teaspoon freshly ground black pepper

1 teaspoon sugar

1 tablespoon Chinese light soy sauce

2 teaspoons fish sauce, *nuoc mam* (or extra soy sauce to taste)

1 tablespoon vegetable oil

1 teaspoon cornflour (cornstarch)

½ teaspoon curry powder

For the final stir-frying:

4 tablespoons vegetable oil

1 medium-sized onion (85 g / 3 oz), peeled and cut into fine half-rings

Garnish:

4–5 tablespoons fresh green coriander leaves

Combine all the ingredients for the marinade. Mix well. Cover and set aside for 1 hour or longer, refrigerating if necessary.

Just before eating, heat the oil in a large wok or frying-pan over highish heat. When hot, put in the onions. Stir and fry for about 2 minutes or until the onions are somewhat browned. Put in the meat and all its marinade. Stir and fry on high heat until the meat is just cooked through. Put in a serving dish. Garnish with the green coriander leaves and serve immediately.

All over Vietnam

VIETNAMESE SAUSAGE ROLL
GIŌ / CHÃ LUA

When my children were small in New York, one of their biggest treats was being taken to the butcher. The reason was that the butcher invariably offered each child a thin slice of cold 'bologna' – fine pork sausage.

This same type of sausage is sold throughout Vietnam. It is called *gio* in the north and *cha lua* in the south. I cannot think of a food that is eaten there with greater enjoyment by people of all ages. It is cut into neat squares or rectangles and eaten with pancakes and salads or just as it is, with drinks. In the markets of the north, I saw it being slapped inside a crusty roll of French bread with lots of black pepper sprinkled on it. In the south, sandwiches made with French bread include this sausage, cucumber, lettuce and red chillies. In fact, while we were filming in Ho Chi Minh City, this is what we were often offered for lunch. The sausage is also cut into slices and fried, just as you might fry a slice of ham. (It is excellent with eggs that way.)

Gio or *cha lua* is just the thing to have in the refrigerator at all times. It keeps for a good week and may also be frozen. I usually keep half in the refrigerator and freeze the rest for later use. What is more, it is quite easy to make.

MAKES A 23 x 7.5 CM / 9 x 3 INCH ROLL

800 g / 1¾ lb lean pork, cut into coarse cubes

200 g / 7 oz pork fat (the butcher will give this to you), cut into small cubes

5 tablespoons fish sauce, *nuoc mam* (or 4 tablespoons Chinese light soy sauce)

2 teaspoons potato flour (potato starch)

1 teaspoon sugar

1 teaspoon salt

1 teaspoon baking powder

Combine all the ingredients in a bowl. Mix well, cover and refrigerate overnight. Next day, put all the marinaded ingredients in a food processor and blend until you have a smooth paste. You may need to do this in 2 batches.

Cut two 33 cm / 13 inch pieces of cling film (plastic wrap). Lay one down on your work surface. Lay the second one down 15 cm / 6 inches below the start of the first one, making for a slightly bigger sheet. Using a dampened rubber spatula, take out all the paste from the food processor and lay it in a rough sausage-shaped roll somewhere below the top of this piece of partially doubled plastic, going left to right. What you are aiming for is a roll that is about 23 cm / 9 inches long and about 7.5 cm / 3 inches in diameter. Use wet hands to pat it into shape. Now roll the sausage within the plastic to enclose it. Twist the ends of the sausage to seal the package. Wrap the package once again in the same way, in a large piece of heavy-duty foil, and twist the ends to seal it.

Bring a large, wide pan of water to a rolling boil. Drop the wrapped sausage into the water. I use a pan that is about the same size as the sausage and wedge it in so that it stays anchored. If yours floats up, put a weight on it so that it stays below the top of the water. Cover partially, turn the heat to medium low and simmer gently for 1½ hours.

A woman prepares her wares at a village stall. Customers select their own combinations of foods from the bowls set out in front of her.

Hanoi, Vietnam
GRILLED PORK KEBABS
BÚN CHÁ

Thin slices of pork are marinated and grilled over charcoal. They are then wrapped inside small bundles of lettuce leaves along with fresh rice noodles, roasted peanuts and herbs, dipped into well-seasoned fish sauce and eaten.

Since fresh rice noodles are very hard to come by in the West, most South-East Asians make do with dried rice sticks, which are thin and vermicelli-like and need pre-soaking, or with *somen*. *Somen* are not made of rice at all but of wheat and are a Japanese product. They are always referred to as 'alimentary paste', whatever that means. They are so well liked by South-East Asians living abroad that many have convinced themselves that they are actually made of rice. When a Thai grocer tried to convince me of this, I looked incredulous and said, 'But look at the label. It says "wheat".' 'Ah,' said the grocer, 'this is only to fool the customs officers. If the packet said "rice", it would not be allowed into the country.'

Somen comes in 450 g / 1 lb packets of five, ribbon-tied portions. If you wish to use it, drop it into boiling water for 1–2 minutes or until just done. Drain it and then wash it off with fresh tap-water to get rid of the extra starch. Dribble a little oil on it and mix.

You may use meat from a pork knuckle or, as I do, use boned pork tenderloin. The grilling can be done outdoors in the summer. For the rest of the year you can pan-fry, a very satisfactory and quick method.

SERVES 4

For the marinade:

340 g / 12 oz boneless loin of pork, cut into 3–5 mm / ⅛–¼ inch thick slices
2 teaspoons Chinese dark soy sauce
1 teaspoon fish sauce, *nuoc mam* (or Chinese light soy sauce)
1 teaspoon sugar
2 spring onions (scallions), cut into very fine rounds all the way up their green sections
Freshly ground black pepper
1 teaspoon vegetable oil

For the noodles:

225 g / 8 oz dried rice sticks

You also need:

Fish Sauce with Lime Juice and Chilli, see p. 56, made without garlic but with carrot, and divided among 4 bowls
Head of soft-leafed lettuce, the leaves separated and washed
Small sprigs of fresh mint
Small sprigs of fresh green coriander
Small bowl of Roasted Peanuts, see p. 201
About 2–3 tablespoons vegetable oil

Cut the pieces of pork into rectangles that are roughly 5 x 2.5 cm / 2 x 1 inch. They will not all be perfectly shaped but that is acceptable. Put them in a bowl. Add all the other ingredients for the marinade and mix well. Cover and leave in the refrigerator overnight.

Soak the rice sticks in warm water for 2–3 hours or until soft. If there are any hard clumps, they should be cut off. Drain. Pour boiling water to cover the noodles. Let them sit for 2 minutes. Drain again. The noodles are now ready to be eaten. Divide them between 4 bowls and set them on the table. Set the Fish Sauce with Lime Juice and Chilli on the table as well. Arrange all the lettuce leaves on one platter and the herbs on another. Take these, and the bowl of peanuts, to the table.

The meat should be cooked just before eating. You may thread pre-soaked bamboo skewers or metal ones in and out of the meat pieces, lengthways, and grill outdoors, or do what I do. I pan-fry. To do this, heat a large, cast-iron or non-stick frying-pan brushed with about 1 tablespoon oil over highish heat.

When very hot, lay down as many meat pieces as will fit in easily. Brown one side – this takes very little time – turn over the pieces and brown the second side. Remove and put on a warm plate. Do all the pork pieces this way, brushing the pan with oil as needed.

To eat, dip a piece of meat in the Fish Sauce with Lime Juice and Chilli and then place it in the centre of a lettuce leaf. Put some mint, coriander, peanuts and noodles on top of the meat. Close up the lettuce leaf package, dip again in the seasoned fish sauce and eat.

Hanoi, Vietnam
SAUTÉD SPINACH WITH GARLIC AND CHILLIES
RAU DỀN XÀO TỎI Ở'I Í

This dish is generally made with swamp morning glory, also known as swamp cabbage or water spinach. You should certainly use it if you can get your hands on it. It is sold in most 'China Towns' around the world, often under the name *kang kung*. (In Vietnam, it is known as *rau muong*.) It is a vine with leaves that are heart-shaped at the top and bottom and very elongated in the middle. The stalks are tougher than the leaves. They are generally split lengthways and put into the wok first. Swamp morning glory cooks very much like spinach and is exceedingly nutritious. In the north, many people survive on just this, a variety of fish sauces and rice.

SERVES 4–6

675 g / 1½ lb spinach
4 tablespoons vegetable oil
5–6 cloves garlic, peeled and finely chopped
1–2 fresh, hot red or green chillies, finely sliced
2 tablespoons chicken stock
1 tablespoon fish sauce, *nuoc mam* (or Chinese light soy sauce)
¼ teaspoon salt

Bring a large pan of water to a rolling boil. Drop in the spinach. As soon as it wilts, drain it and leave in a strainer. Heat the oil in a wok or large frying-pan over medium-high heat. When hot, put in the garlic. Stir and fry until the garlic turns light brown. Put in the chillies and stir once or twice. Put in the spinach, the stock, fish sauce and salt. Turn the heat to high. Stir-fry on the highest heat until the spinach is well flavoured with the other ingredients, another minute or so.

Hanoi, Vietnam

STUFFED TOMATOES
CÁ CHUA NHÔÌ

The stuffing here, made with pork, black fungus and mushrooms, is used commonly to stuff bean curd, cabbage leaves and aubergines (eggplants) as well as tomatoes. Such vegetables are generally served with rice but at times they sit atop a bed of salad greens, dressed with a French vinaigrette. I serve mine over a bed of watercress (a large bunch – about 130 g / 4½ oz), tossed with a dressing containing 1 teaspoon Dijon mustard, 2 teaspoons red wine vinegar, ¼ teaspoon salt, ¼ teaspoon sugar and 4 tablespoons olive oil.

SERVES 4–5

6 dried Chinese mushrooms
1½ tablespoons black fungus
About 4 tablespoons (approx.) cellophane noodles
4–5 large, well-shaped tomatoes (900 g / 2 lb) with stable bottoms
Salt
250 g / 8 oz minced (ground) lean pork
4 teaspoons fish sauce, *nuoc mam* (or Chinese light soy sauce)
Freshly ground black pepper
1 egg, lightly beaten
1 spring onion (scallion), cut into fine rounds all the way up its green section
2 tablespoons vegetable oil

Soak the mushrooms in hot water to cover for 30 minutes or until the caps are soft. Lift out of the water, remove and discard the hard stems. Cut the caps into very thin slices.

Soak the black fungus in plenty of warm water until soft. Feel for the hard 'eyes' and cut them off. Chop the fungus finely.

Soak the cellophane noodles in plenty of warm water until soft. Drain and cut into 2.5 cm / 1 inch lengths.

Cut caps off the tops of the tomatoes. Using a spoon, remove all the inside pulp and seeds without perforating the shells. Sprinkle ⅛ teaspoon salt inside each shell and set aside for 15 minutes. Drain the shell thoroughly and pat the inside dry.

In a bowl, combine the pork, mushrooms, black fungus, noodles, fish sauce, black pepper, egg and spring onion (scallion). Mix well and stuff the tomatoes with this mixture.

Heat the oil in a frying-pan over medium-low heat. When hot, put in the tomatoes, cut-side down. Cover and cook slowly for about 10 minutes. Turn the tomatoes over carefully. Cover and cook another 5 minutes. Serve hot.

Southern Vietnam

SIZZLING PANCAKES
BÁNH XÈO

Pancakes of some sort exist in every nation. Vietnam has a great variety of them. This one, from the south, hints at distant Indian parentage, what with the use of turmeric and mung beans. The stuffing, however, of prawns (shrimp) and pork, is very East Asian as is the sauce and salad it is served with.

The pancakes may be made a few hours ahead of time and then either wrapped in foil and heated in a moderate oven (gas mark 4 / 350 °F / 180 °C) for about 10–15 minutes or they may be heated, unwrapped, in a microwave oven for a few minutes, one at a time.

MAKES ABOUT 6 STUFFED PANCAKES

For the pancakes:

225 g / 8 oz / 1½ cups rice flour
1½ teaspoons sugar
½ teaspoon salt
1 teaspoon baking powder
½ teaspoon ground turmeric
475 ml / 16 fl oz / 2 cups fresh coconut milk, well stirred, see p. 212, or 250 ml / 8 fl oz / 1 cup canned coconut milk, well stirred and mixed with the same amount of water

For the cooked stuffing:

60 g / 2 oz / ½ cup hulled and split mung beans
1½ teaspoons vegetable oil
1 medium-sized onion (85 g / 3 oz), peeled and cut into fine half-rings
115 g / 4 oz lean pork, cut into fine, 5 cm / 2 inch long slivers
12 medium-sized prawns (shrimp), peeled and deveined and cut in half lengthways
1½ teaspoons fish sauce, *nuoc mam* (or Chinese light soy sauce)
A good pinch of sugar
Freshly ground black pepper

You also need:

3 tablespoons vegetable oil
85 g / 3 oz / 1¼ cups fresh bean sprouts
7–8 whole plants of Chinese chives, cut into 5 cm / 2 inch lengths (or 24 stalks of ordinary chives, cut into 5 cm / 2 inch lengths)
Fish Sauce with Lime Juice and Chilli, see p. 56
A plate of fresh vegetables and herbs which should include soft lettuce leaves, sprigs of fresh green coriander and mint, and cucumber slices

Combine the rice flour, sugar, salt, baking powder and turmeric in a bowl. Add half of the coconut milk and mix well with a whisk. Cover and set aside for 3–4 hours or overnight. Refrigerate the remaining coconut milk. One hour before cooking the pancakes, stir the refrigerated coconut milk and add it to the batter. Mix well.

Soak the mung beans in water for 3 hours. Drain and put in a small pan. Add enough water to cover them by 2.5 cm / 1 inch and bring to a simmer. Cook for about 10 minutes or until the beans are just tender. They should remain whole. Drain, rinse under cold water and set aside.

Hanoi Noodles in Broth with Chicken (page 54).

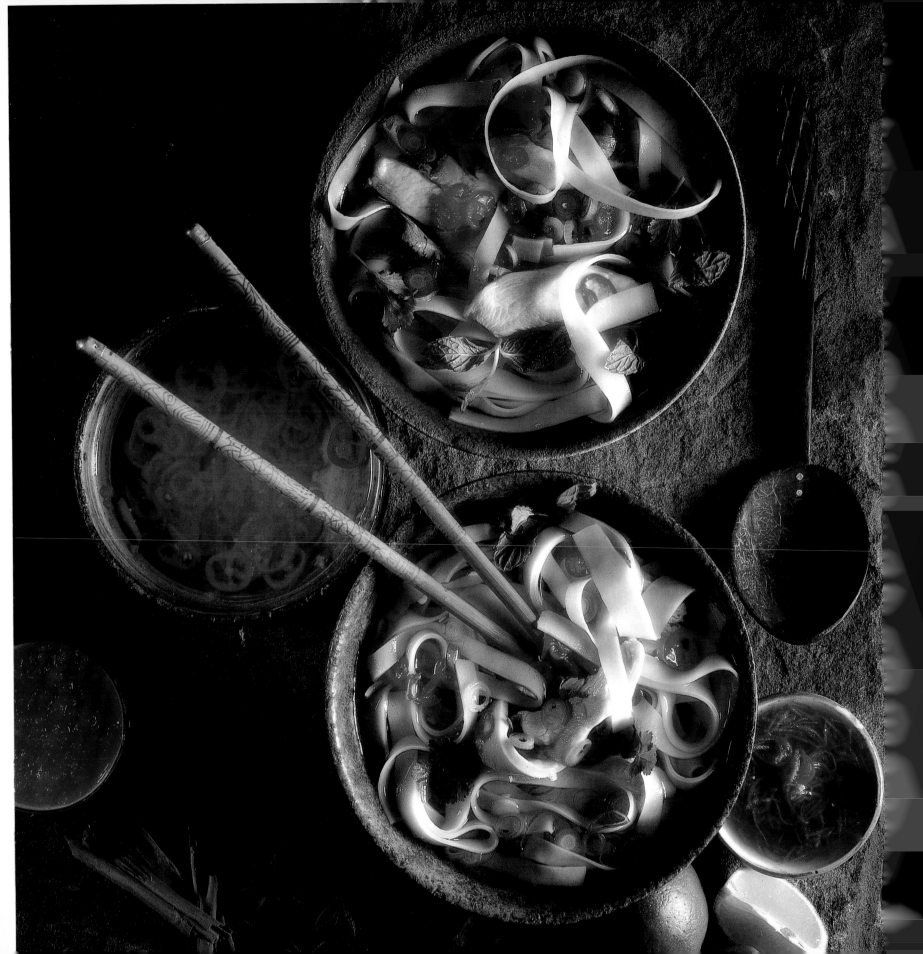

is used in the north and, to my surprise, I noticed that tamarind water was being used for this purpose in the south.

Mustard cabbage, also known inaccurately

Nuoc mam, being prepared above, is made from dried fish and has a special flavour that is all its own.

as mustard greens, is sold under the name *gai choy* by Cantonese-speaking Chinese grocers in the West. It is almost always available and has a mustard-like pungency. Its stems are thick and grooved, the leaves are dark green. If you can find it, do use it.

I have made the pickle here with ordinary green cabbage as the tastes are similar. You may add a clove or two of peeled garlic to the pickle if you wish. Also, you could increase the sugar if you prefer a sweeter pickle. In Ho Chi Minh City, they often add extra sugar to the pickle bowl just before they bring it to the table. My own preference is for the less sweet variety.

These pickled vegetables may be served with Western meals.

SERVES 4

| 4 tablespoons distilled white vinegar |
| 1 teaspoon sugar |
| 2 teaspoons salt |
| 450 g / 1 lb green cabbage, cored and cut crossways into 4 cm / 1½ inch wide strips |
| 2 medium-sized carrots (170 g / 3½ oz) peeled and cut crossways into 3 mm / ⅛ inch thick rounds |
| 1 medium-sized onion (85 g / 3 oz), peeled and cut into 5 mm / ¼ inch thick half-rings |
| 1 fresh, hot red (or green) chilli, halved lengthways (optional) |

Put the vinegar, sugar and salt into a deep glass or ceramic bowl. Mix. Bring 475 ml / 16 fl oz / 2 cups water to a boil and pour into the bowl. Let the mixture cool off to the point where it is barely warm. Now put in all the other ingredients. Upturn a smallish plate over the vegetables and put a heavy weight on top. The idea is to force the vegetables to stay submerged. To improvise a weight, I often fill a large, glass pitcher with water and, for good measure, put some glass paperweights in it as well. Do not use any metal. Leave the pickle this way for 2–3 days or until the vegetables stay submerged of their own accord. You may now put the pickle into jars and refrigerate it. Take out only what you need for a meal. The pickle should last over a month in the refrigerator.

All over Vietnam

FISH SAUCE WITH LIME JUICE AND CHILLI
NUOC CHAM

This is the national sauce. It is the seasoning that appears on every table in Vietnam. It is used as a dipping sauce, dribbled over grilled meats and, in the kitchen, used for braising and flavouring. It tastes a bit like a limeade. The garlic is optional and so are the carrots. I find that the carrots are rather good in dipping sauces.

SERVES 4

| 4 tablespoons fish sauce, *nuoc mam* |
| 2 tablespoons distilled white vinegar |
| 2 tablespoons fresh lime juice (or lemon juice) |
| 2 tablespoons sugar |
| 1 fresh, hot red (or green) chilli, cut into fine rounds |
| 1 clove garlic, peeled and crushed (optional) |
| 2 tablespoons peeled and grated carrot (optional) |

In a work bowl, combine all the ingredients. Add 4 tablespoons water and stir until the sugar is dissolved. Pour into individual bowls or use as needed.

All over Vietnam

BANANAS FLAMBÉ
CHUOI CHIEN

This is a French-Vietnamese speciality, much loved among those who can afford cognac. On our trips to Vietnam, whenever we asked officials what 'gifts' we might bring back, they repeatedly suggested State Express 555 cigarettes and cognac. On our returns, we brought back cognac. The French influence remains strong even though the French themselves have left.

This amount of batter is enough for at least a dozen good-sized bananas, if not more. Start out by making only one banana per diner. I find that many of my guests ask for second helpings. It is very easy to fry up a second batch, if needed.

SERVES 6–8

| 130 g / 4½ oz / 1 cup strong white (unbleached white, all purpose) flour |
| 115 g / 4 oz / ¾ cup plus 1 tablespoon potato flour (potato starch) |
| 2½ teaspoons baking powder |
| 2 teaspoons vegetable oil plus oil for shallow-frying |
| 12 very firm but ripe bananas |
| About 12 tablespoons sugar |
| About 250 ml / 8 fl oz / 1 cup cognac |

Put the white flour in a bowl. All at once, pour in 175 ml / 6 fl oz / ¾ cup water. Stir to mix until smooth. It will be thick and pasty. Cover and set aside, unrefrigerated, overnight.

Next day, mix the potato flour (potato starch) and baking powder in a bowl. Add half of this mixture as well as 1 teaspoon of the oil to the flour batter. Also add 85 ml / 3 fl oz water and mix well. Now add the remaining potato flour (potato starch) mixture and another teaspoon of the oil. Mix well.

It is best to use 2 large frying-pans for frying the bananas. Put about 2 cm / ¾ inch oil in both pans and put over medium-low heat. Allow the oil to get really hot. This will take at least 10 minutes. Peel as many bananas as will fit into the frying-pans without touching. Dip each thoroughly in the batter and lay in the hot oil. They should sizzle immediately. It is important that the bananas not touch each other or they will lock together. Fry until one side is a rich golden-brown and crisp, about 3½ minutes. Turn over carefully with 2 wooden spatulas and cook the second side in the same way. Remove from the pan with a slotted spoon and leave to drain on a plate lined with paper towels. Put the bananas in a large serving dish. Sprinkle about 1 tablespoon sugar over each banana. Heat some of the cognac (allow about 1⅓ tablespoons per banana) in a small pan until a haze appears. Light the cognac with a match and then pour it over the bananas. Keep turning the bananas as you pour the flaming cognac over them. This will keep the flame going and also distribute the brandy.

Serve the first batch of bananas. Make a second batch, if needed, in exactly the same way.

Yellow and green bananas contrast colourfully in a market. The recipe for flambéd bananas on this page is a gastronomic reminder of the French influence in Vietnam.

KOREA

The November day was bright and sunny but the wind, carrying portents of the future, blew icily, picking up drying leaves and blowing them about in circles. In field after field, the Chinese cabbages stood upright in neat raised rows, not a weed in sight, each head carefully tied in the middle with cord so that no erring leaf would drag on the ground and require trimming.

I had been told to return to South Korea in the middle of November if I wished to see an annual ritual which is centuries old: the making of winter *kimchee* (Korean cabbage pickle). So here I was, in the prosperous village of Chilwon, south of Seoul, on the pre-arranged date, watching one of the last farm activities before the onset of winter.

The village women, some in baggy pants, others in skirts, bent down and cut the cabbage heads with a quick snip while the men piled them on motorised carts. Two hundred heads of cabbage, weighing about 1.5–2 kg/3½–4½ lb each, would feed a family of ten for about 3–4 months, I was told, and fill about seven large ceramic jars. This was a village of 450 people, so much work lay ahead.

If there is one food that is found at every meal, on every table, in every season in Korea, it is *kimchee*. In its most common version it is made with cabbages, but *kimchees* of radishes, cucumbers, even ginseng, are also eaten with passion. Addictively tart, garlicky and hot – and rich in minerals and Vitamin C besides – *kimchee* is not a main dish. It is really a condiment. But, along with Japanese-style, short-grained rice which replaced the millet and barley of earlier times, it is a staple here, eaten as a side dish. Korea is perhaps the only country in the world where a condiment has attained such

Opposite: A 19th-century farmhouse in a South Korean folk village.

A woman prepares the ingredients for kimchee.
This condiment is a staple food in Korea.

she reaches the other – a neat trick. These are combined with julienned carrots, spring onion (scallion) pieces, chopped ginger, garlic, fresh oysters, salted shrimp, salt and lots of freshly crushed red chilli powder, brilliantly carmine in colour. The mixture is tasted and pronounced good. The men, who have been standing around, now move in. They cannot resist taking a bite. One tears off a wilted cabbage leaf, wraps some stuffing in it and pops it into his mouth. He looks heavenward with satisfaction. Others follow.

The women put some of the stuffing between each leaf and then tuck the cabbage bundles into a giant ceramic jar. As jars are filled, a few men carry them up a hill and bury them up to their necks in the earth so they do not freeze in the coming months. A plastic collar is put around the necks to

importance that a meal is inconceivable without it.

The motorised carts carry the cabbages into an enclosed, whitewashed courtyard where more women wait, the older ones wearing the traditional long robes, *hanboks*, all squatting near large basins. They set to work. Each cabbage head is trimmed at the bottom

and then split in half, lengthways. It is dipped gently, almost cradled, in salted water, and lifted out again. Coarse sea salt is thrown between each leaf and the cabbage halves left to wilt for 10 hours. The next day they are washed again to rid them of the salt. Meanwhile, the stuffing is prepared.

Giant white radishes are thinly sliced and spread out in an overlapping row like a deck of cards. One woman starts cutting them into fine matchsticks at one end with a well-sharpened cleaver and does not pause until

Aromatic kaenip leaves are used raw to make
morsels of grilled meat and rice.

prevent dirt from getting in, then a lid and
finally a stone is put on top so the bubbling,
seething, fermenting pickle will not ooze
out. This cabbage will be ready to eat in
3–4 weeks.

When all the pickling is done, the entire
village celebrates with *pattok*, steamed rice
flour cakes layered with red beans, secure in
the knowledge that another winter will pass
with a bankable supply of vegetables.

Late autumn may be the time to make and
store large quantities of winter *kimchee*, but in
the crowded cities few have that kind of
space or time. Yet *kimchee* has to be at the
table, winter and summer.

Mrs Han, Chung Kyu lives in a small,
high-rise apartment in Seoul's suburbia. She is
an eldest son's wife. As such, her duties are
clear. She must, with gentleness and humility
– as well as strength – serve her in-laws and
her husband. To this end, she makes two
buckets full of *kimchee* four times a month, all
through the year. One bucket goes to her
in-laws, the other stays with her in the
apartment she shares with her husband and
two children.

In the last two decades, South Korea has,
with hard work and gritty determination,
hurled itself with enviable success into the
modern, industrialised world. I can hardly
recognise Seoul from when I visited it for the
first time in the 1970s. Skyscrapers loom over

Chillies drying outside a farmhouse on the volcanic island of Cheju. In the background are some of the orange trees that provide fruit for the whole nation.

a newly cleaned Han River. Sleek buses glide from stop to stop. Restaurants are expensive and parking is impossible to find. But Confucian values remain ingrained. Mrs Han, who worked as an airline stewardess once, chafes somewhat at her burdens. Yet she does what has to be done. On pickling days, she seats her small children in front of musical and mechanical toys and gets to work in her small but modern, well-equipped kitchen.

She squats on the floor where she has all the space she needs and, wearing rubber gloves over her manicured hands and using electric blenders and food processors where needed, does all the necessary pickling. When she finishes, she tucks her stuffed cabbages into plastic buckets, covers them and leaves them to mature for several days in her small pantry.

Kimchee is not only eaten as a side dish, it goes into soups and stews and is considered so important to the country's heritage that, in South Korea's capital city of Seoul, a whole museum is devoted to it. There was a time when, for the very poor, kimchee and rice could constitute an entire meal. But there are not many such people left in this newly prosperous country. For breakfast most people these days can afford to add a large bowl of beef soup with radishes or bean sprouts in it. The rice, kimchee and soup are then eaten with Korea's unusual cutlery: a pair of thin, knitting-needle-like metal chopsticks and a long-handled spoon. For lunch and dinner, more dishes are added: there may be fish stew, containing chunky pieces of fish, bean curd and briny clams that have just been steamed open, all floating in a fermented bean paste (toen chang) broth; some lightly dressed vegetables, flavoured with sesame oil, which the Koreans do so well – bean sprouts, aubergine (eggplant) or spinach; some stir-

fried squid, fiery with chillies; perhaps a pancake made with mung beans or rice flour; and, best of all, some beef, either grilled or made into a stew.

Rice remains the staple and is always served in individual metal bowls. But ancient likes have not been forgotten so today's rice is frequently mixed with the barley and millet of bygone years.

The seasonings used are not unlike those of China and Japan, Korea's powerful and influential neighbours: sesame seeds, sesame oil, spring onions (scallions), ginger, soy sauce, chillies, vinegar, fermented soy bean pastes and garlic. But the way they are used – and their proportions – are entirely different. Take sesame seeds, for instance. They are used in such quantities that our Mrs Han, Chung Kyu, who pickles for her in-laws, buys them by the tubful in the autumn when they have just been harvested and prices are low. Small quantities at a time are roasted, lightly crushed with salt and kept within reach in a jar, to be sprinkled on foods just as we might black pepper.

Or take garlic. To a Chinese person, raw garlic would be anathema. The Koreans thrive on it, recognising its ability to cleanse the blood and also revelling in its pungent taste. Whole, peeled garlic cloves sit on restaurant tables, to be nibbled on at will or to be grilled whenever the opportunity presents itself. In many stir-fried dishes, garlic is added not at the beginning but towards the end so that its taste is no mere hum in the background. Most markets and supermarkets sell already peeled cloves. The only effort required of the housewife is to throw them into her shopping basket or trolley.

Chillies too are used with a generous hand. Korean chilli powder, roughly pounded and glowingly carmine in colour, is among the best in the world. A cross between paprika and hot chilli powder, it is relatively mild and is used by the fistful, making many foods, from pickles to fish stews, a brilliant, glorious red. Apart from crushing the chilli skins, Koreans – it is usually old women who do

this – painstakingly cut them into hair-thin threads. These are used mainly as a garnish. It is not uncommon to see a mild dish of braised bean curd decorated prettily with a few, scattered red threads. Both the Korean chilli powder and the chilli threads now reside permanently in my spice cupboard to be used in foods that are Korean, and also in foods that are not.

The Korean taste for beef is unusual for this region of East Asia, where fish, poultry and pork are kings. For many people in Seoul today, their Sunday outing consists of a drive with the family to some newly built resort area. It could be by a stream in the hills such as the villa-style restaurant built just near the president's house, surrounded by carefully designed 'rustic' huts. Here, with mothers, grandmothers and children in tow, they first admire the scenery and then settle down at outdoor tables to get on with the serious business of eating bulgogi (marinated and grilled-at-the-table beef) or kalbi chim (beef ribs braised with radishes or with Korea's large, sweet chestnuts).

A taste for beef is said to have galloped in with the Mongols who had already conquered much of Asia and some of Europe as well. Koreans are actually of Mongol descent, owing their heritage to Mongol tribal groups that migrated south from what is now Manchuria in prehistoric times. But it was the warring, pillaging, thirteenth-century Mongol armies that decided that the best place to raise horses and cows was on the pasture lands of Cheju Island in the south. That pastoral tradition continues to this day.

Cheju is a paradisic isle. Carpeted with azaleas and rhododendrons in the early summer and a source of all of Korea's mushrooms and tangerines in the autumn, the island is the volcanic creation of one major mountain, Mount Halla, which rises more than 2000 metres/6000 feet smack in its centre. As streams and waterfalls make their way to the blue sea, they go through vast pasture lands that were once the domain of Korean overlords and kings. Today, divided

Freshly caught fish is unloaded from a boat. Seafood of all kinds from oysters to mackerel has always been an essential part of the Korean diet.

into American-style ranches, they are privately owned and some are set up on as many as 81 000 hectares/200 000 acres. New wealth has brought Charollais, Herefords and Aberdeen Angus to these shores and new silage in the form of Italian eyegrass. While the taste for beef was always present, the money to indulge it was previously restricted. Now, even the fisherman returning in his trawler after 2 weeks at sea wants his *bulgogi* and his *kalbi chim*. These are, to the newly prosperous South Koreans, what steak was once to the newly prosperous Americans.

If the love of beef and the ability to indulge in it is the sign of moving on, then the daily diet of fish and seafood is the sign of constancy. Korea is surrounded by the sea

on three sides and the fruits of the sea are almost mother's milk to the nation. Salted shrimp and oysters are added to *kimchee* not only to hasten the fermentation process but to add mineral value: they melt away almost without trace, leaving only a richness behind. Roe is pickled, octopus is pickled and so are crabs. All sit in tubs in the markets, glowing the Korean chilli red. In the harbour town of Pusan, huge fishing vessels spew out the fish catch from their cavernous bellies through wide, umbilical-cord-like tubes: mackerels, groupers, blow fish, all come flying out, landing in monstrous bins from where they are sent further afield. Some even get as far as *kisseng* houses.

Ah, those *kisseng* houses! I had no right to be there but was taken to one in Seoul out of pity by a businessman who realised that I might burst with curiosity if I were not. Rather like geisha houses in Japan, they cater only to men. The *kisseng* girls, wearing

flowing *hanboks* for dinner and trendy silk pants at more casual lunches, entertain with music, poetry and more. While I was there, two such damsels were seated with us on cushions at a low, lacquered rectangular table in a private room. All they seemed to do was feed my host morsels of food and mop his brow whenever a drop of perspiration made its unwanted appearance. Since the food was fiery, there was much mopping to be done.

We started with cold rice wine (*popchu*) from the south-eastern Kyonju area and six different varieties of *kimchee*, one even made from radish leaves. Then came fish roe cured in a garlicky sauce, chillied crabs' legs, slices of raw, white fish reminiscent of Japanese *sashimi*, some anchovies sautéd with chillies, batter-dipped fish slices, and a whole snapper doused in a sesame-flecked sauce (*saengsun yangyum chang kooee*, see p. 00). Lightly dressed spinach and dried courgettes (zucchini) were set out as well. These were only the first courses. Soups and stews were yet to come: red snapper with leeks and potatoes; beef with fish and bean curd; seaweed with taro; and pork with *kimchee*. The young, pretty *kisseng* girls removed choice pieces of fish from their bony moorings and popped them into my host's mouth. At other times they made bundles in lettuce leaves of rice and roe or fish and *kimchee* and placed them on our small plates. For dessert, there was fruit as there always is in Korea: translucent persimmons from the Seoul area and crisp apples from Taegu, all peeled, cut and ready for devouring.

City slickers depend upon the fish that comes from neighbouring waters but many have lost their ties to the sea. It is perhaps only on islands like Cheju that the lives of the people and the sea are ceaselessly intertwined.

A shaman ceremony is taking place by the sea, in a compound enclosed by a wall of black basalt stones to keep the wind at bay. There are many such walls here on Cheju, stark and utterly beautiful, trailing up and down the moors. Many of the old thatched huts are made of the same stones though they are slowly being replaced by more mundane dwellings. At the ceremony, The Great Female Spirit of the island is offered some of Cheju's harvest – oranges, apples, pears, pineapples and grain cakes – so that she may ensure the safety and harvests of the

Freshly gathered abalone, mussels and sea urchins for sale on a beach.

fishermen and the diving women. The sea too is propitiated. A miniature sailboat with similar offerings is set adrift . . . fruits are cast into the water. As they bob in the waves all thoughts are for those who toil on or in the sea.

The lives of the diving women, called *haenyo* or 'women of the sea', are not easy. When I had seen them in the 1970s, young and all dressed in white, they had seemed like romantic nymphs. This time I was invited to go on the boat with them and was even

taunted to follow them into the water.

In this semi-matriarchal society, it is the women who make a living, diving for whatever the bottom of the sea offers – sea urchins, mussels and the prize, abalone – most of which is eaten raw and accompanied with spicy sauces.

We set out on a cold, foggy afternoon when the tide is going out. The women dive all year, even in freezing weather. They do not eat before they dive. It is only when they return, a good 4–5 hours later, that they sit

A *haenyo*, one of Korea's 'women of the sea', who dive for mussels, abalone and other delicacies. A net attached to the float holds her catch.

down to a reviving bowl of stew made with *toen chang* (bean paste), fish, bean curd and cockles.

The men collect the women from their homes in vans, transporting about 30 of them to the docks that lie in the shadow of flat-topped Songsan Sunrise Mountain. Here they clamber on to three motor-powered boats, with the men working the engines.

Right away, the women start to change their clothes. The white suits are a thing of the past. First, they put on double layers of underwear and then roll on black, spongy wet suits. They are not young nymphs any more, these women. Some are in their late 30s and 40s. Others in their 60s. The workings of wind and weather have etched deep creases in their faces. They complain of headaches, earaches and chest pains. In the old days, one says, diving women used to teach their daughters the craft. At 12 or 13, the girls were already diving for seaweed, the kind that goes into the making of the gelatin, *agar agar*. By 16, many had graduated to abalone. Today's young girls are refusing to join the profession. They prefer to work in beauty salons, even in factories, one diver snorts.

Headgear goes on, flippers go on. Goggles are rubbed with mugwort and sea water so they do not cloud over, and they too are slipped on. By this time, we have lost sight of the shore. The fog is all around us. One by one the women jump off, carrying plastic floats with an attached net to hold the shellfish and a stone to anchor the float. A pair of flippers goes up in the air and one diver has gone 10 metres/35 feet under. The others follow. Many stay submerged for more than 3 minutes. To co-ordinate and space their breathing, they emit high, whistle-like sounds before they dive. Perhaps this also lets their men know where they are. In the fog, the eerie, repeated whistles sound like the lonely calls of whales.

As the women work, the men pull their three boats together, hop on to one of them and settle down to a bottle of *sochu*, a mild, gin-like drink made from potatoes. The women will be in the water for a good 3–4 hours. There is a lot of time to kill.

There is a shout from one of the diving women. I wonder if she is hurt. Many get run over by boats. No, what she wants is a spear. She has spotted something. Within seconds she pops up again, triumphantly holding a speared, red-flecked fish. She tosses it on to the deck. This is her gift to the men.

A knife is sharpened and the fish instantly transformed into *saengsun hwae*, which is the same as Japanese *sashimi* – and served up on a piece of plastic. Would I like some, I am asked. It is the sweetest, most delicate, *sashimi*, or sliced raw fish, I will probably ever taste. The men use a mixture of *kochu chang* (hot, fermented bean paste) and vinegar as a dip and eat and drink as the women dive and dive. The leader of the diving women will, at the end of the day, sell all the shellfish to the Fisheries Cooperative Union. Twenty per cent of the money will go to the men, the rest will be divided among the women.

It is a hard life for the women but many of the divers have done well by it. Some own fields of sesame and rape. Others own tangerine orchards. What is best, they say, is that they can afford to send their sons to college in Seoul!

RECIPES FROM KOREA

A selection of seafood snacks.

All over Korea

AUBERGINE (EGGPLANT) SALAD WITH SESAME SEEDS
KHAJI NAMUL

Considered both a salad and an appetiser, this is generally served at the start of a meal but stays on the table until the very end. (Incidentally, it also goes very well with cold lamb and chicken.)

The ideal aubergines (eggplants) to use for this recipe are the slim, long, oriental variety. If you cannot get them, use the ones that are normally available but get the smallest size.

SERVES 4–6

560 g/1¼ lb aubergines/eggplants (see below left)
2 cloves garlic, peeled and crushed
1 spring onion (scallion), cut into very fine rings all the way up its green section
2 tablespoons roasted, lightly crushed sesame seeds, see p. 217
1 tablespoon sesame oil
3 tablespoons Japanese light soy sauce
2 tablespoons distilled white vinegar
¼ teaspoon salt
1 tablespoon sugar

If using oriental aubergines (eggplants), quarter them lengthways and then cut each piece crossways into half. If using regular aubergines (eggplants), cut them into long sections that are about 2.5 cm/1 inch thick and wide. Steam (see p. 208), covered, for about 15 minutes or until tender. Let the pieces cool slightly and then pull them by hand into thin, long strips. Add all the other ingredients and mix well. Taste and make adjustments, if needed. Serve at room temperature or cold.

All over Korea

BEAN SPROUT SALAD
KONG NAMUL

A crunchy, nutritious and easy-to-prepare salad, this is served in all Korean homes and in many Korean restaurants as a much-loved side dish. In restaurants, it often appears at the start of a meal to be nibbled upon with drinks and *kimchee* as one waits for the more substantial foods.

This salad also happens to be equally good when made with the firmer and larger soy bean sprouts. In the West, these sprouts are generally found only in the 'China Towns' of larger cities. If you wish to use them, you will need to parboil them for about 5 minutes instead of the 30 seconds specified in this recipe.

Needless to say, the quality of the salad will depend upon the freshness of the sprouts.

SERVES 4–6

675 g/1½ lb/7 cups fresh mung bean sprouts (or see above)
5 spring onions (scallions), cut into very thin rounds all the way up their green sections
3 tablespoons sesame oil
2 cloves garlic, peeled and crushed to a pulp or very, very finely chopped
1 fresh, hot red or green chilli, cut into fine rounds (optional)
½–¾ teaspoon chilli powder (cayenne pepper)
¾–1 teaspoon salt, or to taste
1 tablespoon roasted sesame seeds, see p. 217

Break off the tops and tails of the bean sprouts if you feel up to it. Wash well in a bowl of water and drain.

Bring a large pan of water to a rolling boil. Drop in the sprouts and boil rapidly for 30 seconds. Drain immediately and rinse under cold water. Gently squeeze out as much water as possible and then put the sprouts in a bowl.

Add the spring onions (scallions), sesame oil, garlic, sliced chilli, chilli powder (cayenne pepper), salt and sesame seeds to the bean sprouts. Toss well and taste, adding a bit more of any of the seasonings listed above if you so wish.

All over Korea

SQUID WITH CHILLIES AND VEGETABLES
OJHINGU BOKUM

With their homeland surrounded by the sea on three sides, Koreans seem to relish almost every fruit the waters bear, from seaweeds and tiny anchovies to large tuna. Squid is exceedingly well liked: it may be grilled, dried and also made into spicy stir-fries. This is a very spicy, stir-fried dish, using both the hot, fermented bean paste known as *kochu chang* and Korea's excellent, coarsely pounded red chilli powder. This powder, while hot, is not killingly so and its best feature is its excellent carmine colour. In order to

Rows of squid are hung out to dry in the open air. This well-liked food is eaten in a variety of ways: dried, grilled or made into stir-fries as in the recipe on this page.

reproduce this, I have used a combination of bright red paprika and our more ordinary chilli powder (cayenne pepper). If you can get the Korean powder, use 1 teaspoon, or a bit more if you like.

This dish cooks fast so have all the ingredients cut and ready and cook it just before you eat. If you are pressed, you may cook this ahead of time and then re-heat it. The vegetables will lose some of their original crispness but will still taste good.

SERVES 3–4

560 g / 1¼ lb cleaned squid, see p. 207

1 medium-sized carrot (85 g / 3 oz), peeled

1 medium-sized onion (85 g / 3 oz), peeled

1 smallish courgette / zucchini (115 g / 4 oz)

2–3 long, fresh green chillies, preferably of medium heat

2–3 long, fresh red chillies, preferably of medium heat, or a quarter of a red pepper (60 g / 2 oz)

3 tablespoons vegetable oil

1–2 cloves garlic, peeled and crushed

Salt

3 teaspoons Hot Fermented Bean Paste, *kochu chang*, see p. 200

1 teaspoon bright red paprika

½ teaspoon chilli powder (cayenne pepper) – use more or less as desired

Freshly ground black pepper

1 teaspoon sugar

2 spring onions (scallions), cut diagonally into 4 cm / 1½ inch lengths. Quarter the lower white section lengthways first

2 teaspoons sesame oil

2 teaspoons roasted sesame seeds, see p. 217

Cut open the squid's sacklike body so that it lies flat and then cut it crossways into pieces that are about 6 x 1 cm / 2½ x ½ inch. The tentacles can be cut into 6 cm / 2½ inch lengths.

Cut the carrot crossways into 6 cm / 2½ inch chunks. Now cut the chunks lengthways into 3 mm / ⅛ inch thick slices.

Cut the onion into half lengthways, and then crossways into 5 mm / ¼ inch thick slices.

Cut the courgette (zucchini) into half lengthways, and then crossways into 3 chunks. Cut each chunk lengthways into 3 mm / ⅛ inch thick slices.

Cut the green and red chillies into halves lengthways, and remove all seeds and membranes. Cut crossways into 4 cm / 1½ inch lengths.

Bring about 2.25 litres / 4 pints / 10 cups water to a rolling boil. As soon as the water is bubbling, turn off the flame and drop in all the squid.

Stir the squid for about 40 seconds or until it turns white. Drain.

Heat the oil in a large, preferably non-stick, frying-pan over medium-high heat. When hot, put in the garlic, onion, carrots and ⅛ teaspoon salt. Stir and cook for 30 or 40 seconds. Put in the courgette (zucchini), the chillies, 2 teaspoons of the Hot Fermented Bean Paste, ½ teaspoon of the paprika and ¼ teaspoon of the chilli powder (cayenne pepper). Stir and cook for 30 seconds. Put in the squid and turn the heat to medium low. Add the remaining 1 teaspoon Bean Paste, ½ teaspoon paprika, ¼ teaspoon chilli powder (cayenne pepper), some freshly ground black pepper, 1¼ teaspoons salt and the sugar. Stir to mix and cook gently for 2 minutes.

Add the spring onions (scallions) and sesame oil. Stir them in.

Empty the contents of the frying-pan into a serving dish. Scatter the roasted sesame seeds over the top and serve immediately.

Squid with Chillies and Vegetables (page 67).

SERVES 4–6

225 g / 8 oz regular (or medium) bean curd
340 g / 12 oz finely minced (ground) lean beef
2 spring onions (scallions), very finely chopped all the way up their green sections
2 cloves garlic, peeled and crushed
2 teaspoons Japanese dark soy sauce
¼ teaspoon salt
1 tablespoon sesame oil
4 teaspoons roasted, lightly crushed sesame seeds, see p. 217
About 4 tablespoons vegetable oil
75 g / 2½ oz / ½ cup plain (all purpose) white flour
2 eggs, lightly beaten
Seasoned Dipping Sauce, see p. 76

Put the bean curd in the centre of a clean cloth. Gather the ends together and squeeze out as much moisture as you can. Mash the curd with a fork and then push it through a coarse sieve.

Combine the bean curd, beef, spring onions (scallions), garlic, soy sauce, salt, sesame oil and sesame seeds in a bowl. Mix thoroughly. Form patties that are about 5 cm / 2 inches in diameter and a little less than 1 cm / ½ inch thick.

Put about 2 tablespoons oil to heat in a large, non-stick frying-pan and set to heat over medium-low heat. When hot, dip the patties first in the flour and then in the egg and put them into the pan, as many as it will hold in a single layer. Fry slowly for about 2½–3 minutes on each side or until golden-brown. Make all the patties this way, adding more oil to the pan when you need it. Serve with the Seasoned Dipping Sauce.

All over Korea

BEEF WITH WHITE RADISH
KALBI CHIM

Beef is eaten with much passion here. This is one of the most popular ways of preparing it. It is definitely considered festive. Serve it with rice and a selection of Korean *kimchees*, salads and vegetables.

SERVES 4

1.3 kg / 2¾ lb short ribs of beef, separated and cut into 5 cm / 2 inch lengths. Each piece should end up about 4 x 5 cm / 2 x 1½ inches
450 g / 1 lb white radish
8 dried Chinese mushrooms
5 tablespoons Japanese dark soy sauce
Freshly ground black pepper
1 tablespoon sesame oil
2 tablespoons roasted, lightly crushed sesame seeds, see p. 217
4–5 cloves garlic, peeled and crushed
2 tablespoons light brown sugar

Score the meaty sides of the rib sections, making 2 fairly deep slashes going both up and down and from side to side. Bring a large pan of water to a rolling boil. Drop in the meat and let the water come to a boil again. Boil for 1 minute. Drain and rinse off the meat under cold water. Peel the radish and cut it, roughly, into 5 cm / 2 inch cubes.

Put the meat and radish in a large frying-pan along with 450 ml / 15 fl oz / 2 cups water and bring to a boil. (It is best if everything fits in a single layer.) Cover, turn the heat to low and simmer gently for 40 minutes.

Meanwhile, soak the mushrooms in hot water until the caps are soft. Lift out of the water and cut away and discard the hard stems.

Combine the soy sauce, lots of black pepper, the sesame oil, sesame seeds, garlic and sugar in a bowl and mix. When the ribs have cooked for 40 minutes, pour in the soy sauce mixture, stir and bring to a boil again. Turn the heat to medium low and cook with the lid slightly ajar for 20 minutes. Add the mushroom caps to the pan. Turn the meat and radish pieces over gently, baste everything with the juices and cook, partially covered, for another 30 minutes, basting the meat and radish pieces with the juices frequently. If the meat is now tender, remove the cover and turn up the heat to reduce the liquid to a few tablespoons. Keep basting. If the meat is not tender, continue to cook, partially covered, until it is, and then reduce the sauce in the same way.

All over Korea

BRAISED BEAN CURD WITH SESAME SEEDS
DUBU JORIM

In Korea, bean curd is combined with minced (ground) meat to make patties and fillings, it goes into stews and soups and, in the winter, it often appears by itself in hot water, to be eaten with a dipping sauce. In this particular recipe, it is first fried so as to become spongy and absorbent and then braised with gently seasoned soy sauce.

It is a side dish and should be accompanied by rice, vegetables and, if you like, some meat or chicken as well.

SERVES 2–4

For the braising sauce:

2 tablespoons Japanese dark soy sauce
1 tablespoon sugar
2 spring onions (scallions), cut into very fine rounds all the way up their green sections
1 clove garlic, peeled and crushed
¼ teaspoon chilli powder (cayenne pepper)
Freshly ground black pepper
2 teaspoons roasted, lightly crushed sesame seeds, see p. 217

You also need:

200 g / 7 oz regular (or medium) bean curd
1½ tablespoons vegetable oil

Combine all the ingredients for the braising sauce in a bowl. Add 7 tablespoons water, mix and set aside.

Cut the bean curd into 5 mm / ¼ inch thick, rectangular slices. Put the slices in a single layer between 2 sheets of paper towel, top with a large plate and put a weight on the plate. Press for 20–30 minutes.

Heat the oil in a large frying-pan over medium heat. When hot, put in the bean curd slices in a single layer. Fry for about 1½ minutes on either side or until golden-brown. As the slices get done, put them on a plate.

Beef with White Radish (opposite) served with Instant Cucumber Pickle (page 76).

Empty out any oil remaining in the pan and put the bean curd back in, again in a single layer. Pour the braising sauce over the top. Cover partially and simmer on medium heat for 6–7 minutes, turning the bean curd slices over in the middle of this period. Most of the sauce should be absorbed by the bean curd. Put the bean curd slices on a serving plate. Any seasonings left in the pan should be spooned over the top.

All over Korea

COURGETTE (ZUCCHINI) STIR-FRIED WITH BEEF
HOBAK BOKUM

A simple but delicious dish that can also be served with Chinese and Malaysian meals.

SERVES 4

4 small courgettes/zucchini (450 g/1 lb), cut crossways into 5 mm/¼ inch thick slices
Salt

For marinating the beef:

115 g/4 oz minced (ground) beef
1½ teaspoons Japanese dark soy sauce
1 spring onion (scallion), cut into very fine rounds all the way up its green section
1 tablespoon roasted, lightly crushed sesame seeds, see p. 00
Freshly ground black pepper
1 tablespoon sesame oil

You also need:

2 tablespoons vegetable oil
1 tablespoon Japanese dark soy sauce
1 tablespoon sugar
2 spring onions (scallions), cut into very fine rounds all the way up their green sections
2.5 cm/1 inch piece of fresh ginger, peeled and finely grated
2 cloves garlic, peeled and finely chopped
½–1 teaspoon chilli powder (cayenne pepper)
2 teaspoons roasted, lightly crushed sesame seeds, see p. 217

Put the courgette (zucchini) in a bowl. Add ¾ teaspoon salt and rub it in. Set aside for 2 hours. Drain and pat the slices dry.

Mix the beef with all the other ingredients in the marinade. Set aside for 30 minutes.

Heat the oil in a large frying-pan over highish heat. When hot, put in the meat. Stir and fry for 1 minute or until the meat changes colour, breaking up all lumps as you do so. Put in the courgette (zucchini) and stir gently. Put in the soy sauce, sugar, spring onions (scallions), ginger, garlic and chilli powder. Stir gently and cook for about 2 minutes. Turn down the heat and stir-fry gently for another minute or so or until the courgette is crisp-tender.

Sprinkle the sesame seeds over the top just before serving.

All over Korea

CUCUMBER SALAD
OEE SAENGCHAE

Mild and crisp, this is an ideal accompaniment for Korean meats, spicy stews and stir-fries. If you like, roasted and lightly crushed sesame seeds (see p. 217) and some chilli powder (cayenne pepper) may be added to this salad.

SERVES 4

450 g/1 lb good quality cucumbers with small, undeveloped seeds, such as the pickling, English or oriental varieties
1 teaspoon salt
1 tablespoon very finely sliced spring onion (scallion) rings
½–1 clove garlic, peeled and crushed
3–4 teaspoons white distilled vinegar or Japanese rice vinegar
½ teaspoon sugar
2 teaspoons sesame oil

Trim the cucumber ends. You do not need to peel them. Cut crossways into 3 mm/⅛ inch thick slices and put in a bowl. Add the salt, mix well and set aside for 2 hours. Drain well and then pat dry. Add the spring onions (scallions), garlic, vinegar and sugar. Mix and taste, adding more of anything you like. Add the sesame oil just before serving and mix again.

A *kimchee* stall in a street market. Although cabbage is generally used to prepare Korea's favourite condiment, it can be made with ingredients ranging from radishes to ginseng.

All over Korea

RICE WITH BEEF AND VEGETABLES
BIBIMBAB

Here rice is served in large, individual portions, just as pasta might be, topped with an assortment of lightly cooked, or blanched and dressed, meat and vegetables. The toppings are neatly arranged on the sloping sides of the rice mound. Crowning the top is a fried egg. To provide pep, there is a dollop of spicy bean paste (*kochu chang*) which is usually put inside a lettuce leaf 'cup' and tucked somewhere on the plate. Diners mix up everything before they eat or else they pick up small amounts of rice with whatever else they fancy.

Bibimbab is a meal in itself, and is best served in wide, shallow bowls that are about 20 cm / 8 inches in diameter. Old-fashioned soup plates may also be used. Generally, clear beef soup, perhaps with a few well-cooked slices of white radish in it, and pickles are served on the side.

Even though there are several parts to this dish – it is after all a whole meal – it is easy to prepare. Everything can be made ahead of time and served at room temperature except for the rice, beef and eggs. The rice may be made up to 1 hour in advance and kept in a warming oven. The meat and the eggs are best made just before eating – but they take all of 5 minutes.

Before starting to cook, peel and finely chop 2–3 cloves of garlic, roast and lightly crush 4 tablespoons sesame seeds (see p. 217 and finely chop 1 whole spring onion (scallion) – including all the green portion.

SERVES 4

For the courgettes (zucchini):

2 small courgettes / zucchini (225 g / 8 oz), cut into fine julienne strips
½ teaspoon salt
1 tablespoon sesame oil
1 teaspoon roasted, lightly crushed sesame seeds, see p. 217
2 teaspoons finely chopped spring onion (scallion), see above
½ teaspoon peeled, finely chopped garlic
Freshly ground black pepper
1 teaspoon vegetable oil

For the bean sprouts:

400 g / 14 oz / 4 cups fresh bean sprouts
2 teaspoons Japanese dark soy sauce
4 teaspoons finely chopped spring onion (scallion), see above
4 teaspoons sesame oil
4 teaspoons roasted, lightly crushed sesame seeds, see p. 217
About ¼ teaspoon salt

For the spinach:

285 g / 10 oz fresh, trimmed spinach
2 teaspoons Japanese dark soy sauce
1 teaspoon sesame oil
2 teaspoons roasted, lightly crushed sesame seeds, see p. 217
1 teaspoon finely chopped spring onion (scallion), see above
½ teaspoon peeled, finely chopped garlic

For the sauce:

5 tablespoons Hot Fermented Bean Paste, *kochu chang*, see p. 200
1 teaspoon sugar
4 teaspoons sesame oil
2 teaspoons roasted, lightly crushed sesame seeds, see p. 217

For the beef:

225 g / 8 oz lean beef steak, cut against the grain into thin strips about 5 cm / 2 inches long and 5 mm / ¼ inch wide
1 tablespoon Japanese dark soy sauce
½ teaspoon peeled, finely chopped garlic
1 tablespoon finely chopped spring onion (scallion), see above
2 teaspoons sesame oil
2 teaspoons roasted, lightly crushed sesame seeds, see p. 217
Freshly ground black pepper
1 teaspoon vegetable oil

You also need:

Freshly cooked Plain Japanese and Korean Rice, see p. 198
4 cup-like lettuce leaves
4 freshly fried eggs

Make the courgettes (zucchini): Combine the cut strips with the salt. Mix well and set aside for 30 minutes. Drain and gently squeeze out as much liquid as you can easily. Put in a bowl and add the sesame oil, sesame seeds, spring onion (scallion), garlic and black pepper. Mix. Heat the vegetable oil in a non-stick frying-pan over highish heat. When hot, put in the courgettes (zucchini). Stir-fry for 1½–2 minutes. Set aside.

Make the bean sprouts. Bring a large pan of water to a rolling boil. Drop in the bean sprouts. When the water comes to a boil again, cook rapidly for 30 seconds. Drain the sprouts and rinse under cold water. Drain again and gently squeeze out as much moisture as you can easily. Add all the remaining ingredients. Mix well and set aside.

Make the spinach. Drop the spinach into a large pan of boiling water. When the water comes to a boil again, boil rapidly for 30 seconds. Drain and rinse under cold water. Drain again and squeeze out as much moisture as you can easily. Separate the leaves a bit. Add all the remaining ingredients and mix well. Set aside.

Make the sauce. Combine the ingredients in a small bowl, mix well and set aside.

Make the beef. Put the beef in a bowl. Add the soy sauce, garlic, spring onion (scallion), sesame oil, sesame seeds and lots of black pepper. Mix and set aside for 15–20 minutes or longer. Just before eating, heat the vegetable oil in a non-stick frying-pan over high heat. When hot, put in the meat. Stir for about a minute or until the meat changes colour.

To serve, divide the rice between 4 wide bowls, forming a mound in the centre of each. Radiating down from the mound, in somewhat triangular segments, arrange the beef, courgettes (zucchini), bean sprouts and spinach. Leave a little room for the lettuce leaf 'cups'. Tuck those in somewhere and put a dollop of the sauce in the centre of each. Put a freshly fried egg (this would be the time to fry the eggs) at the very top of each mound and serve.

All over Korea

SPRING ONION (SCALLION) PANCAKES
PA'CHON

At fêtes and fairs one can see – and better still, smell – these pancakes sizzling away on cast-iron griddles. Spring onions (scallions) are first laid out on the griddle. Then a batter, made with both rice flour and white wheat flour, is poured over the top and the pancakes are browned lightly on both sides. If one orders a fancier version, chopped oysters are added to the batter. The cooked pancakes are swiftly cut up into squares – so they can be picked up easily with chopsticks – and served with a dipping sauce.

They are heavenly. Koreans refer to them as 'Korean pizzas'. They may, indeed, be eaten as a snack just as pizzas are. This recipe makes three pancakes. My husband and I often have them for breakfast and, between the two of us, devour all three of them. If there are other foods, people might eat smaller portions. They are quite wonderful with scrambled eggs and bacon!

These pancakes are best eaten soon after they are made. However, if you wish to make them ahead of time, wrap them in foil and heat them in a pre-heated, medium oven (gas mark 4/350°F/180°C) for 15 minutes. If you have a microwave oven, heat each one separately, uncovered, for 1 minute.

SERVES 2–4

85 g/3 oz/¾ cup rice flour	
85 g/3 oz/¾ cup plain (all purpose) white flour	
1 teaspoon sesame oil	
½ teaspoon salt	
1 large egg, lightly beaten	
3 tablespoons vegetable oil	
6 whole spring onions (scallions), quartered lengthways, then cut crossways into 7.5 cm/3 inch segments	
Korean Dipping Sauce, see right	

Put the 2 flours in a bowl. Slowly add 250 ml/8 fl oz/1 cup water, mixing as you go until you have a smooth batter that is like flowing cream. You may need to add just a drop more water. Add the sesame oil and salt. Mix. Add the beaten egg and mix again. Cover and set the batter aside for 30 minutes or longer.

Pour 1 tablespoon of the vegetable oil into a large, non-stick frying-pan and let it heat over medium-low heat for a few minutes. When hot, scatter one-third of the spring onions (scallions) evenly at the bottom of the pan in a diameter of about 20 cm/8 inches. Pour one-third of the batter over the spring onions (scallions), making a 20 cm/8 inch

(roughly) pancake. Cover and cook for 5–6 minutes. Turn the pancake over, cover again and cook for 3 minutes. Uncover and cook for another 2 minutes. The pancake should brown lightly in spots. Make all the pancakes this way, adding fresh oil to the frying-pan each time. Cut into 5 cm/2 inch squares (approximately) and serve hot, with Korean Dipping Sauce.

All over Korea

KOREAN DIPPING SAUCE
CHO CHANG

This is an all-purpose sauce that is used for dipping a variety of pancakes, egg dishes, bean curd, and batter-fried foods. Chilli powder (cayenne pepper) and roasted, lightly crushed sesame seeds (see p. 217) may be added to it, if you like.

SERVES 4

6 tablespoons Japanese dark soy sauce	
2 tablespoons distilled white vinegar	
2 teaspoons sesame oil	

Mix all the ingredients for the sauce and divide between 4 small bowls, or as many bowls as there are diners.

All over Korea

SEASONED DIPPING SAUCE
YANGYUM CHANG

This sauce is not only used as a dip, but may also be poured over simply grilled meats and fish or used as a marinade.

SERVES 4

4 tablespoons Japanese dark soy sauce	
2½ tablespoons Japanese rice vinegar	
1 tablespoon very finely sliced spring onion (scallion)	
2 teaspoons roasted, lightly crushed sesame seeds, see p. 217	
¼ teaspoon or more chilli powder (cayenne pepper)	

Combine all the ingredients for the sauce and divide between 4 small bowls.

All over Korea

INSTANT CUCUMBER PICKLE
KHACHORI

This is really a *kimchee*, only it does not need to mature and may be eaten right away – which makes it very convenient. It is prepared in villages in large plastic basins and is generally shared by the whole community.

You could, if you prefer, make this pickle with Chinese cabbage instead of the cucumber in almost the same way. Just cut the cabbage crossways into 5 cm/2 inch sections and leave it in salt with a weight on it for 6 hours.

For this recipe, I have used 1½ teaspoons of the coarsely pounded Korean chilli powder which is of medium heat and is very red in colour. This is sold only in Korean supermarkets. You could use a combination of 1 teaspoon each of bright red paprika and chilli powder (cayenne pepper) – make it as hot as you like.

SERVES 6–8

450 g/1 lb cucumbers. (Use any with tender seeds, such as the pickling, English or oriental varieties)	
Salt	
95 g/3½ oz white radish. (Use a section from a large radish)	
1½ teaspoons coarse Korean chilli powder (or see above)	
1 clove garlic, peeled and crushed	
2.5 cm/1 inch piece of fresh ginger, peeled and grated to a pulp	
2 spring onions (scallions), cut into fine rounds all the way up their green sections	
1 tablespoon sesame oil	
2 teaspoons roasted, lightly crushed sesame seeds, see p. 217	

Cut off the ends of the cucumbers but do not peel them. Cut them crossways into 5 cm/2 inch sections and then cut each section lengthways in half. Now lay each section, large cut-side down, and cut lengthways into rough rectangles. Put the cucumber pieces in a bowl. Add 1¼ teaspoons salt, mix well and set aside for 3 hours. Drain gently but thoroughly, squeezing out as much liquid as possible.

Meanwhile, peel the radish and cut it into 5 cm/2 inch long julienne strips. Put in a bowl. Add ¼ teaspoon salt, the chilli powder, garlic, ginger and spring onions (scallions). Mix well. Add the cucumbers to this mixture after they have been drained. Mix well. Just before serving, drain lightly again and add the sesame oil and sesame seeds. Toss to mix.

All over Korea

WHITE RADISH PICKLE
KAKDOOKI

At Korean tables, there is generally more than one kind of pickle. Here is a favourite of mine. It is made with large, white radishes though, at a pinch, you could make it with small red ones instead. Trim them but do not peel them. Cut them in halves lengthways.

MAKES ENOUGH TO FILL A 900 ML/1½ PINT/
1 QUART JAR

800 g/1¾ lb white radish, peeled and cut into 5 cm/1 inch cubes
2 tablespoons coarse Korean chilli powder or 1½ tablespoons bright red paprika mixed with 1 tablespoon chilli powder (cayenne pepper)
1 tablespoon plus ½ teaspoon salt
2 teaspoons sugar
2.5 cm/1 inch piece of fresh ginger, peeled and finely chopped
1 tablespoon peeled, finely chopped garlic
3 spring onions (scallions), cut into very fine rounds all the way up their green sections

Put the radish cubes in a bowl. Rub with the chilli powder, or paprika and chilli powder (cayenne pepper) mixture, wearing gloves if necessary. Set aside for 30 minutes. Now add the remaining ingredients and mix well. Cover first with a large sheet of cling film (plastic wrap) and then put a plate (or plastic lid or anything else that fits) directly on top of the radishes inside the bowl. Put a weight on the plate (a large bottle of oil usually does the trick) and let it sit until the liquid rises above the radishes, about 48 hours. Remove

the weight. Let the pickle sit until it 'matures' and turns sour. This usually takes about 3 days from the start of the pickling process in summer and up to a week when it is very cold.

Put the pickle in a jar or plastic container, cover and refrigerate. The pickle will keep in the refrigerator for many weeks.

All over Korea

COOKIE TWISTS
MAEJAGWA

What can I tell you about these cookies, other than that I cannot stop eating them even as I write this? My fingers are a bit sticky but that goes with the job! Crisp, and covered with both honey and crushed pine nuts (or sesame seeds), these cookies are the perfect accompaniment to coffee and tea.

MAKES ENOUGH TO FILL A
900 ML/½ PINT/1 QUART JAR

4 tablespoons Japanese *sake*
2 tablespoons sugar
130 g/4½ oz/1 cup plain (all purpose) white flour plus some extra for dusting
120 ml/4 fl oz/½ cup honey. (Make sure it is soft and flowing)
Vegetable oil for deep-frying
2 teaspoons roasted, finely chopped pine nuts, see p. 216 (or roasted, lightly crushed sesame seeds, see p. 217)

Combine the *sake* and sugar in a cup and stir until the sugar has dissolved. Sift the flour into a bowl. Slowly add the *sake*-sugar mixture and gather the flour together to make a ball. Knead the ball on a very lightly floured surface until the dough is smooth.

Roll the dough out, again on a very lightly floured surface, until you have a rectangle that is somewhere between 1.5 and 3 mm/1/16 and 1/8 inch thick. Cut into pieces that are 5 cm/2 inches long and 2.5 cm/1 inch wide. In the centre of each piece, going lengthways, cut a 2.5 cm/1 inch long slit. (See Diagram A.) Take the top of a piece, push it through the slit and pull it up on the

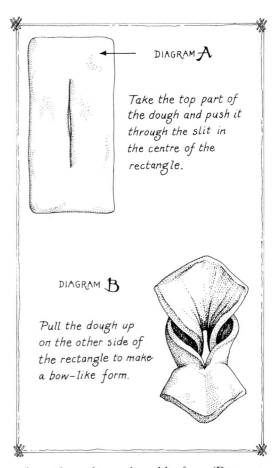

DIAGRAM A

Take the top part of the dough and push it through the slit in the centre of the rectangle.

DIAGRAM B

Pull the dough up on the other side of the rectangle to make a bow-like form.

other side, making a bow-like form (Diagram B). Do this to all the pieces and keep them on a lightly floured plate or baking sheet.

Spread the honey out on a large dinner plate. Line a second plate with paper towels.

Heat the oil in a wok or deep-fryer to about 330°F/160°C. When hot, put in all the cookies. Stir and fry for 4–5 minutes or until a rich, golden-brown. Remove with a slotted spoon and spread out on the plate lined with paper towels. Let the cookies drain briefly and then put them, in a single layer, on the plate with the honey. Turn the cookies around until they are coated with honey. Sprinkle the pine nuts (or sesame seeds) over the top. Transfer the cookies to a clean plate and serve. Any cookies that are not eaten within the next few hours may be stored in a clean, lidded jar or plastic container. They will stay fresh for several days this way.

MALAYSIA

We come upon it rather suddenly: a small village, a *kampung*, hidden among the lush green of the hills on the less populated western side of Penang Island, away from the bustle of Georgetown. Lilting popular music flows out of the loudspeaker, radiating from a cashew nut tree whose tender, astringent leaves will later be eaten with fiery *sambals*. Motor cycles and bicycles, dozens of them, are parked near a rustic gate. Bunting is tied to the fruiting banana trees. A wedding is in progress and we are invited.

A cluster of men is gathered under a translucent tent of red parachute silk left over from the last war. The groom, in flared jeans and a shirt open down his slim chest, glows in the filtered sunlight. The women are all gathered on the porch of the small, thatched home at the back – a typical *kampung*-style hut, made of wood and standing on stilts, distanced carefully from the moist, teeming earth. There is a basin on the ground to wash the feet and then steps leading up to the airy porch where the ladies sit. They seem in charge of a basket filled with aromatic pandanus leaves, rose petals and jasmine flowers. Nestled in the basket are hard-boiled eggs, called *bunga telor*, 'flower eggs' because they are so perfumed, and each painstakingly attached to a gold 'branch' as if it was a bud about to flower. These symbols of fertility will be given out to all the honoured guests. The bridal bed, decorated with more flowers, can be seen in the dim interior.

Behind the house, under the custard apple trees whose fruit are all carefully wrapped in newspaper to save them from voracious birds and insects, are two tents, one for men and the other for women. Long tables, covered with plastic, have been

Opposite: A riverside scene, at dawn, in a small Malaysian village.

laid out and the feasting, in batches, has commenced. As we join in, we are offered *nasi minyak*, rice cooked with cinnamon, cloves and clarified butter, a *kurma* of beef cooked with coconut milk, a curried *pacheri* of pineapples and a *kaliya* of stewed beans flavoured with cumin and coriander. No fish is served. It is considered too ordinary, too everyday, not befitting a feast.

More than half of Malaysia's people, such as these villagers, are simple, god-fearing Muslims, whose ancestors were converted to Islam around the fifteenth century. They measure their days in prayers and rituals and their major, and sometimes only, travel takes the form of a pilgrimage to Mecca. In their eating habits, as with everything else, there are things that religion permits (*halal*) and things that religion proscribes (*haram*). The dietary dos and don'ts clearly insist that all meat be butchered with a clean cut and a prayer. Even a housewife who kills a chicken, first says, 'In the name of God the Merciful and Benevolent.' Pork and alcohol are taboo.

But Malaysia is a true melting-pot and Muslim Malays are not the only people who call it home. Since the earliest times, Indian, Arab and Chinese ships have wafted here with south-west and north-east monsoon winds, aiming mostly for the strategically placed town of Malacca in the straits. Here they exchanged silks for spices and gold for fine cottons and gems, and then waited for the next monsoon to blow them back home. Many of the traders stayed and intermarried with the local women.

Then, starting in the sixteenth century, the Europeans began to arrive in violent spurts – Portuguese, Dutch and English – not just to trade but to control the trade through conquest. The Malays, eating mostly rice and fish, flavoured with aromatic lemon grass and black pepper, ginger, fresh turmeric, coconut milk and shrimp paste (*blachan*), had already begun to incorporate cooking techniques and flavours provided by traders. Noodles were stir-fried with soy sauce, Middle Eastern kebabs were skewered on bamboo sticks and

Scenes from a Muslim wedding. Perfumed hard-boiled eggs, symbols of fertility, are placed in front of the bride and groom (above) and (opposite) rice is prepared for the marriage feast.

grilled, rice pilafs were enriched with clarified butter (*ghee*), and stews turned into curries with the use of cumin and coriander. Thanks to the Portuguese conquerors, they also acquired a serious chilli-habit, adding that New World spice not just to meats and vegetables but to the hand-pounded, chutney-like *sambals* essential to every meal, where it almost stood alone in red, fiery splendour.

If the Malays were adventurous in their eating habits, so were the Chinese and Indian settlers. Many early Chinese traders, known as *babas*, had not only bedded down with Malay women, known as *nonyas*, but had given up chopsticks and learned to enjoy the addition of coconut milk, candle nuts, tamarind and lemon grass to their repertoire of seasonings. This great culinary merger took place mainly in the straits settlements of Penang, Malacca and what is now independent Singapore, and a cuisine, now popularised as *nonya* food, was born.

In the nineteenth century, when labourers were required to work the newly grown rubber plantations and mine the tin, hoards of Indian indentured workers were brought in from South India. Chinese immigrants looking for opportunity were encouraged to come *en masse* from southern China, mainly from the villages in Fukien and Hainan and urban centres like Canton, Swatow and Amoy. It is said that all the British had to do was fire cannons filled with silver coins into the jungles of Malaysia to get them cleared.

Some of the immigrants perished in the swamps but many of them did exceedingly well, building mansions in Penang, in the hill stations, and in the newly emerging town of Kuala Lumpur. They also added a whole range of local cuisines to the Malaysian culinary melting-pot: pancake-like *thosais* from South India, stuffed in gentle vegetarian

fashion with potatoes; Hokkien style pig's feet (from Fukien) stewed with Chinese black vinegar and dark soy sauce to be offered to young, nursing mothers for strength; and Chiu Chow (same as Teochew) style duck (from Swatow), braised with star anise and ginger. While some dishes kept their original forms, others were subtly transformed either by the sauces they were served with – the mild Hainanese chicken rice is served here with an incendiary chilli sauce – or by the addition of seasonings – the Indian-style beef curry, *daging nasi kandar*, is now perked up with lemon grass and soy sauce.

Thirty-five per cent of the population in Malaysia today is Chinese and about 10 per cent Indian. It is the Chinese who dominate the economy, far in excess of their numbers.

Helen and S.K. Ching are a young, successful Westernised couple living in

southern Malaysia, in the town of Johore Bahru, not far from Singapore. In fact their little sons, Kevin and Aaron, go to school there, across the border. They drive a BMW and both sport his and her gold Rolex watches. S.K. is a lawyer. He and Helen also run a superb restaurant, Paradise Seafood Garden, where food and song may be enjoyed at the same time. It is a *karaoke* restaurant, the latest fashion, imported from Japan, where guests may sing to video-taped sound-tracks. To go with the song are superb creations from the kitchen, such as Fragrant Prawns (Shrimp), cooked with curry leaves and chillies (see p. 89), fish heads braised both in Malay and Chinese styles and okra sautéd with a *sambal* sauce containing red chillies and shrimp paste.

In the vast restaurant kitchen, the chef works with a battery of seasonings that vary considerably in their origins. For the prawn dish, for example, he throws in ginger, garlic, shallots, chillies and small, powdered, dried prawns (shrimp) which belong to one culinary tradition, yellow bean sauce, oyster sauce, Chinese rice wine and dark soy sauce which belong to another, and curry leaves

Kuala Lumpur, capital city of Malaysia, where hawkers sell their wares in shopping centres.

Banana leaves on their way to market. They will be used as packages for take-away meals.

little savoury pastries filled with sardines or with curried potatoes, go on to little rice cakes, both sweet and savoury, and end with a stunning *laksa*. It is worth a trip to Malaysia just to have the *laksa*.

Let me try and describe to you what a *laksa* is. Think of the puréed fish soup that you might have in the south of France. Instead of fennel and saffron, imagine it flavoured with chillies, lemon grass, ginger and coconut milk. Now, into that soup, instead of bread, throw a handful of noodles. Do not stop. Top the bowl with a julienne of crunchy cucumbers, aromatic ginger flowers and with pineapple, bean sprouts and mint, and serve it with *sambal blachan*, a kind of *rouille*, but a *rouille* made with red chillies, shrimp paste, shallots and lime juice. *That* is *laksa*. (A recipe for Penang *laksa* is on p. 95.)

Eating at a restaurant or café is only one way of eating out in Malaysia. There are others. You may, if you like, pick up a *nasi lemak* from a perspiring vendor in the market. This banana-leaf-package meal, consisting of coconut rice, a few prawns (shrimp) cooked with fiery *sambal*, some fried whitebait and a few slices of cucumber could be a breakfast or a lunch. You open the package and eat – on the street, if you like, or carry it up to your office.

Street vendors, known as hawkers, have their stands strategically placed in markets, along beaches and river fronts, usually bunched together. Get iced fruit juice from one, stir-fried rice noodles from another. Eat as you walk or sit at one of the few tables the hawkers put out. Do you want a *poh piah*? The *poh piah* maker may wear only an undershirt and drawers but he is a miracle man. He takes the softest of unwieldy doughs, twirls a big ball of it in his hand and then allows it to land for just a second on a hot griddle. It leaves a bare imprint. He does that again and again. An assistant scrapes up the 'imprints'. They are the thinnest pancakes you will ever see and are used to enfold fillings of sliced vegetables and prawns (shrimp). This is a *nonya* speciality.

The hawkers' stalls do not always have official names and numbers but they do build up a reputation if they are good. Pork products and the plates and utensils used for them are kept clearly segregated, though it is quite common for a group of friends – a Hindu who eats no beef and a Muslim who eats no pork and a Chinese who eats everything – to get food from different hawkers and then to sit and eat together at a common table.

In the ultra-modern, spitting-clean capital city, Kuala Lumpur, where mosque minarets, church spires and temple domes all glint in the tolerant sunlight and where cricket is played on the greens, the fine for littering is very high. Hawkers here have been sanitised and moved into hawker centres, their freewheeling spirit controlled by guidelines and rules, wind and weather banished. Medan Hang Tuah is one such centre, spread out on the top floor of a vast, trendy shopping centre. Hawkers, set up in neat rows, sell curried squid and cockles, stir-fried Chinese broccoli with prawns/shrimp (*kailan chow bar*), fried noodles (*mee goreng*), fresh fruit with a peanut sauce (*rujak*) and chilli crabs. Thousands of shoppers and office workers – Chinese-Malays, Malay Muslims, South Indian Hindus – come here daily. Woks and steamers work their miracles. At lunchtime, one can hardly move.

Far away from this hubbub, on the quiet east coast of Malaysia, is the seaside town of Kuantan in the state of Pahang. Here, Datin Rozita, with a group of upper-class ladies, has invited me to a lunch at her home.

The house is large and modern, set within a manicured compound. Cooling breezes from the South China Sea waft in through the many windows. In the living-room, the sofas and chairs, all pale blue and beige, are arranged against the walls in rectangular perfection. Little pillows lean neatly on the sofas. Writings from the Koran illuminate the wall. Birds chirp outside, a fan whirs above and the ladies keep up a quiet, jolly chatter. 'You go and change into a *kurong* (long,

and curry powder which smack of a third. And yet, they all blend into one glorious, harmonious whole. They transform the prawns into a truly Malaysian dish.

Like many other Malaysians, Helen and S.K. eat out with great frequency. They ask me if I would join them for a Malay breakfast that Saturday. It seems that one of the most popular places, on the western fringe of the town, is Warung Saga, owned by a retired customs officer and his wife, both of whom have been to Mecca. He runs the front, she manages the kitchen at the back. It is just a small, simple verandah café but cars are lined up. Fancy decor counts for little here. The food's the thing.

We start out with Curry Puffs (see p. 86),

A pancake stall. Throughout Malaysia pancakes are used to enclose all sorts of fillings such as the chopped peanuts used here.

sarong-like garment),' one lady gently admonishes a young girl just back from school and still in her Western clothes, 'Your knees should be covered when we sit down.' The girl makes a mild protesting face as young girls do, and then runs off.

A mat is rolled on the floor, a batik 'tablecloth' spread on top of it and the ladies all sit down in a circle, legs folded to the left. This is the traditional Malay way of eating. A jug of water and a bowl are passed around to wash the right hand, the hand we are to eat with. I wait for a towel but am told, 'Just leave that hand wet. This way the rice will not stick to it.'

Rice, which is the staple, and all the other foods are placed in the centre. We serve ourselves with our clean – and dry – left hands. There is a simple, delicious chicken soup with potatoes and carrots flavoured with ginger, garlic and aromatic turmeric leaves (*sop ayam kampung*), a grilled fish smothered with a chilli and pineapple sauce (*ikan bakar sambal nenas*), another grilled fish basted with a tamarind and coconut sauce (*ikan percik*), pasties filled with poached, spiced fish (*tembosa*), a lacy pancake (*roti jala*) to be eaten with a thick syrup made from the potent durian fruit, coconut milk and palm sugar (*pengat durian*), a coconut milk 'Bavarian' (*pudding santan gula Melaka*) and *Pudding Di-Raja*, a dish from the royal palace, introduced by the late Sultan of Pahang. It is a glorious, Malay-British concoction of fried bananas embedded in custard.

We eat in a leisurely fashion, the ladies talking about the things that matter to them: their children, the arrangements for Malaysian pilgrimages and the unbeatable quality of local fish. It occurs to me as I feast that of all the great cuisines of the world, Malaysian food is perhaps the least known. We should change that.

RECIPES FROM MALAYSIA

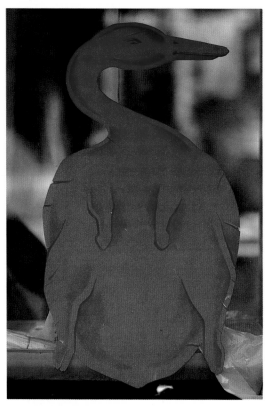

Roast duck is much loved by the Chinese Malaysians.

Johore, Malaysia
CHILLI MUSSELS
CILI KERANG

The small village of Kukup is right by the water on the west coast of Johore. Its main street is lined with seafood restaurants. These – and fishing – would seem to be its main businesses. Customers drive here from as far away as Singapore to eat. The food is that good. One of the restaurants is Kweelim. Its food, a brilliant mixture of Malay and Chinese, is some of the best I ate in Malaysia. This dish is offered there under its local name, *Chili Tartu*.

A similar dish may also be made with lobsters and crabs. They should be bought live, cut up into smaller pieces with a heavy cleaver and cleaned before proceeding with the recipe.

On mussels: Pick mussels that are firmly closed. If they are open, try prodding their flesh with the point of a sharp object. They should close immediately. If they do not, leave them in the shop. Discard mussels that seem too light and those that seem too heavy (the latter are probably filled with sand). You will probably have to bring the mussels home in a plastic bag. As soon as you come home, open up the bag slightly to allow the mussels to breathe and then refrigerate them. Next, they need careful cleaning. Scrub them well with a stiff brush or plastic scrubber under running water. Scrape or pull off their 'beards'. Soak them for 1 hour in a big bowl of fresh, cold water to help them to clean themselves. Lift them out of the water and scrub them once more under running water.

In Malaysia, these mussels would be served at the main meal of the day with rice and vegetables. I like to serve them all by themselves as a first course.

SERVES 2–4

6 dried, hot red chillies, de-seeded

2 teaspoons shrimp paste, *blachan*, roasted, see p. 00 (or 2 canned anchovy fillets, blended with the other ingredients)

4 cloves garlic, peeled and coarsely chopped plus 1 clove garlic, peeled and finely chopped

6–8 shallots or 1 small onion (60 g / 2 oz), peeled and coarsely chopped

1 stick of fresh lemon grass, just the lower 15 cm / 6 inches, cut crossways into very fine rounds (or 1½ teaspoons powdered lemon grass or 2 teaspoons grated lemon rind)

2.5 cm / 1 inch piece of fresh galangal (or fresh ginger), peeled and coarsely chopped

6–8 candle nuts (or 1 tablespoon blanched, slivered almonds)

1 teaspoon bright red paprika

½ teaspoon salt, or more to taste

6 tablespoons vegetable oil

900 g–1.35 kg / 2–3 lb fresh, live mussels, cleaned (see left)

Put the chillies in a small bowl with 4 tablespoons hot water. Soak until slightly soft or, if you have a microwave oven, zap the chillies and soaking liquid for 1 minute.

Combine the chillies and their soaking liquid, the roasted shrimp paste, the 4 coarsely chopped garlic cloves, shallots, lemon grass, galangal, candle nuts, paprika and salt in the container of an electric blender and blend, adding a little extra water only if it is necessary. You may need to push the mixture down a few times with a rubber spatula.

Heat the oil in a large, wide pan over medium-high heat. When hot, put in the finely chopped garlic clove. Stir once or twice or until the garlic just starts to brown. Now put in the paste from the blender. Stir and fry for 3 minutes or until the paste feels well-fried. Put in 350 ml / 12 fl oz / 1½ cups water and bring to a boil. Put in all the mussels and bring to a boil again. Cover tightly and cook over medium-high heat for about 5 minutes or until all the mussels have opened up. Discard any mussels that fail to open. Half-way through the cooking, shake up the pan with a good toss. Serve in deep plates with the sauce.

All over Malaysia
CURRY PUFFS
•

There is a poem, written in the tenth century for the court of the caliph of Baghdad, that extols the virtues of the *sanbusak*, a savoury pastry filled with well-seasoned minced (ground) meat and eaten with a mustard sauce. This same pastry travelled to India soon thereafter and there became the beloved *samosa*, stuffed with spicy minced (ground)

Curry Puffs and Chilli Mussels (both this page).

the heat to low and cook for 2–3 minutes or until the prawns (shrimp) are just cooked through. Uncover and put in the sugar and wine. Turn the heat to high and stir for a few seconds. Taste, adding a little salt only if needed. Serve at once.

Malacca, Malaysia
NONYA CHICKEN
AYAM TEMPRA

An everyday dish from the home of Chinese-Malay *nonyas*, this is both easily made and excellent to eat. Serve it with plain rice and any vegetable. Ideally, the chicken should be cut into fairly small sections. I buy chicken pieces and then ask the butcher to cut each leg into four and each breast into six pieces. If you have a heavy cleaver, you can do this yourself at home. You may use dark or light meat or a mixture of the two.

SERVES 2–4

4 tablespoons vegetable oil
800 g / 1¾ lb chicken pieces (see above)
1–2 fresh, hot red (or green) chillies, cut into thick rounds
1 tablespoon Chinese dark soy sauce
1 tablespoon Chinese light soy sauce
1½ teaspoons sugar
1 large onion (180 g / 6 oz), peeled and cut into 5 mm / ¼ inch rounds

Heat the oil in a non-stick frying-pan over highish heat. When hot, put in the chicken. Brown it on all sides and lift it out with a slotted spoon. Keep in a bowl. Pour out all but 2 tablespoons of the oil and turn the heat to medium. Put in the chillies. Stir and fry for a few seconds. Now put back the chicken and any accumulated juices. Add 4 table-spoons of water. Bring to a simmer. Cover, turn the heat to low and simmer for 10 minutes. Put in the two soy sauces, the sugar and the onion. Stir and bring to a simmer. Cover, turn the heat to low and simmer for another 5 minutes or until the chicken is cooked through. Stir a few times during this period so that the chicken colours evenly.

Kelantan, Pahang and Johore, Malaysia
CHICKEN ROASTED WITH GINGERED SOY SAUCE
AYAM PANGUANG BEEKICAP

An unusually good way to roast a chicken. It turns deliciously dark, almost black. Serve it with rice, accompanied by a vegetable and assorted salads and condiments. You could also serve it with boiled potatoes and a green salad.

This recipe comes from the palace home of Tunku Puan Azizah Iskandar, wife of the heir to Pahang and daughter of the Sultan of Johore.

SERVES 4

1 medium-sized onion (85 g / 3 oz), peeled and coarsely chopped
3 cloves garlic, peeled and coarsely chopped
4 cm / 1½ inch piece of fresh ginger, peeled and coarsely chopped
1.5 kg / 3½ lb chicken
6 tablespoons vegetable oil
3 tablespoons rice wine vinegar – use a mild vinegar, such as Japanese vinegar (or cider vinegar)
3 tablespoons Chinese dark soy sauce
2½ tablespoons sugar
¾ teaspoon salt

Put the onion, garlic and ginger into the container of an electric blender. Blend, adding just as much water as you need to make the machine do its work. Put the chicken in a roasting pan. Rub half of the onion-garlic-ginger mixture all over the chicken, inside and out, and leave for 1 hour. Put the remaining paste in a bowl. Add the oil, vinegar, soy sauce, sugar, salt and 6 tablespoons water. Mix.

Pre-heat the oven to gas mark 4 / 350 °F / 180 °C.

Pour as much of the soy sauce mixture into the cavity of the chicken as it will hold easily. I raise the tail end of the chicken slightly by putting the neck under it so that the liquid will stay in. Bake the chicken for 25 minutes, basting it every now and then with the sauce in the bowl. Now put all the remaining sauce around the chicken. Keep basting it for another 50 minutes or until the chicken is cooked through. If the sauce in the pan begins to dry out and get scorched, add 1 tablespoon or so of water to the pan and scrape it quickly.

A dawn scene in Malacca. The Portuguese first settled here in the 16th century – and stayed. Dishes like the Devil's Curry on this page, which uses the chillies and mustard seeds they brought from their Indian colony of Goa, reflect their influence on Malaysian cuisine.

Malacca, Malaysia

DEVIL'S CURRY

CURRY DEBIL

When the first Europeans – the Portuguese – landed *en masse* in the port city of Malacca around the start of the sixteenth century, the local inhabitants did not know what to make of them. They labelled them 'white Bengalis'. Malacca then was not only a major trade centre for most of Asia, but was perhaps the most important one in the East for a commodity whose monopoly the Portuguese were anxious to take away from the Arabs: spices. The Portuguese stayed to

rule, only to be followed by the Dutch and the English.

During the early Portuguese period, intermarriages with the local Malays – and conversions to Catholicism – were encouraged, as were more casual alliances. The children of such couplings tended to marry each other, communicating mostly in Portuguese. Four hundred years later, the Portuguese Eurasian community still survives, still speaking Cristao, an archaic form of Portuguese. Today, it tends to gather in a Portuguese settlement especially built for it in 1933. At the heart of this settlement is Portuguese Square, Medan Portugis, where, with shops and restaurants and cultural gatherings, these Eurasians try to keep a unique culture alive. It was here, at a restaurant called De Lisbon, that I got this recipe for Devil's Curry.

Most 'devilled' dishes in the West, such as 'devilled' eggs, involve the use of an ingredient that could well be associated with hell-fire: powdered mustard. Mustard is used here, but chillies and mustard seeds are also thrown in to further the potency. The Portuguese had a precedent for this.

Side by side with Malacca, they held another territory, this one on the west coast of India, the colony of Goa. It was here that *vindaloo*, a dish of pork cooked initially with just wine vinegar and garlic, blossomed with local assistance into a volatile composition brimming with chillies and mustard seeds. It is this combination of seasonings that found its way into the 'devilled' Malaccan curry.

This is best served with plain rice, a vegetable such as Okra in a Sambal Sauce (see p. 94) and a condiment.

SERVES 4–6

1.5 kg / 3½ lb chicken, cut into serving pieces (skinned, if you prefer)

Salt

For the spice paste:

10–15 dried hot, red chillies, de-seeded

Half a red pepper (75 g / 2½ oz), de-seeded and coarsely chopped

2 teaspoons bright red paprika

5 cm / 2 inch piece of fresh ginger, peeled and coarsely chopped

2 small onions (115 g / 4 oz), peeled and coarsely chopped

3 cloves garlic, peeled and coarsely chopped

8 candle nuts or 1 tablespoon blanched, slivered almonds

1 tablespoon ground coriander

½ teaspoon ground turmeric

You also need:

1 teaspoon whole black (or yellow) mustard seeds

2 teaspoons dry, powdered mustard

1 tablespoon Chinese dark soy sauce

2 tablespoons rice vinegar – use a mild vinegar, such as Japanese vinegar (or cider vinegar)

8 tablespoons vegetable oil

6 shallots or 1 small onion (45 g / 1½ oz), peeled and thinly sliced

3 cloves garlic, peeled and thinly sliced

4 small potatoes (285 g / 10 oz), peeled and halved

Garnish (optional):

2–4 fresh, red and green chillies

Rub the chicken pieces with 1 teaspoon salt and set aside for 30 minutes or longer.

Put the dried red chillies in a bowl with 5 tablespoons hot water and soak until slightly soft. Alternatively, if you have a microwave oven, you could zap the chillies and their soaking liquid for 1 minute. Combine all the ingredients for the spice paste, including the soaking liquid from the chillies, in the container of an electric blender. Blend until smooth, pushing down when you have to and adding a little bit more water only if necessary.

Put the mustard seeds in the container of a spice-grinder and grind for a second, just until the seeds split. You could crush them lightly in a mortar.

Combine the dry mustard, soy sauce and

vinegar. Mix together well and set aside.

Heat the oil in a large wok or a wide pan over medium-high heat. When hot, put in the sliced shallots and sliced garlic. Stir and fry until they are lightly browned. Now put in the spice paste from the blender. Stir and fry for about 5 minutes or until the paste develops a fried look. If it starts to stick, light sprinklings of water will help. Now put in the mustard seeds and stir once or twice. Put in the chicken pieces. Stir and cook until they lose their outside pinkness.

Add the potatoes, 600 ml / 1 pint / 2½ cups water and 1½ teaspoons salt. Bring to a boil. Cover, turn the heat to low and simmer for 15 minutes. Add the mustard-soy-sauce-vinegar mixture, stir, cover and cook another 15–20 minutes or until the chicken is tender. You should stir gently a few times during this period.

Garnish with red and green chillies if liked when serving.

Kuala Lumpur, Malaysia

PORK CHOPS SIMMERED WITH TAMARIND
— BABI MASAK ASAM —

This dish is normally prepared with streaky pork, the same cut that is used for bacon, or with pork meat from the shoulder. Both are cut into 4 cm / 1½ inch chunks first. You may certainly use either of these instead of the pork chops which I just happen to be very partial to.

Both tamarind and fermented soy beans are rarely found in the same dish, except, of course, in the cooking of the Malaysian-Chinese. And in this predominantly Muslim nation, it is they who would be the ones to eat pork.

I find that the best chops for simmering slowly are loin chops only about 5 mm / ¼ inch thick.

Pork Chops Simmered with Tamarind (above) and Cucumber and Pineapple Salad (page 95).

4–5 dried, hot red chillies, de-seeded

1 stick of fresh lemon grass, just the lower 15 cm/6 inches cut into very fine rounds (or 2 teaspoons powdered lemon grass)

3 slices fresh galangal (or fresh ginger), peeled and coarsely chopped

1 teaspoon shrimp paste, *blachan* (or anchovy paste)

1 medium-sized onion (75 g/2½ oz), peeled and coarsely chopped

¼ teaspoon ground turmeric

1 tablespoon bright red paprika

15 fresh mint leaves

1 teaspoon sugar

1 teaspoon vegetable oil

3 tablespoons tamarind paste, see p. 218

Salt, to taste

You also need:

225 g/8 oz dried rice noodles *bahn pho* (or see previous page)

225 g/8 oz/4 cups lettuce that has been cut into 5 mm/¼ inch wide strips

60 g/2 oz/½ cup fresh pineapple peeled, cored and cut into julienne strips

1 small cucumber (115 g/4 oz), peeled and cut into julienne strips

Half a small onion (30 g/1 oz), peeled and finely sliced

20–30 fresh mint leaves

1–2 fresh, hot red or green chillies, cut into thin rounds

Put the fish in a pan with the chicken stock and bring to a boil. Cover, turn the heat to low and simmer gently for 15 minutes. Take the fish out of the broth and let it cool slightly. Remove all the flesh and mash it. Put the bones back into the broth and bring to a simmer. Simmer on low heat for 15 minutes. Strain the broth and reserve in the pan.

Put the dried chillies in a small bowl with 4 tablespoons water. Soak until the chillies are somewhat soft. Alternatively, if you have a microwave oven, you could zap the chillies and their soaking liquid for 1 minute.

Put the chillies and their soaking liquid, and the lemon grass, galangal, shrimp paste, onion, turmeric and paprika into the

container of an electric blender. Blend until you have a smooth paste. Pour this paste into the pan with the broth. Add the mint leaves, sugar, oil, tamarind paste and 250 ml/8 fl oz/ 1 cup water. Bring to a simmer. Simmer gently, uncovered, for 15 minutes. Make sure that there are no bones in the mashed fish. Put this fish into the broth as well. Stir and bring to a simmer. Simmer gently, uncovered, for 30 minutes. Taste for salt. You will need some if your stock was unsalted. Stir to mix. Turn off the heat. (Bring the soup to a fast simmer before serving.)

Soak the dried rice noodles in hot water for about 15 minutes or until they are soft. Drain. Bring a large pan of water to a rolling boil. Drop the drained noodles in it for about a minute. Keep checking as they cook fast. Drain. Divide the noodles between 3 largish eating bowls. Scatter a third of the lettuce over each lot of noodles. Divide all the remaining ingredients into 3 parts each and scatter one part each over the lettuce in the bowls. Pour simmering soup equally over the raw vegetables and fruit in each bowl. Serve immediately. Eat with chopsticks and a spoon, or a fork and a spoon.

Kuala Lumpur, Malaysia

FRESH MINT SAMBAL
SAMBAL PUDINA

Very similar to the fresh, vitamin-rich, Indian chutneys, this may be served with most curries as a condiment. It goes particularly well with Curry Puffs (see p. 86). This chutney may be frozen and then defrosted, though it will suffer a bit in quality.

MAKES ABOUT 250 ML/8 FL OZ/1 CUP

Bunch of fresh mint (60 g/2 oz after trimming)

1–3 fresh, hot green chillies, coarsely chopped

1 cm/½ inch piece of fresh ginger, peeled and coarsely chopped

1 small onion (60 g/2 oz), peeled and coarsely chopped

4 tablespoons fresh lime or lemon juice

½ teaspoon salt, or to taste

Combine all the ingredients in the container of an electric blender and blend them to a paste. You may have to push them down with a rubber spatula a few times.

All over Malaysia

SHRIMP PASTE RELISH
SAMBAL BELACAN

The best way to make this relish, found on a daily basis in almost every home in Malaysia, is to cut up 8–9 fresh, hot red chillies, remove their seeds if liked, and then pound the chillies in a stone mortar. After they are mashed up a bit, add about 1 tablespoon roasted shrimp paste (*blachan*) and pound some more until the desired consistency has been achieved. Freshly squeezed lime juice, about 2–3 tablespoons, is added at the table.

The problem, of course, is that we do not all have stone mortars and we cannot always get the correct sort of long, hot red chillies. Here is my alternative.

MAKES ABOUT 120 ML/4 FL OZ/½ CUP

2 medium-sized red peppers (225 g/8 oz), de-seeded and coarsely chopped

1 tablespoon shrimp paste, *blachan*, roasted, see p. 217, and crumbled

2½ tablespoons fresh lime juice (or lemon juice)

1½ teaspoons salt

¾ teaspoon chilli powder (cayenne pepper)

Put all the ingredients in the container of an electric blender and blend, pushing down a few times if necessary, until you have a coarse paste. Serve in a non-metallic bowl.

Kelantan and Pahang, Malaysia

QUICK MIXED PICKLE
ACAR RAMPAI

Every state in Malaysia has its own variation on a basic mixed pickle. This is a fairly simple one that is made in vast quantities for weddings. It is usually allowed to mature overnight but I find that it is good enough to eat almost immediately.

An evening market in one of the many China Towns that cater to Chinese and Muslim Malays.

MAKES ENOUGH TO FIT INTO A

900 ML / 1½ PINT / 4 CUP JAR

For the spice paste:

5–6 shallots or 1 small onion (45 g / 1½ oz), peeled and coarsely chopped

3 cloves garlic, peeled and coarsely chopped

2.5 cm / 1 inch piece of fresh ginger, peeled and coarsely chopped

You also need:

4 small carrots (200 g / 7 oz), peeled and cut into sticks

180 g / 6 oz / 2 cups cauliflower that has been broken into delicate florets

3 small cucumbers (180 g / 6 oz), unpeeled, cut into sticks the same size as the carrots. (Use pickling or long English cucumbers, if possible)

3 tablespoons vegetable oil

3 cloves garlic, peeled

2 small shallots or small pickling onions (20 g / ¾ oz), peeled

4 thin slices of peeled ginger, cut into fine strips

½ teaspoon whole black (or yellow) mustard seeds

1 tablespoon curry powder

1 teaspoon chilli powder (cayenne pepper)

½ teaspoon ground turmeric

4 tablespoons rice vinegar – use a mild vinegar, such as Japanese vinegar (or cider vinegar)

2 teaspoons sugar

1¾ teaspoons salt

1 tablespoon sesame oil

1 tablespoon roasted sesame seeds, see p. 217

Put the shallots, garlic and ginger for the spice paste in the container of an electric blender and blend, using as little water as possible to make the machine do its work.

Bring a large pan of water to a rolling boil. Drop in the carrot and cauliflower for just 30 seconds. Drop in the cucumber and boil rapidly for another 3 seconds. Drain immediately.

Heat the oil in a large, preferably non-stick, frying-pan over medium-high heat. When hot, put in the spice paste and fry for 1 minute. Put in the garlic cloves, shallots and ginger shreds and fry for 15 seconds. Turn the heat down to medium low. Put in the mustard seeds and stir once. Put in the curry powder, chilli powder (cayenne pepper) and turmeric. Stir once. Put in the vinegar and all the blanched vegetables, sugar and salt. Stir to mix. Add the sesame oil and sesame seeds. Mix well and turn off the heat. Let the pickle cool and then put it in a jar. Leave it out for 8–10 hours and then store it in the refrigerator.

All over Malaysia

PINEAPPLE CAKE
KEK NENAS

Columbus not only discovered America, he discovered pineapples. He found them growing abundantly in the West Indies where they were used in cooking and for making wine. By the mid-sixteenth century, thanks mainly to the Portuguese, pineapples were shooting up throughout most of the tropical world. They were easy enough to grow: Portuguese sailors took the fresh fruit on board ship with them to eat and the thick, succulent tufts were removed and stored. Then, when the sailors landed, the tufts were planted in the soil. It was as simple as that.

Malaysia has thousands of pineapple plantations and pineapples are used in daily cooking almost as much as coconuts are. Pineapple is put into curries along with prawns (shrimp), put into salads and made into hot *sambals*, and its sweet-sour juice is squeezed into curries. It also finds its way into dozens of tarts, pastries and cakes.

SERVES 6

A little vegetable oil and white flour for dusting the baking pan

2 large eggs

155 g / 5½ oz / ¾ cup sugar

120 ml / 4 fl oz / ½ cup corn or peanut oil

140 g / 5 oz / 1 cup plain (unbleached) white flour

1 teaspoon baking powder

¼ teaspoon ground cinnamon

¼ teaspoon salt

100 g / 3½ oz / ½ cup crushed pineapple with liquid (or canned, crushed pineapple, preferably unsweetened in its own juice)

1 medium-sized carrot (100 g / 3½ oz), peeled and grated

3 tablespoons coarsely chopped walnuts

2 tablespoons sultanas (golden raisins)

Pre-heat the oven to gas mark 4 / 350 °F / 180 °C. Use a 20 cm / 8 inch round or square baking tin that has a height of 4–5 cm / 1½–2 inches. Rub it with oil and then dust it very lightly with flour. Upturn the tin so all extra flour falls out.

Beat the eggs in a bowl until mixed. Add the sugar, beating as you do so, and incorporate it into the eggs. Keep beating as you slowly pour in the oil. Now add the flour, baking powder, cinnamon and salt and beat until all are mixed well. Add the pineapple and its juice and fold in gently. Put in the carrot, walnuts and raisins. Fold those in as well. Pour into the prepared cake tin and bake in the pre-heated oven for 40–45 minutes or until the cake is done. A tooth-pick, when inserted, should come out clean.

Imagine walking shoeless into a spare, *tatami*-matted room. You lower yourself on to floor cushions. Clear glass sliding-doors on three sides help to enclose you in an autumnal mountain scene – all around are hills, bursting with flaming maples and oaks. Vaporous mists are followed by sun, only to be overtaken by the mists again.

A waitress in a kimono comes in bearing purplish-black ceramic plates which she sets on a lacquer table. On the plates, still lolling in their half-shells, are fresh, briny rock oysters from the cold waters of Miyagi prefecture. Each oyster has a dollop of *momiji-oroshi* on it, a pungent mixture of grated white radish spiked with red chillies. You pick up an oyster with your chopsticks, dip it into a lime and soy-based sauce (*ponzu*) and then roll it in your mouth before allowing it to slither down your throat.

To heighten the ecstasy, there is *sake*, the national rice wine. It is ladled straight from a cedar cask into squarish wooden cups. As you sip from a corner, you feel you are drinking the sweetest, cedar-flavoured, spring water. But this 'water' carries a deceptive kick.

The next course comes in a covered china cup. You lift the lid. Steam, bearing the clean smells of earth and sea, rushes up. When it clears, you see a pale yellow custard with embedded slivers of wild mountain mushrooms. The 'custard' is savoury and is actually a steamed 'soup' known as *chawanmushi*. It is as close to being liquid as a custard could ever get. There is not a single bubble to mar its satiny finish.

All this could well be the start of a traditional Japanese meal – tiny portions that are both ascetic and aesthetic in a very Zen Buddhist way, served in a series of courses that might also

Opposite: A temple and Mount Fuji, symbols of timeless Japan.

include raw slices of sea bream, eaten with green horseradish; chicken legs, marinated in *sake*, soy sauce and grated citrus rind and then grilled; tiny aubergines (eggplants) fried and then simmered in a spicy broth; and, of course, the unvarying staples but always of the highest quality, *miso* (fermented soy bean paste) soup, rice, pickles and tea.

Such a meal, where seasonality, tradition, religion, art and craft are all celebrated, where substance and form merge as the freshest of ingredients are cooked for a minimum length of time, and then laid out as three-dimensional paintings on a 'canvas' of rare plates and bowls – this is what Japanese food at its most exquisite is all about.

However, such food today can only be afforded by the super-rich, by magnates of industry, royalty, top-ranking bankers, designers, conductors and actors. Freshness and a labour-intensive striving for perfection carry a heavy price, so this food is to be found at high-class inns (*ryokan*) such as the Tawaraya in Kyoto or in restaurants serving traditional *haute cuisine* (*ryotei*). Still, its spirit can be seen in humbler quarters, in the perfect bowl of noodle soup topped with the wild spring greens or in a winter serving of silken bean curd cubes in a steaming bath of kelp water.

There is a second trend in Japan that is changing eating habits and causing younger Japanese to live shorter lives than their parents – and that trend is Westernisation.

On my last trip to Japan, I arrived in Tokyo around the time that Emperor Akahito was to ascend the Chrysanthemum Throne. Every major world leader was in town. The national papers were filled with the details of a mysterious, 1500-year-old enthronement ritual which marked the actual consecration.

Called The Festival of Great Eating (*Daijosai*) it involved, among other things, a procession of foods: rice, *sake*, seaweed broth and fruit, all borne aloft in vessels of oak leaves and unglazed red earthenware. The emperor was to make an offering of them to the Sun Goddess and then partake of some rice dumplings and *sake* himself.

That same day's paper also carried an item headlined, 'Security Frustrates Japanese Beaujolais Lovers'. It seemed that all incoming air cargoes, including the 2.2 million bottles of Beaujolais Nouveau which trendy Japanese are now used to drinking on the actual day of its release in France, were being held up by nervous security officials. The Japanese who, in a new seasonal ritual, rush to the Narita Airport Hotel to celebrate with the wine the minute it lands, were visibly annoyed.

Japan's days of isolation are definitely over.

HOKKAIDO

Akita

MIYAGI

Sea of

Japan

Tokyo

Kyoto

Osaka Matsusaka

PACIFIC

OCEAN

East

China

Sea

KYUSHU

Shoes are left at the entrance to one of Japan's high-class inns, the Tawaraya Inn.

Traditional Japan and a very modern, Westernised Japan are now beginning to merge and nowhere is this more apparent than in the revisions of the culinary world. The old foods are by no means lost. But, with a financially powerful Japan able to scour the world for its needs, there are many new ones. And many old foods now have fashionable new marinades, accents and trimmings.

Until the late nineteenth century, the Japanese consumed hardly any red meat or dairy products. Traditionally, breakfast was a healthy soy bean paste soup (*miso-shiru*), a bowl of rice (*gohan*), perhaps some dried fish, maybe a mouth-puckeringly sour preserved plum, filled with Vitamin C (*umeboshi*), some pickles (*tsukemono*) and green tea (*ryokucha*). Lunch and dinner were fairly similar but with more dishes. A soup with three dishes – not counting the rice, tea and pickles which were *de rigueur* – would be considered an average meal. There would certainly be fresh fish in some form and perhaps fowl as well as seasonal vegetables. Fruit might well conclude the meal. Noodles, always popular, could be had cold in the summer and in hot soups in the winter. The stock for these soups was generally made with dried fish and kelp, although fowl was sometimes used as well. Dried beans, used in ancient times to pay taxes, were sprouted, made into bean curd and scores of fermented pastes and seasoning sauces. Some beans, such as the *aduki* red bean, were made into a sweet paste that performed all the functions chocolate does in the West.

This way of eating still exists. But Western foods and ingredients have made deep inroads.

Take red meat, for instance. The Japanese were themselves keen to introduce it to their country at the end of the last century. They wanted their people to grow tall and strong like Westerners. So dishes such as *sukiyaki* and, much later, *shabu shabu* were invented. These called for thinly sliced beef being cooked briefly in flavoured liquid. Such slices could be picked up easily with chopsticks.

'Kobe beef' is meltingly tender – and very expensive. Thin slices are frequently cooked in a broth along with vegetables.

Being perfectionists, the Japanese then proceeded to raise the most marbled meat – *shimofuri* or 'frosted' beef – in places like Matsusaka. This is known generally as 'Kobe beef' and practically melts in the mouth. But it is so expensive that it is sold in grams rather than kilograms.

Rice, a staple for centuries, is being replaced at breakfast by bread, specially for the younger generation. In many families, grandparents still eat rice in the morning while the youngsters eat fresh bread made at home by new, plug-in machines which require only measured flour and water and do the rest on their own. The consumption of rice has gone down 40 per cent, though it remains the emotional heart of most lunches and dinners and of many religious ceremonies. Japanese rice is short-grained, sweet flavoured, slightly sticky and, it must be confessed, highly addictive.

Because it is just not done to drink *sake* while eating rice, the grain is always served at the conclusion of a meal rather than with it. Drinking can thus continue till the very end – and certainly does at most banquets. On my earlier trips to Japan, *sake* was being replaced by whisky and now French wines seem to have taken over.

Takashimaya, one of Tokyo's leading department stores, has its own temperature-controlled wine 'cellar' and a major interest in the French Romanée-Conti vineyard. Mr Okura, the store's managing director, told me that 40 years ago, during the Japanese seasons of gift-giving in July and December, the gifts would most likely have been *sake* or expensive seaweed or salted salmon. Twenty years ago they had already changed to whiskies, hams, coffees and English teas. Today it is mostly wine – sets of red and white wine or, better still, Dom Pérignon champagne.

On the whole, Japanese seasonings have not changed much. They consist mainly of light and dark soy sauces, ginger, white radish (*daikon*), green horseradish (*wasabi*), sweet *sake* (*mirin*), *sake*, fermented bean pastes (*miso*), sesame seeds, spring onions (scallions), vinegar, sour plum paste (*bainiku*), *sansho* pepper, red pepper and various local citrus, lime-like fruits such as the *yuzu*, *kabuso* and *sudachi*.

But cognac has begun to replace *sake* as a marinade in chic restaurants and garlic is slowly being added to the repertoire. Garlic, because of its associations with health, is now the newest rage among the trendy. There is a restaurant in Tokyo that serves nothing but garlic-flavoured dishes. My Japanese translator on my last trip there – who was also an excellent cook – gave me a recipe for grilled pork strips, marinated first in dark soy sauce and ginger, *buta no shoga yaki*. He added with a smile, almost as if he were suggesting something naughty, 'Of course, you could substitute garlic for the ginger, in which case the dish would be called "stamina'-yaki"!'.

In the land of the tea ceremony, coffee is

fast becoming the most fashionable drink, especially for breakfast and for mid-morning and afternoon breaks. I think it can be said quite unequivocally that coffee here is among the tastiest in the world. The Japanese can afford to buy the world's best beans. They are fanatical about roasting them freshly, and

Wasabi paste, made from a pungent, green Japanese horseradish, for sale in one of Tokyo's leading department stores.

equally fastidious about the brewing. With the coffee, cakes and pastries that rival the best of Europe are served. Shizuo Tsuji, who heads an academy for professional chefs in Osaka, once offered me the best cake I have probably ever eaten – passion-fruit flavoured and utterly ethereal. The Japanese seem to approach their pastry cookery with the same meticulous care that they give to their construction of cameras. And they are beginning to beat the world at it.

To see how East and West, old and new,

combine in everyday lives, it may be best to look at individual Japanese.

Sakae Takita, a friend, is a renowned actor with matinée-idol looks. He has played the lead in the Japanese version of *Les Miserables* and had just opened in a translation of *King Lear*, in the title role. His wife, Taeko, is a ballet dancer. They have three children. Unlike most people in crowded Tokyo, where land seems to cost as much as gold, they own a multi-storey house tucked into the quiet back lane of a fashionable district.

Madhur Jaffrey with a young girl dressed for Children's Day in a traditional kimono.

For breakfast, Sakae likes to have salted dried fish – it could be sardines – that he stocks in the freezer. They are grilled and then eaten with rice. There is also *miso* soup, some fermented glutinous beans, strong as a ripe cheese, called *natto*, a raw egg, pickles and tea. He never stoops to the instant *miso* soups that much of Japan now eats.

Lunch is late, at around 3.30 p.m. and is usually a *nabemono* – things cooked in a single pot. The tradition for this goes back to Japanese farmhouses where a single kettle hung over the central open hearth known as the *irori*. That particular day's *nabemono* bears the marks of another country as well, the Mongolian hotpot of China, which found its way into Japan in this century as *shabu shabu*.

When Sakae is performing, he likes to eat *nabemonos* of fish and vegetables. They are light and satisfying and they give his body 'good balance', he says. He can also put into them the best foods of the season.

Many Japanese talk about 'eating the season', or 'tasting the season' as if the season were a food that they could roll around the tongue. They mean many things by this. In the autumn, for example, they not only eat chrysanthemum leaves and petals which grow at that time but they also cut other vegetables – such as turnips – to resemble chrysanthemums. It is this same spirit that makes them go, *en masse*, to look at the cherry blossoms in the spring and, more recently, rush to enjoy the first of the Beaujolais Nouveau in the late autumn. It is an almost religious immersion of all the senses in the joys of a season. A poet writes in late autumn:

As I tie together
The Kyoto (winter) greens
There is the sound of frost

Perhaps because I am present that chilly November day, Sakae is serving a lunch of *shabu shabu* made with the very special

Matsusaka beef. We sit on chairs at a table. On the centre of the table, attached to an umbilical-cord-like hose, is a gas burner, a modern *irori*. There is a bowl of simmering kelp (*konbu*) broth on top of it.

Taeko comes in with a large platter of thinly sliced beef arranged in overlapping layers. We take a slice of beef, swish it in the simmering liquid to cook it slightly and then dip it into our choice among four sauces. There is a sesame sauce; a vinegar sauce; *shotsuru*, a fish sauce from Akita flavoured with fresh green coriander and the naturally brewed, bonito-flavoured, Tosa soy sauce to which are added squeezes of *kabuso* lime juice. As a change from the meat, Sakae turns to an even larger platter of vegetables: tender chrysanthemum leaves, trefoil (*mitsuba*), wild grasses, just-picked mountain *shimeji* mushrooms and slim leeks (*negi*) which are dropped into the now very well flavoured broth and then retrieved at appropriate times. Other complementary foods arrive, such as *sengiri*, a salad of hair-thin shreds of carrot and white radish, which Sakae dresses very simply with a few dashes of a herb-flavoured French white wine vinegar. At the very end, some rice and a beaten egg are folded into the broth which is still simmering on the burner. We accompany this gruel (*zosui*) with pickles and tea.

Sakae does not drink during lunch. He has a performance to think about. But after the show is over, in his dressing-room, he drowns out Goneril and Regan with a can of chilled Sopporo beer and, when he comes home, with an ice-filled glass of *nigori sake*, a fresh, milky variety that does not travel.

When Sakae goes out to eat, it is to places where he is assured of the highest quality. He was raised that way by his father who took him into the mountains to live off fresh fish, game and wild greens.

Tenharu is a place he approves of. It serves *tempura*, fried morsels of fish and vegetables encased in gossamer-thin batter. Here it is not only freshness and seasonality that are important, but the quality and temperature of

Sign in a Tokyo department store. Fish is central to the Japanese diet.

the oil. The top grade *tempura* establishments use their oil once and then sell it to lesser *tempura* places. The oil temperature needs constant adjustment so that aubergines (eggplants) do not lose colour or red snapper overcook.

Sakae also has an enduring relationship with a *sushi* restaurant, Taikou. *Sushi* is the Japanese canapé-like sandwich – sometimes open, sometimes closed and sometimes rolled up in toasted seaweed (*nori*). Rice replaces bread, and the toppings or fillings are mostly raw fish pieces with omelette sections, some grilled eel and even pickled and plain vegetables.

It seems that *sushi* in its earliest forms came into Japan from South-East Asia. Sixth-century records from China describe a method of preserving raw fish by wrapping it in boiled rice. The fermenting fish formed

amino acid while the fermenting rice formed lactic acid. This combination preserved the fish, sometimes for several years. The rice was thrown away and only the fish eaten. Such recipes began to be seen in Japan in the eighth century, under the name of *nare-zushi*. By the sixteenth century, the pickling process had been hastened to a few days and both fish and rice were eaten.

It was only in the early nineteenth century that residents of Edo (Tokyo after 1868), ever in a hurry to snack and move on, came up with the idea of vinegared rice fingers topped with pieces of the freshest fish, to be eaten with dips in soy sauce and occasional bites of pickled ginger. Today, this very popular form of *sushi* – *nigiri-zushi* – exists alongside some of the earlier ones.

The street stalls of the nineteenth century have given way to restaurants and one can sit instead of standing, the best place being on stools at a counter. At Taikou, the chef trained for nine years before becoming the master he is. As he deftly makes up *sushi* of

105

Frozen tuna, which now comes from seas around the world, for sale in Tsukiji's auction sheds.

along Tokyo's dark and empty streets. The market sits on a wide waterway that connects the Sumida River to Tokyo Bay.

Even though the city is empty at this hour, the fish market is a hive of activity. Cars, trucks, forklifts, handcarts and about 100 000 people are milling around. Tatsuko tries four large parking lots before seeing an empty space. It is almost time for the tuna auction to start and she cannot afford to be late. Her dealer will bid for the tuna and she will buy it from him moments later.

The auction sheds, vast and numerous, are just by the water's edge. Even I, who have been travelling to Japan regularly for the last 20 years, can remember a time when all the tuna was fresh and came from local waters. Today Japan must send its ships to seas off the coasts of Peru, Chile, Angola, Alaska and India to satisfy the cravings of the populace.

Much of the tuna unloaded here is frozen solid and is destined, once defrosted, to be eaten raw, as *sashimi* – small, rectangular slices of fish eaten with *wasabi* (Japanese horse-radish) and soy sauce – or as *sushi*. Tuna freezes well enough to satisfy all but those who are both very finicky and very rich.

The frozen tuna, tails and flippers clipped for convenience, lie in rows on the floor, each weighing over 100 kg/45 lb and looking like the monster eggs of Spielbergian aliens. They emit a smoky, ghostly haze which rises for about 30 cm/1 ft and then breaks away in little wisps. Before sun-up, each tuna will be numbered with red paint and then offered to the commodity dealers by a fast-talking auctioneer with a permanently hoarse voice, who is reputed to sell 40 tunas in a minute.

Potential buyers hack out little pieces of meat from a flap cut near the tail. The meat is mashed between the fingers to check for fat content. The fattier the meat, the better the price. *Maguro*, the flesh nearest the spine, is deep red, meaty and very well liked – but not as much as the fattier and pink *chutoro* or *toro*, the very pale pink and fattiest meat of all near the stomach. One piece of good *toro sushi* can cost upward of 2000 yen.

delicate white snipe, salmon eggs and *ama-ebi* (a glutinous shrimp), he states that at *his* restaurant, all the fish must be fresh.

This is not always the case today. The Japanese consume over 12 million tons of fish annually. It is central to every meal. Some is, of necessity, frozen. To see how fish is supplied, I accompany Tatsuko Shiotani to Tokyo's largest wholesale fish market in Tsukiji. Tatsuko owns the Yutaka restaurant in the fashionable Akasaka area. She depends on a regular supply of fish.

The chilly November day has barely begun when Tatsuko can be seen, speeding west

Most of the fish at the market is not frozen at all. It is fresh and clear-eyed, sometimes alive enough to be jumping around in tanks. Tatsuko has her list but she picks whatever looks good: there are freshwater eels (*unagi*), ready for grilling, to be eaten with a slightly sweet sauce and liberal sprinklings of Japanese *sansho* pepper (Japan Airlines serves an excellent version of this); there is devil's fish and, better still, devil's fish liver which will be salted, moulded in foil, steamed and then eaten rather like *foie gras*; there is plump mullet roe which can be salted and pressed to produce the caviare-like *karasumi* – some people, like Mr Okura of Takashimaya, like to prepare this themselves; and, best of all, there are those oysters from the Miyagi prefecture.

This wealth from the waters finds its way into Tatsuko's Yutaka restaurant that same morning. It also finds its way into another Yutaka restaurant in Tokyo, this one in Shibuya. It is owned by my hosts for the evening, the Hoshiyas, and is tucked into a tiny basement. Almost all the seating here is along a small counter. But the food, prepared in the delicate Kansai or Kyoto style right in front of the diners, is exquisite.

We fatten ourselves on fresh turtle soup, cod roe simmered in stock (*dashi*), with grilled and deep-fried oysters and with the wonderful *kinki* fish from the waters of northern Hokkaido. After the end of the meal, generous and irrepressible Mrs Toyomi Hoshiya invites me to her home for dinner the day before I am to leave.

The Hoshiyas live in an apartment. Their living-room is divided into two parts, diagonally. One half, comprising the kitchen and eating area, is dominated by a triangular dining-table, the other half by a piano and television set. The dining-table has a built-in gas burner which can be covered up when not in use.

Toyomi's mother, in an indigo-patterned kimono, has already prepared a persimmon salad and two simmered dishes, one of white beans, calcium-rich *hijiki* seaweed and

vegetables and another of *shiratake* noodles and cod roe. A special rice, flavoured with the season's *matsutake* mushrooms, is already in the large, electric rice cooker. Toyomi grates some glutinous mountain yam for another salad and stews some white radish with minced (ground) chicken. A daughter comes in and plays her own composition on the piano for us. Toyomi's sister, an English teacher, drops by too. During all this pleasant, family commotion we have the raw fish course: a *sashimi* of bonito, a tuna-like fish. Toyomi has stuck fragrant *shiso* leaves between the slices and scattered shreds of ginger over the top. For the dip, she quickly

Karasumi, made from salted and pressed mullet roe, is similar to caviar. Here it is served plain with rice and a broth.

mixes some very coarse mustard from a Fortnum & Mason jar with soy sauce. It is superb.

We drink a special *sake* from Kyushu and go on to a *nabemono* of mixed seafood – shellfish, crustaceans and fish – cooked at the table. We eat through the evening and some of the night. As I get ready to leave, Toyomi scoops up two lumps of mushroom rice, stuffs some sour plum paste into the centre of each and forms triangular *onigiri* which she wraps in foil. She also wraps sheets of toasted seaweed (*nori*) in plastic. She encloses these two packets in an embroidered napkin, a *fukin*, made by her mother. 'Fold the *nori* around the rice and have it for breakfast,' she says, 'and remember not to refrigerate it.'

As I head back to my hotel I glow in the warmth of Japanese hospitality. And I look forward with great pleasure to my *onigiri*.

RECIPES FROM
JAPAN

An illuminated sign above a store entrance.

Japan

GLORIOUS RAW OYSTERS WITH A DIP
── NAMAGAKI ──

There is nothing quite like raw oysters in season and November in Japan seems to mean the best of rock oysters. These can be grilled on beds of *konbu* seaweed or crumbed and deep-fried but they are wonderful just raw, served as they were at the Yutaka restaurant in Tokyo's Akasaka area, with grated radish spiked with chillies and with a lemony dipping sauce.

The greatest difficulty with raw oysters is

opening them. Sea gulls are known to drop them from great heights to crack their shells and sometimes mortals are tempted to do the same. Oysters are stubborn. The professional way is first to insert an oyster knife and pry the two shells apart and then use the same knife to cut the adductor muscle. An innovative method used by the American cookery expert, Julia Child, involves using a beer-can opener. The triangular end, point facing up, is inserted into the hinge end of the oyster and then it is pried apart. If the worst comes to the worst, you can always put the oyster, rounded side down, on a low flame for a brief minute. This does not cook it but it does force the rotter to open up. You could also get your fishmonger to open up the oysters. Ask him to put them and their juices in a closed container which you can refrigerate until needed. Bring the shells home as well, especially the bottom shell which will act as a container. To serve, embed the bottom shells in crushed ice to steady them and then spoon in an oyster each and some juice.

You can allow anywhere from 3–6 oysters per person for this recipe. I have allotted 5 as a first course.

SERVES 4

2 spring onions (scallions)
Red Maple Relish, see p. 121
Simple Lemon-Soy Sauce, see p. 121
Extra lemon wedges
20 fresh oysters

Cut the spring onions (scallions) crossways into very, very fine rounds all the way up their green sections. Put in a bowl of cold water for 30–60 minutes. Drain. Put in a dishcloth and squeeze out extra water.

Pour the Simple Lemon-Soy Sauce into 4 small bowls for dipping and then set them on the table.

In 4 small saucers, make little heaps of the spring onions (scallions) and the Red Maple Relish. Put a wedge of lemon on each plate.

Serve the oysters as suggested above, in their shells, embedded in crushed ice (or set

on napkin rings) to keep them steady. Each diner should mix some of the spring onions (scallions) and some of the relish in the sauce, then dip the oysters in it and eat. Extra lemon may be squirted on as well.

Japan

A STEAMED SOUP-CUSTARD WITH CHICKEN AND PRAWNS (SHRIMP)
── CHAWANMUSHI ──

I urge you to try this. It is a silken soup that is allowed to set – but just barely. As you make your way down to the bottom of the cup, nuggets of chicken and prawn (shrimp) lie in wait.

Versions of this dish can be found in China, where it probably originated, and in Korea. But it is the Japanese who have perfected it, lowering the proportion of eggs to liquid in order to achieve the most delicate of jells. I have been making this soup for over two decades now. Of all the methods I have used, this one, which calls for steaming at two different temperatures, achieves the most perfect result. This is an ideal dish to serve to the family on a winter night or to friends when you entertain. All the ingredients may be prepared ahead of time and the soup put together and set to steam about 18 minutes before you are to eat it. In the summer, you could prepare the soup ahead of time in its entirety and serve it cool.

For the steaming, I use a large, lidded wok into which I fit a round steaming tray. *Chawanmushi* is traditionally cooked and served in individual cups especially made for the purpose. They have lids to prevent condensation from dripping on to the soup, and no handles. Oriental utensil shops often carry the cups. What may be substituted without any loss of style are egg coddlers or

Clockwise from top left: **Salmon Roe Sushi** (page 112); **Smoked Salmon Sushi** (page 112); **Cucumber Rolls** (page 113); **Glorious Raw Oysters** (opposite); **Pickled Ginger** (page 110); **Sushi Dipping Sauce** (page 111).

Fish in a Tokyo department store. The main ingredient in sushi, when it is served raw with vinegared rice, it is also often combined with vegetables or soused, as in the recipe here.

trench and then lay some of the cucumber strips in it as well.

Begin rolling the mat tightly away from you. Do one roll, keeping the cucumber strips in place with your index fingers, if necessary. The first roll should take you just past the cucumbers. When the edge of the mat touches the rice, squeeze lightly all along the length of the mat to firm up the roll. Keep rolling, this time making sure that the edge of the mat stays on top of the roll and does not get rolled into it. Once the roll is made, press the mat on all sides to flatten the roll and square it off slightly. Remove the mat. Using a sharp knife wiped with a dampened cloth, cut the roll in half crossways, and then cut each half into 3 sections. Stand the pieces on end. Use up all the seaweed this way. Serve with Sushi Dipping Sauce and Pickled Ginger on the side.

Japan

SOUSED FISH
NAMBANZUKE

Namban is the Japanese word for 'Southern savages' and refers to the Spaniards and Portuguese who came from the south in the sixteenth century. As they brought red chillies with them, dishes with this fiery spice often carry their appellation.

Nambanzuke, a dish where cooked fish are left to bathe in a vinegary marinade, is generally made with small fish such as horse mackerel. It is served as an appetiser. I have decided to use a trout instead. Any white-fleshed fish, specially from fresh waters, is best. I had my fish cut by the fishmonger into round chunks but you could use fillets with skin instead.

A Japanese portion would consist of just one piece of this fish, sitting in solitary splendour on a small plate. I serve it just that way at dinner parties, making this my first course. I tuck a small lettuce leaf on one side as a garnish.

SERVES 2–5

Whole fresh trout (450 g / 1 lb or a bit more), cleaned and cut crossways into 2.5 cm / 1 inch sections – you may keep the head or not, as liked (or see above)

Salt

450 ml / 15 fl oz / 2 cups Japanese Soup Stock, see p. 198, freshly made or instant (or light chicken stock)

6 tablespoons Japanese rice vinegar

6 tablespoons *mirin*, see p. 214

6 tablespoons Japanese light soy sauce

2–3 dried red chillies

45 g / 1½ oz / ⅓ cup plain (all purpose) white flour

Vegetable oil for deep-frying

2 very thin, round slices (15 g / ½ oz) cut from a peeled onion

2 tablespoons fine matchsticks (15 g / ½ oz) cut from a peeled carrot

2 tablespoons fine matchsticks (15 g / ½ oz) cut from a firm, peeled cucumber

Spread the fish pieces out on a plate or board and salt lightly on all sides. Set aside for 30 minutes.

Meanwhile, combine the stock, vinegar, *mirin*, soy sauce and dried chillies in a pan. Bring to a boil. Turn off the heat and set aside.

Pat the fish dry and then dredge the pieces in flour. Dust off as much flour as will flake off easily. Heat the oil until it is about 160 °C / 325 °F and then fry the fish for about 6 minutes or until it is golden-brown. Drain for a minute on paper towels. As you do this, heat the marinade. Put the fish in a bowl

while it is still very hot and pour the hot marinade over it. Add the onion, carrot and cucumber. Allow to cool and then cover and refrigerate for at least 4 hours or overnight. This dish may be served up to 3 days later.

To serve, lift a piece of fish out of the marinade and place it in the centre of a half plate or shallow bowl. Arrange a few pieces of the vegetables on top. A thin round of the red chilli could be sliced off and placed prettily somewhere. You may also put a small lettuce leaf to one side. A very little liquid from the marinade, perhaps 1 tablespoon, may be spooned over the top.

Japan
QUICK-GRILLED CHICKEN WITH GINGER
TORI NO YUAN-YAKI

What an easy and delightful way to grill chicken, either outdoors or indoors. In Japan, chicken legs are preferred for the obvious reason that they are much more moist. You may use breasts, but remember that they will be a bit drier. I often serve rice and a salad with this chicken.

SERVES 4

4 chicken legs, boned, see p. 207, but not skinned

8 tablespoons Japanese dark soy sauce

8 tablespoons *sake*

8 tablespoons *mirin*, see p. 214

2 teaspoons finely grated, fresh, peeled ginger

A little ground *sansho* pepper (optional)

Prod the chicken skin with a fork. Combine the soy sauce, *sake*, *mirin* and ginger in a bowl. Mix. Put in the chicken pieces and let them marinate for 30 minutes.

Heat your outdoor grill or indoor grill (broiler). Spread the chicken pieces neatly on a grilling surface, skin-side facing the source of heat, rearranging each piece so it looks more whole than ragged (you do this by swinging the drumstick section around to lie beside the thigh section). Grill the skin side for 5–6 minutes. Do not let it burn. Turn the

chicken pieces over and grill the second side for about the same length of time. The chicken should be done. If it is not cooked through to your satisfaction, either distance it from the source of heat and cook for another minute or so, or, if cooking indoors, turn off the heat and let the chicken just sit under the grill (broiler) for another minute.

Serve immediately, skin-side up, with a light dusting of *sansho* pepper. If serving Japanese style, use a very sharp knife and cut each piece neatly into 2.5 cm / 1 inch sections. Then re-form the sections into the original shape of the leg.

Bonus: If there are any left-overs – I generally make extra chicken to create these – they are wonderful cold. Just slice the chicken at a slight diagonal and have it on toast, which you should first butter lightly if you like and then smear with a thin layer of French mustard.

Japan
PAN-FRIED DUCK AND SCALLOPS
SUMIBIYAKI

This is a right royal dish. I mean that quite literally. It was served to Their Royal Highnesses the Prince and Princess of Wales at the Tsuriya restaurant in Kyoto on May 9, 1986 as part of a special banquet hosted by Japan's Minister for Foreign Affairs.

It seems that Prince Charles had requested a dish he might cook himself at the table, a commonplace phenomenon in Japanese cuisine. Tsuriya, a *ryotei* (restaurant serving traditional *haute cuisine*) obliged by presenting this superb creation among a host of others. (I got to eat the entire meal at a later date.) There was a modern touch in the royal dish. Cognac had replaced the *sake* in the marinade.

Japanese shops sell small, individual braziers that come with removable 'grills' made out of firm netting. Burning hardwood charcoal is put in them at the appropriate time and they are placed on the dining-table. Raw meat slices, marinaded or otherwise, follow on a plate. Then each diner cooks his or her own food to the doneness they like and eats it right away.

You may want to try and acquire these braziers. Most of us would probably find it all too cumbersome. You might, in the summer do a cook-out and have all your friends standing around a larger single grill, each person making their own food. But if you want to bother with none of this, there is a way to do it all in a pan in the kitchen.

The main ingredient here is duck breasts. In some countries, it is quite easy to get boned duck breasts, even in supermarkets. Where you cannot, you will need to buy a whole, good-sized duck to get about 900 g/2 lb of unboned breast (450 g/1 lb of boned, trimmed breast). Have the butcher joint it and then ask him to bone the breasts but to leave the skin on.

If necessary, you can bone the breasts yourself. Use a sharp boning knife. Just follow the bone structure starting with the thinner ribbed side and make your way below the meatier section. There are the odd single bones you will have to work around. Once the bones are out, cut off the flap where the ribbed section was and remove all extraneous blobs of fat. You should end up with a neat, trim, oval shape.

To cut the breasts into slices, wrap each piece well and freeze it for 1–1½ hours. Use a very sharp knife and cut at a slight diagonal, holding the knife facing not down but to one side. This way you will get wider slices. Each slice should have a thin strip of fat at the top, almost like icing on a slice of cake. Your first slice will probably have more. Trim the fat on that one so it looks like all the other slices.

SERVES 4

400–450 g/14 oz–1 lb boned duck breast, cut into 5 mm/¼ inch thick slices (see above)

8 large scallops

4 fresh *shiitake* or plain white mushrooms

One-third of a green pepper (70 g/2½ oz)

6 tablespoons *mirin*, see p. 214

10 tablespoons Japanese light soy sauce

3 tablespoons cognac

A few tablespoons vegetable oil

2 spring onions (scallions)

Simple Lemon-Soy Sauce, see p. 121

Red Maple Relish, see p. 121

Place the duck neatly in a row of slightly overlapping slices on a large plate which has a little depth to it. Cut the scallops in half crossways, making medallions, and lay them around the duck. Cut away the mushroom stems. Drop the caps in a little boiling water and boil for 1 minute. Remove the caps and place them over the duck, or to one side. Cut the green pepper into 8 strips, each 5 cm/2 inches long and 1 cm/½ inch wide. Drop them into boiling water for 20 seconds. Drain and place over the duck. Mix the *mirin*, light soy sauce and cognac and pour it over the duck and the other ingredients on the plate. Make sure each is properly submerged. Set aside for 30–60 minutes.

Cut the spring onions (scallions) into very fine rounds all the way up their green sections and leave to soak in cold water for 30 minutes. Drain. Put in a dish towel and squeeze out all the moisture.

Just before eating, divide the Simple Lemon-Soy Sauce between 4 small bowls and put them on the table for dipping. In 4 saucers, place small mounds of the spring onions (scallions) and the Red Maple Relish and put these on the table.

Brush a large frying-pan (I use cast-iron) with a little oil and set it over highish heat. When very hot, lift up one piece of duck at a time and lay it in the pan. Do not crowd the pan. The duck will brown fast. Turn it over and brown the other side. The centre of the slice should remain pink. Remove the duck pieces as they get done and keep on a warm serving plate. Do the scallops, mushrooms and pepper the same way and arrange prettily on the same plate. As soon as they are done, take the plate to the table.

To eat, each diner should put some spring onions (scallions) and some Red Maple Relish

into the Simple Lemon-Soy Sauce. All the cooked foods should be dipped into the sauce before eating.

Japan

BEEF AND VEGETABLES COOKED AT THE TABLE
— SHABU SHABU —

It is a convivial way to eat, sitting around a table, a hotpot of stock simmering in the centre and everyone picking up bits of raw meat and vegetables, dipping them first into the common stock to cook them briefly, and then into a deliciously tart sauce, before gobbling them up. *Shabu shabu* (the name comes from the sound of foods being swished around in hot stock), owes its ancestry to the Chrysanthemum Pot and Mongolian Hot Pot of China, and was introduced to Japan about a century ago, around the same time as Western diplomats introduced beef. Until then only the meat of two-legged creatures – birds and poultry – was consumed.

It is a dish for cold days. The first time I had it, we were at the Ugenta restaurant, way up in the hills just outside Kyoto. It was spring and drizzling endlessly. We were asked to sit around a low table that had spread over it – as you might spread a table-cloth – a large, generous quilt. On top of the quilt, anchoring it down, was a second table-top. As I sat down, I was encouraged to pull the quilt over my legs. There was extra heat emanating mysteriously from under the table. Then hot *sake* arrived. As we drank it, a gas plate was set up on the table and on it was placed a beautiful *donabe*, a rough ceramic pot that can withstand direct heat. There was *konbu* (dried kelp) stock in this pot. A platter of thinly sliced, well-marbled beef was placed nearby, as well as a platter of beautifully arranged vegetables, fungi and noodles. We lifted the meat first with our chopsticks,

Pan-fried Duck and Scallops
(page 115).

swished it around in the hot stock, cooking it just as much as we liked, and then ate it after dipping it into a choice of sauces. We picked up the vegetables next and dropped them in the stock. They took longer to cook and could be retrieved a little later. Noodles and fungi followed. The broth was skimmed many times by a patient attendant. At the end, the broth was poured into bowls, lightly salted, and offered to us as a soup. There were bowls of rice and pickles to round off the meal.

To cook *shabu shabu* at home, you can improvise with an electric frying-pan set on your dining-table, or a fondu pot if you happen to have one. You could also use an electric hotplate on which you place a casserole-type pan. The broth should be brought to a boil and then kept at a bare simmer.

The beef used here is cut into very, very thin, large sheets about 10 x 7.5 cm / 4 x 3 inches. It is best if the butcher does this for you. If he has done any cutting for Italians, try asking him to cut it as he would *carpaccio*. I sometimes manage to cut somewhat less than paper-thin slices myself at home by partially freezing the meat first for about an hour. I tend to keep my pieces a bit smaller, about 7.5 x 5 cm / 3 x 2 inches.

SERVES 4

450 g / 1 lb very tender, well-marbled beef, either from a boneless rib-roast or tenderloin, or boneless sirloin steak, cut, preferably by the butcher, as above

225 g / 8 oz well-trimmed, fresh spinach leaves

225 g / 8 oz Chinese cabbage (or Chinese leaves / celery cabbage)

225 g / 8 oz mushrooms

115 g / 4 oz watercress

150 g / 5 oz medium bean curd

12 spring onions (scallions)

Simple Lemon-Soy Sauce, see p. 121

Sesame Sauce, see p. 121

Red Maple Relish, see p. 121, made just before eating

10 cm / 4 inch square of *konbu* if available, or light, unsalted vegetable or chicken stock

On a large serving plate, arrange the meat in neatly overlapping slices. Cover with cling film (plastic wrap) and set aside, refrigerating if necessary.

Some people like to blanch the spinach leaves by dropping them into boiling water for 1 minute and then rinsing them in cold water. You may do so, if you wish, and then pat the leaves dry or leave the spinach raw, which is how I prefer it.

Cut the Chinese cabbage into 10 cm / 4 inch lengths. Trim the mushrooms and cut them in half lengthways. Trim away the coarse stems from the watercress. Cut the bean curd into 2.5 cm / 1 inch cubes. Cut 20 cm / 8 inches off the top of all the spring onions (scallions). This is most of the green section. Wash these green sections and cut them into 10 cm / 4 inch lengths. Pat dry. Reserve the white portions.

Arrange the spinach, Chinese cabbage, mushrooms, watercress, bean curd and spring onion (scallion) greens next to each other on a large serving plate. Use more than one plate if necessary. Cover with cling film (plastic wrap) and set aside, refrigerating if necessary.

You now have the white portions of several spring onions left. You need only four of them. Slice these four crossways into very fine rounds. Soak the rounds in cold water for 30 minutes or longer. Drain and pat dry.

Make the Simple Lemon-Soy Sauce and pour into 4 individual bowls. Make the Sesame Sauce and pour into 4 bowls.

Grate the chilli-stuffed radish for the Red Maple Relish and divide into 4 portions, making a mound of each portion. Place each mound on a small saucer. Divide the sliced spring onions (scallions) into 4 portions and place a portion on the same saucers as the radish mounds. Keep the onions (scallions) and radish separate.

Wipe the *konbu* with a damp cloth and put into a pan with 1 litre / 1¾ pints water. Bring to a simmer. Just before the water boils, remove the *konbu*. Put the *konbu* stock (or other light stock of your choice) into the pan

you are using to cook the *shabu shabu* and bring to a simmer at the table.

You are now ready to serve. Bring the plates of meat and vegetables, the bowls of sauces and the saucers with the relish and spring onions (scallions) to the table. Small amounts of relish and/or spring onion (scallion) should be mixed into Simple Lemon-Soy Sauce by each diner. You can now start cooking your meat and vegetables by dipping them into the stock. Dip each mouthful into either the Lemon-Soy Sauce or the Sesame Sauce before you eat it.

Japan

QUICK-COOKED PORK WITH GARLIC
BUTA NO 'STAMINA'-YAKI

Here is a modern Japanese dish that uses both cognac and garlic. Sometimes, these days, a little butter is swirled into the pan juices at the very end.

SERVES 4

3 tablespoons vegetable oil

Eight 5 mm / ¼ inch thick slices cut from a boneless tenderloin of pork

3 cloves garlic, peeled and very finely chopped

3 tablespoons cognac

2 tablespoons *mirin*, see p. 214

2½ tablespoons Japanese dark soy sauce

Heat the oil in a large frying-pan over highish heat. Put in as many slices of pork as the pan will hold in a single layer and brown them on both sides. The meat should cook through. If you are concerned, turn the heat down and cook another minute on one side. Do all the slices this way, arranging them in a warm serving dish as you go. When the last slice is out, turn the heat to medium low if it was high, and put in the garlic. Stir once or twice. It should turn golden. Now pour in the cognac, *mirin* and soy sauce and mix with the

A selection of vegetables, generally cut up and served at the end of a meal with rice and tea.

pan juices, scraping them up as you do so. The sauce will bubble vigorously and thicken. Stir to mix again and pour the sauce over the pork slices. Serve immediately.

Japan

SATIN AUBERGINE (EGGPLANT)
NASU NO NIBITASHI

This is my version of a melt-in-the-mouth dish served at the Yutaka restaurant in Tokyo's Shibuya area. Small, tender aubergines (eggplants) are fried quickly at just the right temperature to preserve their colour, and then briefly braised. The temperature of the oil should be around 160 °C/325 °F. It helps to have either an electric deep-fryer or a thermometer. If you have neither, aim for a medium temperature.

Since I cannot find the very small aubergines (eggplants) that are used for this dish, I use the equally tender pinkish-purple, long, Japanese aubergine (eggplant). If only the larger variety is available, halve or quarter the vegetable lengthways and then cut it into 4 cm/1½ inch chunks.

In Japan, very small portions are eaten. You can double the recipe if you require larger servings.

SERVES 4
For the simmering sauce:
450 ml/15 fl oz/2 cups Japanese Soup Stock, see p. 198, freshly made or instant (or light chicken stock)

2 tablespoons Japanese dark soy sauce

1 tablespoon sugar

You also need:
225 g/8 oz slim, long Japanese aubergines (eggplants), or a section of the same weight from a larger vegetable

Vegetable oil for deep-frying

1 teaspoon very finely grated, fresh, peeled ginger

Combine all the ingredients for the simmering sauce and stir until the sugar has dissolved completely.

Going lengthways, peel off two 1 cm/2½ inch wide strips from the skin of the aubergines (eggplants), leaving purple and white stripes. This will help them to cook better. Now cut each crossways into 4 cm/1½ inch long chunks.

In a deep-fryer or wok, heat the oil to about 160 °C/325 °F or to a medium temperature. When hot, put in the vegetable pieces. Stir and fry for 5–7 minutes or until lightly browned. Remove with a slotted spoon and drain briefly on paper towels.

Bring the simmering sauce to a boil in a small pan. Drop in the aubergine (eggplant) pieces and adjust the heat so that they simmer gently for 3–4 minutes or until they are tender. Do not let them fall apart. Turn off the heat.

To serve, take the aubergine (eggplant) pieces out with a slotted spoon and arrange them in the centre of 4 saucer-like dishes. Spoon 1 tablespoon of the simmering liquid over each serving. Divide the ginger into 4 little hillocks and put one hillock on the edge of each saucer. The aubergine (eggplant) may be dipped into the ginger before eating, or each diner can mix the ginger into the sauce and then roll the aubergine (eggplant) in it.

Japan

GLAZED CARROTS
KIMPIRA

If preparing Western-style meals, try this with duck, pork and chicken. It cooks in about 5 minutes.

SERVES 4
1 tablespoon vegetable oil

4 medium-sized carrots (340 g/12 oz), peeled and cut into 5 cm x 5 mm x 5 mm/2 x ¼ x ¼ inch sticks

1½ tablespoons *sake*

1 tablespoon sugar

1½ tablespoons Japanese dark soy sauce

½ teaspoon roasted sesame seeds, see p. 217

Heat the oil in a non-stick frying-pan over medium-high heat. When hot, put in the

carrots. Stir and fry for 1 minute. Put in the *sake* and sugar. Cook until all the liquid has disappeared. Now put in the soy sauce and cook until that too has mostly gone. Turn off the heat.

Sprinkle the sesame seeds over the top of the carrots and serve.

Japan

OKRA WITH JAPANESE HORSERADISH
OKURA NO WASABI AE

Perhaps no nation revels in the natural tastes and textures of foods as much as Japan. Take okra. Most people in the world are at pains to hide its viscous quality so they fry or sauté the vegetable. Not so the Japanese. Since okra is naturally viscous, it is that very quality that they celebrate. Here is a thoroughly Japanese way of preparing okra, with a hint of nose-tingling Japanese green horseradish (*wasabi*). Even my husband, who learned to loathe okra as a child because of its texture, adores this dish. This is best served as an appetiser or side dish.

Make sure that the okra pods are young, small and tender. Look for pods that are 5–6 cm/2–2½ inches in length. Since not many are needed, you can actually pick out the pods, one by one, as I do.

SERVES 4
About 28 small okra pods (100 g/3½ oz)

¼–½ teaspoon *wasabi* paste, see p. 218

2 tablespoons Japanese dark soy sauce

1 teaspoon *mirin*, see p. 214

Bring a small pan of water to a rolling boil. Drop in the okra pods. Boil for 2 minutes and drain. Run under cold water and drain again. Cut crossways into 5 mm/¼ inch thick rounds. Discard the caps. Set aside, covered in the refrigerator, if necessary.

Just before serving, combine the *wasabi* paste, soy sauce and *mirin*. Mix. Add the okra and toss. Pile the okra in the centre of 4 small bowls or deep saucers. Serve at room temperature or cold.

Japan

PARENT AND CHILD RICE BOWL
OYAKO DONBURI

If you want a quick, cheap meal in Japan, ask for a *donburi*. A *donburi* is actually a bowl with a lid, used for serving individual meals-in-a-bowl. It is larger than normal Japanese rice bowls as it has to accommodate a full helping of rice as well as a topping of meat or fish and/or vegetables, and some sauce. Both the meal and the bowl are referred to as *donburi*. In this recipe the rice is topped with eggs and chicken, hence its name. It is very easy to put together. The Japanese like to start out with fairly runny eggs. As the topping is ladled over very hot rice, the eggs tend to keep cooking a bit.

I serve this in an old-fashioned soup plate.

SERVES 4

Plain Japanese and Korean Rice, see p. 198, freshly made (the entire amount)
1 chicken leg, boned, see p. 207, and skinned
4 spring onions (scallions)
600 ml / 1 pint / 2½ cups Japanese Soup Stock, see p. 198, freshly made or instant (or light chicken stock)
6 tablespoons Japanese dark soy sauce
2½ tablespoons sugar
1 tablespoon *sake*
4 eggs

Cut the chicken meat into 5 mm / ¼ inch pieces. Cut the spring onions (scallions) into 4 cm / 1½ inch lengths. Now cut each piece lengthways into halves or quarters to make strips. Combine the stock, soy sauce, sugar and *sake*. Beat the eggs lightly.

Just before serving, put the flavoured stock into a 20–23 cm / 8–9 inch frying-pan and bring to a simmer. Add the chicken and spring onions (scallions) and simmer for 3–4 minutes. Pour the beaten egg into the centre. As the eggs begin to curl on the outside, use a fork and gently pull the ends towards the edges of the pan so that you cover the top with a sheet of egg. Cover, turn the heat to low and cook until the eggs are done to a consistency you like.

Divide the hot rice between 4 bowls or soup plates, giving people what they think they are able to eat. Now ladle some egg, chicken and liquid over the rice and serve immediately.

Japan

RED MAPLE RELISH
MOMIJI-OROSHI

This Japanese condiment, a combination of grated white radish (called *mooli* in Indian shops and *daikon* by the Japanese) and dried red chillies, gets its name from its flecked hue. It is served with seafood casseroles and bean curd, and added to a variety of sauces. It is quite wonderful on raw oysters as well. You should prepare the radish for grating and then grate only what you need as the relish does not keep well. The unused portion of the radish, if well-wrapped in cling film (plastic wrap), will keep in the refrigerator for a few days.

In Japan, the radish is grated on a grater with little hair-like spikes. If you have access to a Japanese store, ask for a grater to make *oroshi*. If you cannot get one, use the finest part of your grater. You need a soft pulp.

MAKES ABOUT 7 TABLESPOONS

3 dried, hot red chillies
10 cm / 4 inch length of long white radish, about 5 cm / 2 inches in diameter

Cut off the stem end of the chillies. Hold one of them, stem end down, and slowly rotate it between a finger and thumb, pushing in gently. This should remove the seeds. Do this with the other 2 chillies.

There should be one cut end on the radish. Burrow 3 long holes, starting at this end. The Japanese push in with a chopstick but you could use a metal skewer. Push the red chillies into these holes.

Set the radish aside for 30 minutes or longer. It can be covered with cling film (plastic wrap) and refrigerated. Just before you eat, grate what you need and then cover and refrigerate the remaining radish.

Drain lightly. The radish should remain fluffy. Servings, usually 1 tablespoon or less per person, are formed into little heaps.

Japan

SIMPLE LEMON-SOY SAUCE
PONZU

In Japan, special *kabuso* limes are used for this sauce. You may use lemons as a substitute or, better still, a half and half combination of lemon and lime.

This dipping sauce is very popular all over Japan.

SERVES 4

8 tablespoons Japanese dark soy sauce
4 tablespoons lemon juice or 2 tablespoons each lime and lemon juice
10 tablespoons Japanese Soup Stock, see p. 198, freshly made or instant (or light, unsalted chicken stock)
4 tablespoons *mirin*, see p. 214

Combine all the ingredients. Cover well and refrigerate, if necessary. The sauce will last for several days in the refrigerator.

Japan

SESAME SAUCE
GOMA-DARE

This is an excellent sauce for dipping. Use it with beef, chicken, vegetables and bean curd.

SERVES 4

4 tablespoons roasted sesame seeds, see p. 217, freshly prepared
5½ tablespoons Japanese Soup Stock, see p. 198, freshly made or instant (or light chicken stock)
2 teaspoons *mirin*, see p. 214
1 teaspoon sugar
2 teaspoons *sake*

Allow the sesame seeds to cool slightly and then grind them in a clean coffee-grinder or other spice-grinder. Empty into a bowl. Add all the other ingredients slowly and mix thoroughly with the back of a wooden spoon.

HONG KONG

As soon as I arrive in Hong Kong I call up old friends, Grace and Kendall Oei. They know why I am in town once again and suggest that I meet them for Sunday lunch at a new restaurant, One Harbour Road. 'It is in the new Grand Hyatt Hotel,' they inform me. 'Just take the lift.'

The hotel lobby shimmers with painstakingly buffed marble and granite. A grand staircase winds its way up to some unknown splendours. I am directed towards a lift which is like no other. Circular and all brass, it carries me in its quiet womb to a two-tiered pavilion high in the sky, a sunroom-cum-conservatory filled with flowering orchids and camellias. Arranged graciously among the verdure are round tables, large and small, draped with crisp white linen and set with the finest Ginori plates. The chairs are made of pale, pickled wood and have, I notice, very comfortable, upholstered seats. The place is in some ways traditional, in others modern and, in every way, opulent.

Prosperous families, little babies included, come to this very elegant, expensive establishment for Sunday lunches, dressed in exquisite weekend casuals. *Amas* (nannies) are welcome too. There is as much sound of crockery and cutlery as there is of well-behaved children.

At the table next to mine, a toddler in denim rompers sits on a pickled wood high chair. Next to his Ginori bowl, he has arranged his German toy truck and assorted cars and boats. Between sips of chicken-rice soup, he peers out of the window at the Hong Kong harbour. We are so far up that the cars and

Opposite: Hong Kong at night – the view from Victoria Peak.

boats below could well be toys, just like the ones near his bowl.

My friends, young and already very successful in Hong Kong's financial world, come in with their seven-month-old baby, Christian, and his *ama* and, in their generous fashion, order up a banquet. How about frogs' legs, known as paddy chicken, with chestnuts. And have I ever tried barbecued chicken liver skewered with alternating pieces of pork fat (the fat provides lubrication) and shrimp balls encrusted with walnuts? And I must have a seasonal speciality: young green shoots of mange tout (snow peas) cooked with wine, ginger and just a dollop of chicken fat, as well as roast duck braised with aubergines (eggplants) in a yellow bean sauce. And, for dessert, how about pear balls stewed with white fungus, very good for combating dry winter skin as well as coughs and colds?

This is Hong Kong – or one aspect of it anyway. Leased to the British since the nineteenth century, this modern, bustling, harbour city will revert to its mother country, China, in this decade. Its citizens, who are mostly Cantonese, now represent much of the mainland. Many residents who fear the merger have already left. Others, smart as whistles, left, found a second passport and then returned, keeping all options open. But most have stayed, tied with fierce bonds to their heritage and their city.

In such times of uncertainty, one might expect Hong Kong to slow down, show signs of apprehension. But it cannot seem to contain itself. It is exploding with energy and vitality. It also keeps growing – not outwards as much as upwards and inwards. Massive renovations make many blocks unrecognisable from one year to the next. Hong Kong already has one of the world's most efficient underground train systems. Now there is I.M. Pei's new Bank of China, the tallest building in the city, rising up like a bamboo thicket with massive crossbands of anodised aluminium set among mirrored glass. Across the harbour is the Regent Hotel, all done up in russet granite, with a wrap-around view of the

South China Sea. How many more banks, hotels and shopping malls can the city put up? And who eats in the thousands of new restaurants that seem to be the natural outgrowth of the new malls and hotels?

The Chinese, of course. In most of the world, according to American anthropologist Professor Eugene Anderson, as incomes increase food generally accounts for a decreasing percentage of a family budget. The chief exception is Hong Kong, where people spend increasingly higher percentages on food as they prosper. (It is also true, though to a lesser extent, in Chinese communities around the world, even on the mainland where the greatest resistance to government-enforced asceticism comes in the area of banquets.) In Hong Kong, whether it is a small stall (a *dai pai dong*) with crude tables and stools on the sidewalk, or a ritzy restaurant where the waiters wear white gloves, it brims with humanity.

In crowded Hong Kong where in some areas, such as Mongkok, there is a density of 362 000 people to a square mile, and where most residents live in small quarters, it is understandable that people want to go out to eat. Breakfast, often a fast bowl of meat-flavoured rice gruel eaten with a cruller, can usually be found around the corner at a neighbourhood *dai pai dong*. Lunch could be a bowl of noodles from a restaurant near the office and dinner, at its simplest, could be some stir-fried squid or pork with rice – or it could be a more elaborate meal with fish and beef and prawns (shrimp) added. Restaurants offer tremendous variety and the freshest of ingredients, just as they did in the sixteenth century, to the astonishment of European travellers. Their clients, then as now, would not settle for anything less. But this is not the only reason why the ebullient enjoyment of food and eating out are national pastimes.

According to Professor Anderson, food acts as a great social cement and lubricant for the

Traditional junks in Aberdeen harbour.

Left: Hong Kong's modern waterfront is symbolic of the city's wealth. As its people prosper, they spend more of their money on food.

Chinese, a marker for many rites of passage. This is no recent phenomenon but can be traced to the dawn of civilisation in China. Gods and ancestors were always offered the best of feasts which mortals could eat later themselves: pigs, always China's premier meat, ducks, rabbits and fish. Not only was asceticism rarely invoked in the name of religion, good foods and plenty of them were actually approved of. The advent of Buddhism, and Communism on the Chinese mainland, made a dent in this thinking but, luckily for all concerned, only a shallow one.

Today, with more than three-quarters of women working, most celebrations tend to take place in restaurants. A promotion at work, a birthday, especially a 60th birthday when a whole cycle in a Chinese calendar has been completed, or a wedding where the bride wears Western white at the ceremony and traditional red at the banquet that follows, all tend to find their most joyous expression at an eatery of choice.

Some dishes are almost required at such times. At birthday celebrations, whatever else one may order, there have to be noodles for longevity. At weddings, after the obligatory games of *mah-jong*, expect roast pork for chastity (in earlier times, the groom sent a roast pig to the bride's house on the third day of the wedding to confirm that she was a virgin), fish for harmony and lotus roots to encourage couples to hold together. There may also be shark's fin soup, dried abalone and roast duck because, rather like champagne in the West, they are expensive and connote a sense of occasion. There will be more food than most people can manage and many cries of, 'Oh, I just cannot eat another thing'. But courses will keep coming – and everyone will keep eating. A successful banquet will not only offer a large selection of dishes but, by the end of it, the tablecloth

A cemetery in Hong Kong. Ancestors are offered cakes, fruit, roast duck and steamed chicken.

will look, as the Chinese like to say, as if a rooster had dipped its feet in the foods and walked all over it. Plenty is combined with unfettered enjoyment. Rice will be served at the end and most guests will not bother to eat it. It is associated with everyday sustenance. No water will be served, just tea and one or more soups. Alcohol is not particularly associated with celebrations.

China, anxious to feed its multitudes, learned to grow its crops using seeds pretreated with natural fertilisers as early as the first century BC. It borrowed cooking ideas and foods from around the world: noodles and dumplings probably came from the

Middle East, as did sesame seeds, broad beans and lemons; Professor Anderson thinks the wok may well have come from India where, in ancient times, it was used for reducing milk to make sweets for the gods – and still is today; mung beans, aubergines (eggplants) and tea probably also came from there; rice moved northwards from South-East Asia; vitamin-rich chillies, corn and peanuts came from the New World with the 'southern barbarians', the Europeans.

The origins of foods hardly matter today. As soon as they were subjected to Chinese demands for freshness and purity, to equipment such as cleavers and woks, to cooking techniques such as stir-frying, braising and steaming and to Chinese seasonings such as soy sauces, sesame oil, vinegar, ginger, rice wine, garlic, star anise

A dragon dance at a Hong Kong festival. The spectators will continue to celebrate after the performance, at one of the city's many restaurants.

and salted soy beans, they were all rendered thoroughly Chinese. And the process of exchanges and borrowing is not over. In Hong Kong, new additions such as broccoli, asparagus and iceberg lettuce have been adapted to Chinese styles of preparation.

Chinese cuisine, as we know it today, settled firmly into its present patterns around the Sung dynasty (960–1379 AD). It was probably the patronage of wealthy merchants that encouraged innovation and experimentation. Also, as civil servants and traders travelled, there was an enormous dispersal and blending of culinary ideas.

The same situation is true of present-day Hong Kong. A wealthy banker who eats out several nights a week is looking for fresh titillation. So how about going to the Lai Ching Heen restaurant in the Regent Hotel and trying their new delicacy: a scallop, a slice of pear, a sliver of Yunnan ham and a leaf of green coriander, all held together with a ground shrimp paste and deep-fried? The Regent also offers a hamburger with a salted black bean sauce, served on a bed of lettuce. According to Willi Mark, Hong Kong's leading food authority, as chefs move around and refugees from all over the mainland start work in Hong Kong's kitchens, cuisines are getting a little mixed up. A northern restaurant may have Peking duck and a dozen breads but it may also use ingredients from western China in its kitchens. A Cantonese restaurant may spice up some of its dishes to suit palates that like a little heat. And the effect of 'nouvelle cuisine' and 'California cuisine' is not to be discounted either.

By now, most of us are aware that Sichuan and Hunan foods from western China are heavily flavoured with chillies, garlic and Sichuan peppercorns, that northerners eat more breads, that Shanghai is famous for its noodles and its cold appetisers, that Cantonese food is mild and gentle – and that one of its strongest flavourings is salted black beans. A cuisine that was less familiar to me, and which was mentioned repeatedly by friends on my last few visits, was Chiu Chow cookery. So I decided to give it a try.

My friends said that I would never find the restaurant in question on my own so perhaps we should meet at the Culture Club and go on from there. Of course I would never have found it. You enter a simple office building, go up to the fourth floor in a lift, open an office door and enter – an office. Only, in the evening the small room is cleared – the files, however, are left on the shelves – and two tables squeezed in. You have to order in advance so that the chef-cum-office manager can cook what you have ordered. The name of the restaurant, if it can be called that, is the name of the office, and I cannot reveal it because this is a hush-hush operation. But can the manager cook!

The Chiu Chow people come from the Swatow region north of Hong Kong. One of their specialities is braised goose. The entire bird comes on a large platter, all sliced in the Chinese manner, the parts sitting on a pile of

fried bean curd and generously oozing their good juices over and into it. I have since watched this exquisite goose dish being prepared at a more legitimate restaurant. A dozen or more geese simmer together in a huge cauldron. The braising liquid, enriched from re-use and daily additions, contains stock, Sichuan peppercorns, star anise, tangerine peel, soy sauce, ginger, cassia bark and liquorice sticks – the real ones. After the birds have cooked for about 1½ hours, they are made to hang by their necks. Then they are boned and sliced. The goose is served at room temperature. Only the braising liquid, which becomes the sauce, is heated, before being poured over the bird. It is a grand dish. And you can have the webbed feet too, if you want.

On my last day in Hong Kong, Willi Mark takes me to the Flower Lounge to have a lunch of seasonal delicacies. I ask Willi what they might be. He gets a very naughty look in his eyes. 'Snake for one,' he says and laughs loudly, 'in a soup, with shark's fin and chrysanthemum leaves.' It is the start of winter and snake shops around town have come into their own. Snake meat is 'warm' and is highly recommended in Chinese medicine for the winter months.

In Chinese cuisine, the distinction between food and medicine is somewhat unclear. Since antiquity, the medicinal properties of foods have been carefully categorised and noted. Ginger, for example, rich in Vitamin C, was kept on board by the earliest sailing vessels as it prevented scurvy. It also prevented seasickness (a fact recognised by the West only in this decade). The concept of 'cooling' and 'heating' foods may well have come into China with the humoral theory, which originated in ancient Greece. Once it came, it stayed as *yin* and *yang*, the two opposites that are needed to keep the body in harmony.

Today it is abundantly clear that Hong Kong residents are hell-bent on keeping their bodies 'well balanced'. They do not necessarily read books on the subject, though books with the collected knowledge of 3000

years do exist and there are many scholars and local doctors who know their contents well. It is more a kind of folk knowledge, acquired through osmosis, that tells them to eat almonds if they wish to stay fair and clear-skinned, walnuts to keep the brain sharp, cooked apricot kernels to soothe the throat and chrysanthemum tea to 'cool' the body after eating barbecued meat. Irene Ho, a lifelong resident of Hong Kong, and also with us at Willi Mark's lunch, is about to emigrate to America. She is genuinely worried. She and her husband have already bought a condominium in Boston. 'Will it be very cold there?' she asks. She already knows the answer. 'I shall be fine,' she goes on, 'as long as I can get snake. Will I be able to get snake?' In America, she might have to catch it first. I invite her to our country home, 2½ hours out of Boston, to try.

The snake meat sold in this shop is a 'warm' medicine and comes into its own during winter.

simplified the dish somewhat. I noticed that during its preparation the chef threw in a dollop of a sauce I did not recognise at all. When questioned, he explained that it was 'Satay Sauce'. There are hundreds of 'satay sauces' in South-East Asia. What was in it? I examined the bottle with its list of ingredients. Then I tasted it all by itself. I

found that the flavour of the sauce can be approximated by combining ingredients that you probably have on hand or can get: ½ teaspoon bean sauce with chilli (available from Chinese grocers), 1 teaspoon sesame paste (or peanut butter) and ½ teaspoon sugar.

All the cutting and preparation of this dish can be done ahead of time. You can fry the rice sticks and keep them in a tightly closed container. You may deep-fry the squid up to an hour ahead of time. Do not refrigerate. The final cooking of the squid and watercress is best done at the last minute.

SERVES 4–6
For marinating the squid:

About 4 medium-sized squid, cleaned, see p. 207, and skinned (250 g / 9 oz after cleaning)

2 teaspoons peeled, very finely grated, fresh ginger

2 teaspoons cornflour (cornstarch)

2 teaspoons Chinese rice wine (or dry sherry)

For blanching the watercress:

3 bunches watercress (400 g / 14 oz)

1 teaspoon vegetable oil (preferably peanut oil)

120 ml / 4 fl oz / ½ cup Chicken Stock, see p. 197

An evening view of Cheung Chan harbour in Hong Kong. The waters of the South China Sea are a rich source of fish – and seafood like the squid used in the recipe on this page.

1 teaspoon salt

1 teaspoon sugar

For the lining for the watercress and squid:

Vegetable oil for shallow-frying (preferably peanut oil)

45 g / 1½ oz rice sticks

About 8 crisp iceberg lettuce leaves

For the sauce:

About 2 teaspoons *'Satay* Sauce' (see opposite)

2 teaspoons cornflour (cornstarch)

250 ml / 8 fl oz / 1 cup Chicken Stock, see p. 197

¼–½ teaspoon salt

You also need:

6 tablespoons vegetable oil. (Oil for frying rice sticks may be re-used)

1 tablespoon peeled, very finely chopped garlic

1 tablespoon peeled, very finely chopped, fresh ginger

1 dried, hot red chilli, crumbled

Cut the body of the squid into 5 mm / ¼ inch squares. Cut the tentacles and head into pieces of about the same length or size. Put the squid into a bowl. Hold the ginger over the squid and squeeze as much juice out of it as you can. Discard the remaining ginger. Add the other ingredients for marinating the squid, mix well, cover and set aside, refrigerating if necessary.

Chop up the watercress fairly coarsely, stems and all. In a wok or pot, put all the ingredients for blanching the watercress *except* the watercress. Add 450 ml / ¾ pint / 2 cups water and bring to a boil. Throw in the watercress and bring to a boil again. Boil vigorously for 1–2 minutes or until the watercress is completely wilted. Drain. If not cooking immediately, rinse the watercress under cold water, drain again and set aside.

Heat the oil for shallow-frying in a frying-pan over medium-high heat. When hot, throw in a few of the rice sticks. They will expand in seconds. Remove with a slotted spoon and lay in a plate lined with paper towels. Fry all the rice sticks this way.

Just before eating, spread the iceberg lettuce on a serving plate. Lightly crush the rice sticks and scatter over the lettuce.

Combine all the ingredients for the sauce and set aside. It should be adequately salted. Check by tasting.

Heat the 6 tablespoons oil over high heat in a wok or large frying-pan. When hot, put in the squid. As soon as it turns colour, remove it with a slotted spoon and put it in a bowl, leaving the oil behind. Put the ginger, garlic, and red chilli into the hot oil. Toss a few times. Now put in the blanched watercress and squid. Stir a few times and turn the heat off. Stir the sauce ingredients and pour in. Mix. Turn the heat to low and cook until the sauce thickens. Empty the watercress, squid and sauce over the lettuce and rice sticks. Serve immediately.

Hong Kong

PRAWNS (SHRIMP) WITH GARLIC AND OYSTER SAUCE
HO-YAU SUEN-YUNG HA

This is a dish of the Chiu Chow people who come from the region around Swatow, north-east of Hong Kong. They specialise in duck, geese and seafood. The simple seasoning here allows the seafood itself to shine through.

SERVES 4

450 g / 1 lb unpeeled, medium-sized prawns (shrimp), peeled but with tails left on, and deveined, or 340 g / 12 oz peeled and deveined prawns (shrimp)

Coarse or kosher salt

2 tablespoons lightly beaten egg white

2 teaspoons cornflour (cornstarch)

2 teaspoons sesame oil

⅛ teaspoon salt

6 tablespoons vegetable oil (preferably peanut)

3 cloves garlic, peeled and very finely chopped

1½ tablespoons oyster sauce

1 spring onion (scallion), cut into very, very fine rounds all the way up its green section

Sprinkle the prawns (shrimp) liberally with the coarse salt – rub well and then wash off. Repeat the process. Drain and pat dry.

Combine the prawns (shrimp) with the egg white, cornstarch, sesame oil and salt. Mix well. Cover and set aside for 30 minutes or longer, refrigerating if necessary.

Just before eating, heat the oil in a wok or large frying-pan over high heat. Put in the prawns (shrimp). Stir and cook until they barely turn pink. Remove the prawns (shrimp) with a slotted spoon and keep in a strainer.

Remove all but 3 tablespoons of the oil. Heat on high heat. Put in the garlic. Stir once or twice. Put in the oyster sauce. Stir and put in the prawns (shrimp). Stir and cook for 1 minute or until they are cooked through. Throw in the spring onion (scallion) and toss a few times. Serve immediately.

Hong Kong

CHICKEN AND ASPARAGUS WITH PORTUGUESE SAUCE
PO-JUP LO-SOUN GAI

The sauce here is based on curry powder which was probably brought to the Canton-Hong Kong region by the early Portuguese.

Curry powders have appeared frequently in Chinese cuisine – in soups and pastries, in dumplings and, indeed, in stir-fried dishes. This modern dish owes its origins to the inspired efforts of executive chef Cheung Kam Chuen. It is served at one of Hong Kong's finest restaurants, Lai Ching Heen, at the Regent Hotel. An unusual ingredient here is canned evaporated milk, which supplies a creamy texture. All in all, this is a magnificent dish, just perfect for entertaining.

Note: The chicken stock used for blanching the asparagus may be re-used later in the recipe whenever stock is required.

SERVES 4–6

For marinating the chicken:

450 g / 1 lb boned, skinned chicken breast meat

½ teaspoon salt

1 tablespoon Chinese rice wine (or dry sherry)

1 egg white, lightly beaten

2 teaspoons cornflour (cornstarch)

2 teaspoons sesame oil

For blanching the asparagus:

450 g / 1 lb green asparagus

250 ml / 8 fl oz / 1 cup Chicken Stock,
see p. 197

2 thin slices of peeled fresh ginger,
lightly mashed

1 teaspoon sugar

1 teaspoon salt

For frying and stir-frying:

Oil for deep-frying (preferably peanut oil)

1 tablespoon peeled, finely chopped garlic

1 tablespoon peeled, very finely chopped,
shallots or onion

1 dried, hot red chilli, crumbled

2 tablespoons curry powder dissolved in 4
teaspoons sesame oil

120 ml / 4 fl oz / ½ cup Chicken Stock,
see p. 197

4 tablespoons canned evaporated milk

1 teaspoon sugar

1 teaspoon salt

1 teaspoon cornflour (cornstarch) dissolved in 4
tablespoons chicken stock or water

The chicken breasts need to be cut
crossways, with the knife held at a slight
diagonal, into 3 mm / ⅛ inch thick slices. It
helps if you partially freeze the breasts first.
Since the breast pieces need to be about
5 cm / 2 inches long, you will need to halve
some of them. Put the chicken in a bowl and
combine with all the ingredients for its
marinade. Mix well, cover and set aside for
30 minutes or longer. Refrigerate if necessary.
You can do this several hours in advance.

Trim away the coarse ends of the
asparagus. Peel away the skin from the lower
third of each stalk. Cut each asparagus spear
into 3 parts. Combine all the remaining
ingredients for blanching the asparagus (but
not the asparagus) and bring to a boil in a
small pan or wok. Drop in the asparagus and
cook, turning the heat to medium, for 1–2
minutes or until it is crisp-tender and still
bright green. Drain, saving the stock for later
use. Discard the ginger. If not proceeding
immediately, rinse the asparagus under cold
water, drain and set aside.

Just before you eat, collect everything you
need and arrange it near you. Chicken breast
stays tender in the stir-frying process if it is
'passed through' oil for a few seconds. Heat
the oil for deep-frying in a wok or fryer and
keep a bowl with a sieve atop it at hand. I
like to line the sieve with a clean cloth or
paper towel so the oil is instantly re-usable.
The temperature of the oil should be medium
low – about 275 °F / 140 °C. When it is hot,
empty all the chicken with its marinade into
it and separate the pieces. The chicken
should just turn white. Empty the oil and
chicken into the strainer.

Put 3 tablespoons of the oil back into the
wok and heat over high heat. When hot, put
in the garlic, shallots and chilli. Stir once or
twice. Put in the curry paste. Stir once or
twice. Put in the stock. Stir once or twice.
Put in the evaporated milk, sugar and salt.
Stir once or twice. Lower the heat a bit, put
in the cornflour (cornstarch) mixture and
stir until it thickens. Put the chicken and
asparagus into the sauce and fold them in,
stirring a few times. Serve immediately.

Hong Kong

DICED CHICKEN WITH PEANUTS IN CHILLI SAUCE
GUNG BO GAI-DING

This old restaurant standby is as good as it is
simple. It comes from the Sichuan Garden
Restaurant. You will need 1½ chicken legs if
they are large, two whole ones if they are
small. After boning, you should have
450 g / 1 lb meat with skin.

SERVES 4

For marinating and pre-cooking the chicken:

450 g / 1 lb boned chicken meat from leg,
see p. 000, cut into 2.5 cm / 1 inch dice

1 tablespoon Chinese light soy sauce

1 tablespoon Chinese rice wine
(or dry sherry)

1 large egg white, lightly beaten

1 tablespoon cornflour (cornstarch)

2 teaspoons sesame oil

Vegetable oil for deep-frying (preferably peanut
oil)

For the sauce:

2 teaspoons cornflour (cornstarch)

1 tablespoon Chinese black vinegar
(or red wine vinegar)

1 tablespoon Chinese light soy sauce

1 teaspoon sugar

1 tablespoon Chinese rice wine (or dry sherry)

6 tablespoons Chicken Stock, see p. 197

For stir-frying:

2–3 cloves garlic, peeled and
finely chopped

4 cm / 1½ inch cube of fresh ginger, peeled and
finely chopped

4 dried, hot red chillies

½ teaspoon roasted and ground Sichuan
peppercorns, see p. 217

1 teaspoon chilli paste with garlic (available
from Chinese grocers)

6 spring onions (scallions), cut into 4 cm / 1½
inch lengths, their white parts halved
lengthways

1 teaspoon Chilli Oil, see p. 199

30 g / 1 oz / ¼ cup Roasted Peanuts, see p. 201

Combine the chicken with all the ingredients
for marinating. Mix well. Cover and then set
aside for 30 minutes or longer, refrigerating
if necessary. Next the chicken needs to be
passed through moderately hot oil, after
which it should not be refrigerated. So do it
an hour or so before eating.

Heat the oil in a wok or deep-fryer at
medium-low heat, about 275 °F / 140 °C. Put
in the chicken with its marinade. It should
not sizzle. Separate the pieces and, when
they turn white, remove with a slotted spoon
and keep in a bowl. This oil may now be
strained and re-used.

Combine all the ingredients for the sauce,
mix and set aside.

Just before eating heat 2 tablespoons of the

**Chicken and Asparagus with Portuguese Sauce
(page 133).**

For marinating the beef:

115 g / 4 oz beef from a lean beef steak, cut against the grain first into 3 mm / ⅛ inch thick slices and then into strips 4–5 cm / 1½–2 inch long and 3 mm / ⅛ inch wide

1 teaspoon Chinese dark soy sauce

1 teaspoon oyster sauce

½ teaspoon cornflour (cornstarch)

1 teaspoon sesame oil

1 teaspoon Chinese rice wine (or dry sherry)

½ teaspoon sugar

For the vegetables:

6 dried Chinese mushrooms

75 g / 2½ oz / ⅔ cup bamboo shoots that have been cut into strips the same size as the meat

75 g / 2½ oz / ⅔ cup carrots peeled and cut into strips the same size as the meat

98 g / 3½ oz / ⅔ cup broccoli stems (or kohlrabi) that have been peeled and cut into strips the same size as the meat

2 spring onions (scallions), cut into 4–5 cm / 1½–2 inch lengths all the way up their green sections, with the white parts quartered lengthways

For the sauce:

1½ tablespoons cornflour (cornstarch)

450 ml / 15 fl oz / 1¾ cups Chicken Stock, see p. 197

1 tablespoon oyster sauce

2 teaspoons Chinese dark soy sauce

1 teaspoon sugar

2 teaspoons sesame oil

For the final cooking:

8 tablespoons vegetable oil (preferably peanut oil)

4 thin slices of fresh ginger, peeled and finely chopped

2 teaspoons peeled, finely chopped garlic

Add the 2 teaspoons salt to about 1.85 litres / 3¼ pints / 8 cups rapidly boiling water. Throw in the noodles, separating them with a fork or chopsticks. When the water comes to a boil again, throw in 250 ml / 8 fl oz / 1 cup cold water. Do this 2 more times. When the water comes to a boil yet again, drain the noodles and rinse under cold water until they

have cooled completely. Leave to drain for 1 hour. Pat dry with paper towels, spread the noodles out on a large plate and leave until no moisture can be seen.

Combine all the ingredients for marinating the beef. Mix well, cover, and set aside for 30 minutes or more, refrigerating if necessary.

Soak the mushrooms in hot water for 30 minutes or until soft. Remove from the liquid. Cut off and discard the hard stems. Cut the mushroom caps into fine slivers. Put the mushrooms together with the cut bamboo shoots, carrots, broccoli stems and spring onions (scallions). Cover and set aside.

Combine all the ingredients for the sauce. Mix well and set aside.

About 10 minutes before eating, make sure you have everything assembled near you. You need a large non-stick (or well-used, cast-iron) frying-pan for the noodles. Take out a large, round serving plate to receive the crisp pancake, which will be the size of the frying-pan. Set up your wok or other large frying-pan for stir-frying the meat and vegetables.

Heat 4 tablespoons oil in a non-stick frying-pan over medium heat. Let it get very hot. Now put in the noodles, spreading them out until they reach the edges of the pan. Fry them for about 4 minutes, or until they are medium-brown. Then turn the pancake over with a wide spatula and fry the second side the same way. Lift the pancake out and put on the serving plate.

Heat 2 tablespoons oil in a wok over a high flame. When hot, put in the ginger. Stir once or twice and put in the vegetables. Stir for a minute or so or until the vegetables are tender-crisp. Empty into a bowl. Give the wok a quick wipe and put in the remaining 2 tablespoons oil. When hot, put in the garlic. Stir once or twice. Put in the beef. Stir a few times until the beef changes colour. Now put back the vegetables. Stir to mix. Turn off the heat. Stir the sauce and pour it in. Turn the heat back to medium low. Cook until the sauce thickens, stirring as you go. Pour the beef, vegetables and sauce over the noodle 'pancake' and serve at once.

Hong Kong

SICHUAN-STYLE SHREDDED BEEF WITH SPRING ONIONS (SCALLIONS)
—— SEI-CHUEN YEUNG-CHUNG NGAU-YUK-SI ——

Here is a dish most of us love to order in Chinese restaurants. It seems to be as popular in Hong Kong as it is in restaurants around the world.

SERVES 4–6

For marinating the beef:

340 g / 12 oz lean beef steak

1 teaspoon Chinese dark soy sauce

1½ teaspoons cornflour (cornstarch)

2 teaspoons Chinese rice wine (or dry sherry)

1½ teaspoons vegetable oil (preferably peanut oil)

For the sauce:

1 teaspoon cornflour (cornstarch)

5 teaspoons Chinese dark soy sauce

1 tablespoon Chinese rice wine (or dry sherry)

4 tablespoons Chicken Stock, see p. 197

2 teaspoons Chinese red vinegar (or red wine vinegar)

1 teaspoon sugar

2 teaspoons sesame oil

For blanching the beef in oil:

About 250 ml / 8 fl oz / 1 cup vegetable oil (preferably peanut oil)

For the final stir-frying:

1 tablespoon peeled, finely chopped garlic

1 tablespoon peeled, finely chopped fresh ginger

1 tablespoon finely sliced rounds of spring onion (scallion)

75 g / 2½ oz / ¾ cup bamboo shoots that have been cut into delicate julienne strips

1 tablespoon bean sauce with chilli (available from Chinese grocers)

Half a red pepper (75 g / 2½ oz), cut into thin, long strips

6 spring onions (scallions), cut into 6 cm / 2½ inch lengths all the way up their green sections, then cut lengthways into thin strips

Cut the beef against the grain into 3 mm / ⅛ inch thick slices, holding the sharp edge of the knife at a slight angle in order to get wider slices. Cut the slices into 2 or 3 parts crossways, and then cut each piece lengthways into 3 mm / ⅛ inch wide strips. It is easier to do all this if the meat is first frozen for 1 hour.

Combine the meat with all the ingredients for the marinade. Mix well. Cover and set aside for 30 minutes or longer, refrigerating if necessary. Combine all the ingredients for the sauce and mix well. Set aside.

Heat the oil for blanching the beef in a wok or large frying-pan over medium-high heat. When hot, put in all the meat with its marinade. Stir to separate the pieces and remove with a slotted spoon as soon as the meat changes colour (about 1 minute). Strain the oil and reserve. Clean out the wok or frying-pan. This can all be done up to an hour ahead of time.

For the final stir-frying, heat about 3 tablespoons of the reserved oil in the wok or frying-pan over high heat. Put in the garlic, ginger and spring onion (scallion) rounds. Stir and fry for a few seconds. Put in the bamboo shoots and bean sauce with chilli. Stir a few times. Put in the beef and red pepper. Stir a few times. Put in the spring onion (scallion) strips and toss for a few seconds. Turn off the heat. Stir the sauce well and pour it in. Turn the heat back on to low and cook, tossing and mixing, until the sauce thickens. Serve immediately.

Hong Kong
AUBERGINES (EGGPLANTS) WITH MINCED (GROUND) PORK
NGEI-GWA YUK-SUNG

This is one of the meltingly smooth dishes served by the Flower Lounge restaurant in

A street in central Hong Kong. There are more than 360 000 people to a square mile in some parts of the city.

Hong Kong. Aubergine (eggplant) fingers are first fried in oil which turns them buttery and then quickly stir-fried with well-seasoned minced (ground) pork.

SERVES 4

For marinating the pork:

60 g / 2 oz minced (ground) pork	
½ teaspoon cornflour (cornstarch)	
1 teaspoon Chinese light soy sauce	
1 teaspoon Chinese rice wine (or dry sherry)	
1 teaspoon sesame oil	

For the sauce:

1 teaspoon Chinese light soy sauce	
1 teaspoon Chinese dark soy sauce	
1 tablespoon oyster sauce	
3 tablespoons Chinese rice wine (or dry sherry)	
2 teaspoons Chinese black vinegar (or red wine vinegar)	
1 teaspoon sugar	

For frying the aubergine (eggplant):

Oil for frying (preferably peanut oil)	
340 g / 12 oz aubergine / eggplant (preferably the slim, long oriental type), cut into fingers 6 cm / 2½ inches long and 2.5 cm / 1 inch wide and thick	

You also need:

3–4 cloves garlic, peeled and finely chopped	
2.5 cm / 1 inch cube of fresh ginger, peeled and finely chopped	
1 dried, hot red chilli, crumbled	
1½ teaspoons cornflour (cornstarch) dissolved in 1½ tablespoons water	
2 spring onions (scallions), cut into fine rounds all the way up their green sections	

Combine all the ingredients for marinating the pork. Mix well, cover and set aside for 30 minutes or more, refrigerating if necessary.

Combine all the ingredients for the sauce with 300 ml / 10 fl oz / 1¼ cups water. Set aside.

Heat about 2.5 cm / 1 inch oil in a wok or frying-pan over medium-high heat. When hot, put in the aubergine (eggplant). Stir and fry until lightly browned. Remove with a slotted spoon and drain on paper towels.

Empty out all the oil except about 1–2 tablespoons. Heat that oil over high heat. When hot, put in the garlic, ginger and chilli. Stir briskly once or twice. Put in the pork. Stir briskly again until the pork changes colour. Now put in the aubergine (eggplant) and the sauce. Bring to a simmer. Turn the heat to low and simmer for 2–3 minutes. Stir the cornflour (cornstarch) mixture and mix it in. Stir gently once and cook until the sauce thickens. Add the spring onions (scallions) and gently stir once or twice, being careful not to break the aubergine (eggplant).

A Hong Kong street market selling budding chives, aubergines (eggplants) and sections of pumpkin. The ingredients for traditional Chinese cuisine came from all over the world.

Hong Kong

BRAISED BEAN CURD, HUNAN-STYLE
MA-LA DAU-FU

The bean curd here remains soft, silken and mild while around it, to give it pep and zest, a sauce brimming with garlic, ginger, chillies and Sichuan peppercorns provides a titillating contrast.

SERVES 4

About 450 g / 1 lb medium bean curd	

For the pork:

About 115 g / 4 oz lean boneless pork	
1 teaspoon Chinese light soy sauce	
1 teaspoon Chinese rice wine (or dry sherry)	
1 teaspoon cornflour (cornstarch)	

You also need:

1½ tablespoons salted black beans	
1–2 fresh, hot green chillies	
4 spring onions (scallions)	

For the sauce:

250 ml / 8 fl oz / 1 cup Chicken Stock, see p. 197, or Beef stock, see p. 197
2 tablespoons Chinese dark soy sauce
1 tablespoon Chinese rice wine (or dry sherry)
½ teaspoon sugar

You also need:

2 teaspoons cornflour (cornstarch)
3 tablespoons vegetable oil (preferably peanut oil)
2.5 cm / 1 inch cube of fresh ginger, peeled and finely chopped
3 cloves garlic, peeled and finely chopped
1 tablespoon chilli paste with garlic (available from Chinese grocers)
1 teaspoon roasted and ground Sichuan peppercorns, see p. 217
2 teaspoons sesame oil
2 teaspoons Chilli Oil, see p. 199

Put the bean curd in a pan and cover with water. Bring to a simmer and cook gently for 2 minutes. Leave to cool in that water. Drain just before cooking and cut into 2.5 cm / 1 inch cubes.

Cut the pork into slivers that are 2.5 cm / 1 inch long and 3 mm / ⅛ inch thick and wide. Mix well with all the other ingredients for the pork and set aside for 30 minutes.

Wash the salt off the black beans, drain and chop coarsely.

Cut the chillies into long slivers, about the same size as the pork. Cut the whole spring onion (scallion), including the green section, into 2.5 cm / 1 inch lengths and then cut each lengthways into fine slivers.

Combine all the ingredients for the sauce and set aside.

Mix the cornflour (cornstarch) with 2 teaspoons water and set aside.

Heat the oil in a wok or a large frying-pan over high heat. When hot, put in the ginger and garlic. Stir a few times and put in the salted black beans. Stir once or twice and put

in the spring onions (scallions) and green chillies. Stir a few more times and put in the pork. Stir, separating the meat, until all the pinkness has disappeared. Put in the chilli paste with garlic. Stir once or twice, blending it with the pork. Pour in the mixed sauce ingredients, stir and bring to a simmer. Put in the bean curd and spread it around gently in the sauce. Bring to a simmer. Cover and simmer gently for 4–5 minutes. Turn off the heat. Stir the cornflour (cornstarch) mixture and pour it in. Mix. Put back on the heat and bring to a simmer. As soon as the sauce thickens, put in the Sichuan peppercorns, sesame oil and Chilli Oil. Stir once and serve immediately.

Hong Kong

BROCCOLI AND CHINESE MUSHROOMS IN BLACK BEAN SAUCE
DAU-SI SAI-LAN-FA DOUNG GU

You may make this with Chinese broccoli (*kailan*) if you can get it. Pull it apart into segments and then cut the segments into halves lengthways.

SERVES 4

8 dried Chinese mushrooms
675 g / 1½ lb broccoli
1 tablespoon salted black beans
6 tablespoons vegetable oil (preferably peanut oil)
1½ tablespoons peeled, finely chopped garlic
1 dried, hot red chilli, crumbled
1 teaspoon salt
175 ml / 6 fl oz / ¾ cup Chicken Stock, see p. 197

For thickening the sauce:

1 teaspoon cornflour (cornstarch) mixed with 4 tablespoons chicken stock

Soak the mushrooms in hot water for 30 minutes or until soft. Remove from the water. Cut off and discard the coarse stems. Leave the caps whole.

Cut the coarse stems off the broccoli

spears. Cut the remaining broccoli into smaller, delicate spears, that are no more than 5–6 cm / 2–2½ inches long.

Wash the salt off the black beans and chop them finely.

Heat the oil in a large wok or large frying-pan over high heat. When hot, put in the garlic, black beans and red chilli. Stir a few times or until the garlic just begins to change colour. Put in the broccoli and mushrooms. Stir and fry until the broccoli turns bright green. Put in the salt and chicken stock, cover and then turn the heat to medium low. Cook for 2–3 minutes or until the broccoli is crisp-tender. Uncover, turn off the heat and pour in the cornflour (cornstarch) mixture. Turn the heat back on to low and cook until the sauce has thickened. Serve immediately.

Hong Kong

SICHUAN CUCUMBER SALAD
MA-LA WONG-GWA

A spicy salad with the unusual taste and aroma of Sichuan peppercorns.

SERVES 4

675 g / 1½ lb cucumbers (preferably slim, oriental cucumbers or English long cucumbers or small pickling ones)
2 teaspoons salt
1 large clove garlic, peeled and cut lengthways into thin slices
1 teaspoon roasted and ground Sichuan peppercorns, see p. 217
1 teaspoon bean sauce with chilli (available from Chinese grocers)
2 teaspoons Chilli Oil, see p. 199
4 teaspoons sugar
2 tablespoons Chinese red vinegar (or cider vinegar)
2 tablespoons sesame oil

Quarter the cucumbers lengthways and cut into 5 cm / 2 inch segments. Rub with the salt and set aside for 1 hour or longer. Drain and mix with all the other ingredients. Taste for balance of sweet, hot, sour and salty, adding a bit more of anything you wish.

Hong Kong

SPINACH WITH CHINESE SAUSAGE
LAP-CHEUNG BO-CHOI

In much of the Far East, greens are often flavoured with odd bits of shellfish, fish sauces or meat. Here it is Chinese sausage that gives its own special sweet flavour to spinach. You may use either duck liver sausage or a plain pork one.

In case you are unfamiliar with Chinese sausages, you have a treat awaiting you. They can be seen hanging, all tied in bunches, in Chinese grocer shops. The lighter ones are pork and the darker ones are duck liver. The liver sausages have a deeper, liver-like flavour. Since they are dry and shrivelled, they are best prepared by steaming. Very often the Chinese just lay them over their rice as it cooks. (Put the sausage in quickly after the first 5 minutes of cooking, when all of the water has been absorbed.) This flavours the rice and cooks the sausage at the same time. The sausage can then be sliced and either eaten as it is or cooked with other foods.

If you are unable to get Chinese sausage, combine 30 g/1 oz minced (ground) pork with ½ teaspoon each of sugar, Chinese dark soy sauce and Chinese rice wine, mix well and set aside, covered, for 30 minutes. This way, you will approximate the taste of the pork sausage.

SERVES 4

1 Chinese sausage (about 30 g/1 oz), or see above

For the sauce:

2 teaspoons cornflour (cornstarch)

175 ml/6 fl oz/¾ cup Chicken Stock, see p. 197

1 tablespoon oyster sauce

1 tablespoon Chinese rice wine (or dry sherry)

You also need:

5 tablespoons vegetable oil (preferably peanut oil)

900 g/2 lb fresh spinach, washed and trimmed

½ teaspoon sugar

¼ teaspoon salt

4 cloves garlic, peeled and finely chopped

2 thin slices of peeled fresh ginger, finely chopped

If the sausage is still attached to its rope, cut it off. Now steam the sausage over medium-high heat for 15–20 minutes. (If general steaming instructions are needed, see p. 208.) Chop the sausage finely.

Put the cornflour (cornstarch) in a bowl. Slowly add the stock, mixing as you go. Now add the oyster sauce and rice wine. Mix and set aside. This is the sauce.

Heat 3 tablespoons of the oil in a large wok (or a large wide pan) over high heat. When hot, put in the spinach, sugar and salt. Stir once or twice. Cover for 30–60 seconds or just until the spinach begins to wilt. Uncover, continue to stir until the spinach is completely wilted and cooked through. Remove with a slotted spoon and place in a warm serving bowl. Discard the liquid in the wok. Clean out the wok quickly.

Heat the remaining 2 tablespoons of the oil in the wok over highish heat. When hot, put in the garlic and ginger. Stir-fry for a few seconds and put in the chopped sausage. Stir-fry for another few seconds. Now turn the heat to very low. Stir the sauce well and pour it in. Stir and cook on a low heat until the sauce thickens. Pour this over the spinach and serve immediately.

Hong Kong

RICE CONGEE WITH BEEF BALLS
NGAU-TUK YUEN DJOU

If there is one food that spells soothing comfort to the Chinese of Hong Kong, it is *tchuk* – rice porridge. Most commonly eaten for breakfast, it is sometimes made at home but, more often than not, bought cheaply from a neighbourhood *dai pai dong* (stall), where, during the early hours of the morning, it steams away in large kettles. A variety of sauces and seasonings are set up on the *dai pai dong* tables.

Rice porridges are savoury and can be topped with anything one wishes, from stewed innards to bits of minced (ground) pork and beef: stalls tend to have their own specialities.

This congee has seasoned beef balls as well as crisply fried rice sticks. Rice sticks are fine rice noodles which puff up when fried. They add a wonderful texture to the porridge.

SERVES 4–5

Long-grain rice, measured to the 120 ml/4 fl oz/½ cup level in a measuring jug

1.6 litres/2¾ pints/7 cups Chicken Stock, see p. 197, or Beef Stock, see p. 197, *very lightly* salted

For the beef:

100 g/3½ oz minced (ground) beef

1 teaspoon Chinese dark soy sauce

½ teaspoon sugar

1 teaspoon Chinese rice wine (or dry sherry)

½ teaspoon peeled, finely grated fresh ginger

½ teaspoon sesame oil

You also need:

Oil for shallow-frying (preferably peanut oil)

15 g/½ oz/⅓ cup rice sticks. (If long, break into 4 cm/1½ inch long pieces)

About 140 g/5 oz/2½ cups finely shredded iceberg lettuce

About 8 tablespoons green coriander leaves

About 2 teaspoons very, very fine fresh ginger shreds

2 spring onions (scallions), cut into very fine rings all the way up their green sections

Combine the rice and the stock in a heavy pan and bring to a boil. Turn the heat to medium low and cook for 15 minutes. Cover, leaving the lid slightly ajar, turn the heat to low and simmer gently for another hour. Do not stir during the cooking.

Meanwhile, combine all the ingredients for the beef, mix well, cover and set aside for 2 hours or longer.

Heat about 5 mm/¼ inch oil in a frying-pan. While it heats, dip the rice sticks in water and then drain. When the oil is hot, throw in the rice sticks. They will sizzle and expand a bit and cook in seconds. They should stay pale in colour. Remove with a slotted spoon and drain on paper towels.

Use soup bowls for serving. In each, put some shredded lettuce, some green coriander, some ginger and some spring onions (scallions). Just before eating, pick up small bits of the meat – about ½ teaspoon size – and without bothering to shape them, throw them into the boiling soup. Cook them to the doneness you like. Now ladle the soup over the fresh seasonings and sprinkle rice sticks over the top.

As condiments, offer soy sauce, sesame oil, Chilli Oil, see p. 199, and, if you like, a hot sauce made by combining 1 tablespoon chilli paste with garlic (available from Chinese grocers) with 1 tablespoon Chinese dark soy sauce, 2 teaspoons sugar and 1 tablespoon sesame oil.

Hong Kong

PANCAKES WITH SWEET BEAN PASTE AND BANANA
DAU-SA HEUNG-JIU BENG

I was served this dish at the Hunan Garden restaurant. Crisply fried pancakes, filled with a melting filling of bean paste and bananas, is one of their specialities. This place is rather unique, even for Hong Kong. It started out as a neighbourhood restaurant and failed miserably because the Cantonese, on the whole, detest spicy foods, especially for everyday family meals. Then it opened again, rather grandly, in the middle of town, where it was deluged by an international clientele. Today, it is hard to get a booking there.

The traditional Chinese pancake, made with just flour, eggs and water – no milk – is filled with a sweet paste of either beans or dates and then deep-fried. At the Hunan Garden, a special yellow bean paste is combined with a slice of banana to make what I think is among the best Chinese desserts for Western palates. I have used sweet red bean paste as it is readily available,

fully prepared, in cans from Chinese grocers. You can make a third or half of the recipe.

MAKES 12 PANCAKES AND SERVES 6–12

For the batter:

3 eggs

130 g / 4½ oz / 1 cup plain (all purpose) white flour

1 tablespoon sugar

1 tablespoon vegetable oil (preferably peanut oil)

You also need:

Vegetable oil (preferably peanut oil), a little for making the pancakes, more for deep-frying

2 tablespoons sweet red bean paste (see below left)

2 bananas, firm but ripe

Combine the eggs, 250 ml / 8 fl oz / 1 cup water and the remaining ingredients for the batter in the container of an electric blender. Blend briefly until smooth. Refrigerate for 3 hours or longer.

You now need to make 12 thin 'crêpes', but with this difference. You will cook them only on one side. Each crêpe needs to be about 18 cm / 7 inches in diameter so you should have a crêpe pan or other frying-pan of that size. (If you do not, adjust the crêpes to suit your pan.) Put a heavy crêpe pan or any non-stick pan to heat on medium heat. Brush the pan with a little oil. When the pan is hot, pour in just enough batter to coat the pan lightly. Tilt the pan in all directions so that the batter flows to the edges. Cook for about 45 seconds or until the batter is set. Lift the pancake out and put it on a plate, cooked side down. Spread 1 tablespoon of the sweet red bean paste in the centre, making a strip that is about 7.5 cm / 3 inches long and 4 cm / 1½ inches wide. Cut a 7.5 cm / 3 inch piece off the banana and then cut that lengthways into 4 parts. Lay one part over the bean paste. Now close up the pancake like an envelope. Pull the bottom flap over the banana, then the left side and then the right side. Put a little fresh batter all along the edges of the last side and pull that over

as well, making sure that it sticks closed. Make all the pancakes this way.

Just before eating, heat oil for deep-frying in a wok, large frying-pan or deep-fryer over high heat. When hot, put in as many pancake rolls as will fit in easily and fry until golden-brown and crisp, about 2 minutes. Turn a few times. Remove and drain well on paper towels. Fry all the pancake rolls this way. Cut each roll crossways in thirds and serve immediately.

Hong Kong

SPRING ONION (SCALLION) BREAD
CHUNG YAU BENG

There are many versions of this northern bread, some pan-fried in a home style, others made a bit more professionally. This is the professional version – and it is very good indeed. The outside of the bread stays very crisp while the inside is filled with soft layers. It needs to be shallow-fried and eaten soon after it is made. I have included some diagrams here to make the rolling-out process a bit clearer. Since the ratio of water to flour is worked out by volume – there must be half as much water as flour – it is best to put the flour in a measuring jug, measure it and then measure out half as much water.

You may eat this bread with a Chinese meal or with Chinese Dipping Sauce containing soy sauce, vinegar and sesame oil (see p. 199).

SERVES 6

250 g / 9 oz / 2 cups plain (all purpose) white flour plus extra for dusting and roux

4 teaspoons sesame oil

About 7–8 spring onions (scallions)

Vegetable oil (preferably peanut oil) for shallow-frying plus a bit extra

Salt

Measure out 125 g / 4½ oz / 1 cup of the flour by the method suggested above and put it in a bowl. Add half as much volume of water (about 120 ml / 4 fl oz / ½ cup). Mix, knead until smooth. Form the dough into a ball.

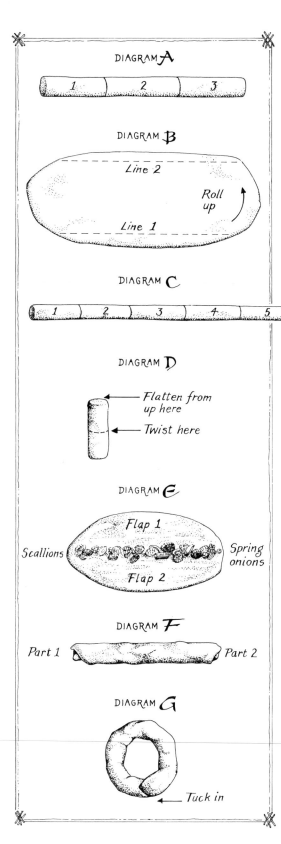

DIAGRAM A

DIAGRAM B

Line 2

Roll up

Line 1

DIAGRAM C

DIAGRAM D

Flatten from up here

Twist here

DIAGRAM E

Flap 1

Scallions   Spring onions

Flap 2

DIAGRAM F

Part 1   Part 2

DIAGRAM G

Tuck in

Measure another 125 g/4½ oz/1 cup of flour as suggested above and put it in a bowl. Pour in half as much volume of boiling water (about 120 ml/4 fl oz/½ cup). Mix with a wooden spoon. Knead until smooth, and form a ball.

With your hands, make a patty out of the cold-water dough. Put the ball of hot-water dough in the middle of it and then enclose it with the cold water dough.

Now you have a ball. Put the ball down on your work surface. Using both hands, proceed to roll the ball into a log about 30 cm/12 inches long. Mark off the log into 3 parts as shown in Diagram A. Fold part 1 over part 2 and then part 3 over part 2 as well. You now have a chunky, squat log. Pull it so it stretches a bit in length and again, using just your hands, make another 30 cm/12 inch log. Again mark off 3 parts and fold parts 1 and 3 over part 2. Repeat this 7–8 times or until the dough feels very smooth and elastic. Make a ball. Rub the ball with 1 teaspoon of the sesame oil and slip it into a plastic bag. Let the dough rest for at least 2 hours.

Cut the spring onions (scallions) into very fine rounds all the way up their green sections.

Put 1 tablespoon flour in a bowl. Heat 2 tablespoons oil until very hot and pour over the flour in the bowl. Stir to mix. This is the roux.

After the dough has rested for 2 hours, flour your work surface lightly, place your ball of dough on it and, using a rolling-pin, roll out an oval shape about 3 mm/⅛ inch thick. First spread the flour-oil roux over it evenly and then dust it very lightly with flour. Now put aside the rolling-pin. Using both hands, roll up the oval crossways, going from line 1 in Diagram B to line 2. You now have a long sponge roll.

Stretch this sponge roll with your hands so it becomes even longer. Put it down on the work surface and roll it with your hands until it is 45 cm/18 inches long and evenly rounded. You now have a snake without a head or tail.

Cut the snake into six 7.5 cm/3 inch long sections (Diagram C).

Pick up one section and stand it on end (Diagram D). Twist it in the middle a full 360° and then flatten it to form a double patty. Do this with all the sections. Cover five of them with a cloth while you work with the sixth.

Roll out this double patty into an oval that is about 25 cm/10 inches at its longest and about 13 cm/5 inches at its widest. Dribble ½ teaspoon vegetable oil and ½ teaspoon sesame oil over it, spreading the oils out evenly with your fingers or a brush. Now sprinkle just a little salt over it. Put a ribbon of spring onions (scallions) – about 1 heaped tablespoon – going, lengthways in the centre, from one end to the other (Diagram E). Fold flap 1 over the onions, then flap 2 over flap 1. Keeping this long bread flat on your work surface (Diagram F), bring part 1 to meet part 2 to make a ring, a kind of flattened dough-nut. Tuck one inside the other, sticking it down with a little water, if necessary (Diagram G). Flatten the bread with your palm so it becomes about 13 cm/5 inches in diameter. Make all the breads this way and keep them covered.

Heat 2 cm/¾ inch oil in a frying-pan over lowish heat. When hot, put in the bread. Fry slowly until one side is golden, about 2½ minutes, pressing the bread down into the oil every now and then. Adjust the heat, if necessary, so that the bread does not brown too fast. Turn over and cook the second side for about 1½ minutes or until golden. Lift out with a slotted spoon and drain well on paper towels. Keep warm.

Make all the breads this way. Cut each bread into 4–5 pieces before serving.

Spring Onion (Scallion) Bread (page 143).

We enter their 'village' outside Manila through a guarded gate. All drivers must hand in their licences here. Our car meanders along wide, newly built boulevards and side lanes until we come to the 'cottage' of Ruby and Buddy Roa. This could be Beverly Hills. Beverly Hills with taste.

The cottage, with its solid wooden gate overhung with vines, is part rustic, part ranch-style palatial; indigenous stone and wood is used to create a home of the utmost luxury, complete with swimming-pool and with miniature ponies grazing on the grass. 'I saw them in the States and I just had to have them,' Ruby says of the ponies. The entire compound is enclosed by a thick, stone wall, delightful in its asymmetry, built specially by northern tribesmen to whom such work is second nature. Sod has been placed on the top of the wall, along its entire length. It is neatly clipped, soft as green velvet. Orchids and ferns sprout from the crevices in the wall.

To keep the Spanish chairs with mother-of-pearl inlay all gleaming and the Spanish tiles scrubbed – indeed, to run this establishment – there is a housekeeper, Norma, and a small army of about eight others.

Today Ruby and Buddy, who proudly declare themselves to be Marcos loyalists, are throwing a party. They like to entertain in the privacy of their own home. With all the help they are able to summon up, their parties can be lavish, yet casual, as many Filipino parties are. It is hard to get too stuffy when the weather is hot.

Opposite: Rice terraces, source of one of the Philippines' staple foods.

LUZON

Philippine

Sea

Manila

South

China

Sea

BATANGAS

Batangas

BICOL

PACIFIC OCEAN

Visayan

Sea

PANAY

Silay

ILOILO

Iloilo

Bacolod

Sittio Maninihon

NEGROS

NEGROS
OCCIDENTAL

Sulu

Sea

MINDANAO

Zamboanga

Celebes

Sea

The women, in summery Western clothes, are cooling themselves with Spanish fans. There is a ceiling-fan whirring overhead but it cannot seem to cut through the thick humid air. Limeade made with the juice of the small *kalamansi* lime, melon juice and coconut water help somewhat.

Ruby comes from a family of beauties. One of her sisters, who is present, was a Miss Universe. Ruby herself could win a few awards in my book. She strolls into in her large, modern kitchen, to sort out the details of her lunch. Some of the dishes, such as the *paella*, a Spanish rice pilaf studded with prawns (shrimp), mussels, clams, sausages, and peppers, will be prepared by her staff in a small, outdoor pavilion designed for grilling and barbecuing. Others, such as the *pikadilyo*, a superb creation combining fish with coconut milk, ginger, onions, tomatoes and black pepper, she will prepare herself.

American nicknames, Spanish last names and Chinese-Malay faces pretty much tell the story of the Philippines and of Filipino food as well. The Chinese, who have traded here since ancient times, came to settle in the eleventh century AD though, according to food historian Doreen G. Fernandez, they may well have started settling and intermarrying with the local Malays as early as the ninth century AD. With them came soy sauce and all their basic, everyday foods – bean curd, noodles, *wontons* and spring rolls. The Filipinos already had plenty of seafood – the archipelago consists of more than 7000 islands – as well as rice, poultry and pigs, to say nothing of coconut-eating crabs, fruit bats and other exotica, all of which could be cooked in Malay, Chinese or Chinese-Malay styles.

Malays have always loved to grill and roast outdoors. Their climate almost cries out for it. Roasted pigs stuffed with lemon grass or

Stilted houses on a reef in the Sulu archipelago. The Philippines consists of more than 7000 islands and seafood has always been plentiful.

A village of houses on stilts. Much of the fish caught by its fishermen will be washed in tubs of water and then dried.

tamarind leaves, and roasted fish and chickens wrapped in banana leaves, all predate the coming of any Westerner and here I include the Arabs. 'Western', after all, is only a relative term. Many of the roasted, steamed and grilled foods were served with sour dipping sauces (*sawsawan*) which could be as simple as coconut water vinegar with crushed garlic in it or fish sauce (*patis*) enlivened with juice from the *kalamansi* lime. Sour sauces are

cooling, so when fish or vegetables were poached a little sourness, perhaps a crushed green tamarind, went into the poaching liquid. These soured stewy dishes were known as *sinigang*.

There was no dearth of vegetables. Banana flowers, plantains, hearts of palm, swamp morning glory (called *kangkong* here) and young coconuts were all pressed into service. For seasoning, there was ginger, garlic, lemon grass, tamarind leaves, fresh turmeric and black pepper as well as various fish sauces and sour fruit. And there was both cane sugar and palm sugar to make sweet cakes with glutinous rice.

The Arabs were the next to hit these shores but, the shores being many, their influence was limited to Mindanao and the southern islands. They brought with them Islam, cumin and coriander, breads and the total ban on pork. They also brought in names for foods and utensils that they had picked up along the way in India. The wok was the *karahay* (from the Indian *karhai*), a name which seems to have travelled through the entire nation along with the Indian word for pickles: *achara*. The South Indian name *appam* was given to the pancakes made in the woks. This last name, and much of the Arab influence, stayed only in the south.

Then came the Spaniards. They colonised much of the country, gave it the name of one of their kings, Philip II, converted it to Catholicism and ruled it with an iron hand from 1521 until 1898. Their influence on the culinary heritage of the Philippines was to be profound, greater perhaps than that of any other colonial power in the East.

Certainly it was greater than that of the British in India and Malaysia and the Dutch in parts of Indonesia. Westernised Indians may eat roast lamb with mint sauce every now and then and have tea with cucumber sandwiches but, basically, Indian food remains completely Indian at all levels of society, with its principal influences coming from other Asians: the Arabs and Persians. British food in India always existed side by side with Indian food. It did not alter it. The Anglo-Indians, who mixed British and Indian culinary traditions, were only a small minority. The story in Indonesia is much the same. Dutch cakes and pastries, even Dutch stews and fish dishes, can be found in many parts of Indonesia. But the Dutch presence did not alter Indonesian food for the masses or supplant the names of local dishes with foreign ones.

It was different in the Philippines. The rule of the Spaniards and, following them, the Americans, who controlled the country until 1946, was to make much deeper inroads.

On Sundays and for Christmas, the upper classes began serving *pochero*, a stew of boiled meats such as beef shank and sausages, cooked with potatoes, cabbage, aubergines (eggplants) and chick peas; for breakfast they had rolls called *pan de sal* or airy buns (*ensaimadas*) dusted with sugar and cheese which they often ate with butter; to go with the buns, there was hot chocolate, well beaten to a froth and served from porcelain pots; for parties, they feasted on Andalusian *paella*, crammed with chunky lobster bits, clams, mussels and prawns (shrimp); and for dessert, there was *leche flan* (caramel custard).

The poorer Filipinos could not afford the rich diet of the upper classes. So, while they continued to eat *paksiw*, fish poached with a little vinegar and garlic, and rice, they learned to add New World foods, such as tomatoes and sweet potatoes to their vegetable stews. At fiestas, or when there was money, they too celebrated with *rellenong manok*, whole, boned and stuffed chickens; with whole roast pig which was now called *lechon*; and, when they could, they offered their children *empanadas*, stuffed, savoury turnovers; and *banadas*, large cookies with white icing.

As Spanish and Malay foods were being mixed and matched, what was happening to Chinese foods? They were indigenised and sometimes even given Spanish names. The spring roll became the *lumpia* and, at its best, was stuffed with fresh heart of palm; Chinese rice gruel (*congee*) became *arroz caldo*, and, when it was served, diners added *kalamansi* lime juice and fish sauce to give it a more Filipino flavour; cellophane noodles, when sautéd with chicken, onions and garlic were now known as *sotonghon guisado* (from the Spanish *guisar*, to sauté).

Among the many dishes at Ruby Roa's feast, all laid out on a counter decked sparingly, and stunningly, with orchids in a round earthen pot, there is a wooden platter of these very noodles sautéd with pork and chicken. There is also *lumpia*, the spring roll. So two dishes are decidedly of Chinese origin. Mediterranean culture is evident in her very Spanish *paella* which has been cooked with imported olive oil. The rest of the dishes show more mixed parentage. There is a grilled fish stuffed with onion, tomatoes and ginger; a pork and chicken *adobo* which is a kind of Mexican-Spanish dish of meat, semi-pickled with garlic, vinegar, black peppercorns and bay leaves – but it also contains soy sauce; and *pikadilyo*, fish cooked with Swiss chard, onions, ginger, tomatoes and coconut milk.

To give all this food coherence and unity, there is plain, boiled rice.

As we eat in a leisurely manner, the servants, all in white, whisk away the flies above us. Our implements are forks and spoons. For drinks with our meal, we are offered water, *kalamansi* juice or Coke. The Americans were the last rulers here and had until recently large army, navy and air force bases. The country is awash with Coke and 7-Up, with canned fruit cocktails, evaporated milk, bottled mayonnaise and hot dogs. When Ruby speaks with her children in Spanish, they reply in English.

The talk in Ruby's house is mostly political with great anger expressed at what are considered to be duplicitous dealings of the government.

The talk on the island of Negros, in the Visayas region of the central Philippines, is also political and equally filled with anger. I have flown south to Bacolod where I am told that a major political assassination, planned

Preparing a sweet snack with ube, a purple-fleshed root, and shredded coconut.

151

Houseboats in the Sulu archipelago.

for that Sunday, has just gone awry. From Bacolod, I have driven to the village of Sitio Maninihon. This seems to be a twin settlement. The side on the sea is an old fishing village. Here, as soon as it is dark, the men go out in their boats, sometimes 10 miles out to sea. They return in the morning and fling their catch first into large tubs of water to be washed, and then on to long, mat-topped tables on the beach where they drain off and start to dry. The dried fish has a vast market as much of the country subsists on it. The major business here is to take these semi-dried fish and put them into large cement tubs with salt. Here they are macerated with the feet and left for 2 months to ferment, transforming them into *bagoong*, a fish paste that compares with the *terasi* of Indonesia and the *kapi* of Thailand. This paste can also be made with tiny shrimp and is

excellent in sauces with lime juice or when eaten with slices of sour, green mango. The last, when offered to me, proved to be so delicious that I can taste it as I write.

The part of the settlement lying between the fishing village and the road is an old potters' village. I am sitting with Emma Ferraris in her small house on stilt-like foundations. Milky-white *tuba* (coconut water) sits outside in the sun in bottles, transforming itself into a deliciously mild vinegar even as we watch it. Emma is a potter. Her works line her tiny living-room. She is also a community worker with a pulse on the anger and frustration of her people. Everyone around her is poor. Emma herself has been seriously ill but, optimistically, cheerfully, she carries on, feeding other members of her family who have even less than she does. On weekends, she holds open house. What she has to offer are the very basics, but they are beautifully prepared.

She has thrown a lace tablecloth over her

simple, oval table. On its centre is placed a large plate of rice. This has been cooked in a pot lined with banana leaves so that not a single grain will stick and get lost. To go with the rice, there is *laswa*, a dish of long green beans stewed with onions, ginger, tomatoes and small clam-like molluscs. Sometimes Emma adds pumpkin to this dish to give its sauce even more flavour. There is *paksiw*, fish poached lightly in vinegared water and flavoured with garlic; some fried fish; and *torta*, a round omelette with prawns (shrimp). There is no meat, only a healthy, sustaining diet of vegetables, rice and fish. Everyone eats with their hands.

Stretching beyond Emma's village towards Silay and beyond, there used to be nothing but sugar-cane fields. Today, the sugar-cane workers are restless and violent. The price of sugar-cane has been down since 1977 and many sugar barons are converting their sugar-cane fields into prawn (shrimp) farms which require fewer hands. Much of this new produce will end up in Japan which seems to be vacuuming up much of the fish in this region.

Sugar was once one of the Philippines' most lucrative exports and Negros, with its one-crop economy, was the very heart of prosperous sugarland. In the nineteenth century, it was neighbouring Iloilo, just across the water on the island of Panay, that had the sugar. The farmers there eyed the rich, underpopulated lands across the strait and sent their sons over to Negros Occidental to carve out enormous farms. It is said that as much land as a horse could cover in a day became the size of a farm. The first generation worked hard and got the earth to yield all the cane it could produce. The second generation, already spoiled with easy money, left the work to foremen and took to travelling abroad and gambling at home.

Fish drying in Manila. Semi-dried fish is fermented and then made into a paste that is used in sauces or served with sour fruit.

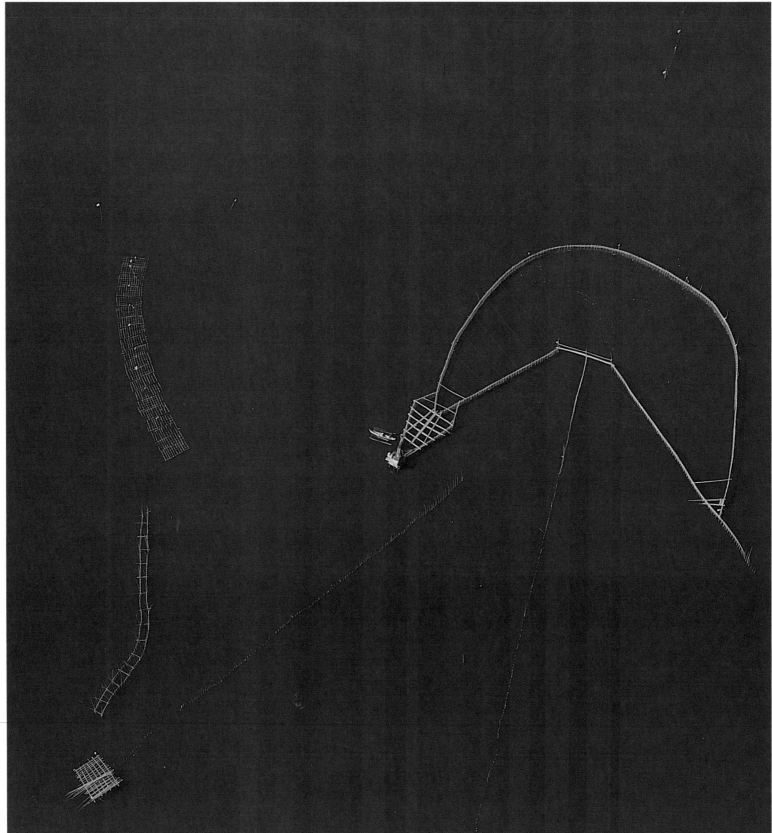

Left: A pen for fish in Manila Bay — a traditional
way of making sure fish is fresh for the table.

Food historian Doreen G. Fernandez, who is from this area, remembers the last of the gambling days when haciendas, jewellery, cars and land titles were lost in one impassioned day. As the men could not leave their *mah-jong*, *panguingue* or *monte* tables, the food naturally had to come to them. It also had to be finger food which could be picked up without disturbing the game. So women came in bearing wide 'flying saucer' baskets, lined with the local speciality, *lumpia*, spring rolls stuffed with the freshest local heart of palm, each wrapped individually in waxed paper; and *piaya*, a flat, sesame-seed-encrusted, cracker, filled with palm sugar. There were also *empanadas*, little pastries stuffed with chicken; tiny tarts (*pastels*) dabbed with banana or mango jam; coconut sweets (candies) called *butong butong*; and wonderfully chewy *dulce gatas*, a candy made from boiled-down buffalo milk.

I was able to taste most of these exquisite Silay creations in the colonial, Spanish-style home of Mrs Hofilena and her son Ramon. They live on Fifth of November Street where the rebellion against Spanish rule began. The ladies with the 'flying saucer' baskets still exist though their numbers seem to be diminishing. They still meet in the town square to exchange gossip and divide up their specialities. They then hawk their bounty of mixed goodies either in the city of Bacolod where they sell in beauty salons, schools and restaurants or they go to the homes of the old families of Silay, such as the Hofilenas, who put in orders for them whenever they feel like *merienda*.

Merienda, though of Spanish origin, fits into the Filipino life-style like a foot in a comfortable slipper. Filipinos love to eat. Breakfast, lunch and dinner do not seem to suffice. What about the long hours between these meals? To fill the tedium and satisfy hunger pangs, there is *merienda*, a mini, in-

A harbour scene at Zamboanga in Mindanao. The
boat's red and black sail adds a splash of colour.

between meal of snacks, usually eaten in the late afternoon and sometimes in the late morning as well. What qualifies as a snack, I wanted to know, seeing a large table groaning with *bibingkas*, cakes of ground rice and eggs, studded with cheese; small glutinous rice cakes in shades of purple and red and green; luscious coconut pies; corn lozenges rolled inside little horns made of leaves; those wonderful *piayas*; noodles; stuffed *empanadas*; a version of *wonton* soup called *pancit molo*; hot, frothy chocolate; *kalamansi* lime juice and every tropical fruit the town could muster up? 'Anything that is not eaten with rice is a snack,' I was told.

These, of course, are the more traditional snacks. Among the newer creations, as I found out on a trip to Manokan Country (Chicken Country), a stretch of eateries in Bacolod where they display their wares in the front and cook at the back, there are chicken

intestines on sticks, sold as 'I.U.Ds'; day-old chicks, sold as 'Day-O'; chicken wings, sold as 'airports'; cocks combs, sold as 'helmets'; pigs' ears, sold as 'Walkmans' and chicken feet, sold as 'Adidas'.

In this country of great contrasts and blends of culinary traditions, one of my happiest moments was a trip to a small island off the shores of Zamboanga in Mindanao. We had taken a small outrigger across the dark blue waters of the Sulu Sea with the intention of having a picnic. Fires had been lit under the palms, and fish and chicken wrapped in banana leaves were being grilled. As we swam and frolicked on those pink coral beaches, divers went down to find us one of the Philippines' greatly treasured seaweeds: *lato*.

A vegetarian caviar, this consists of crystalline green sea-grapes, luminous with the goodness concealed in each little capsule, all held together in small clusters. All we had to do was sprinkle some *kalamansi* juice on them and then drop them into our mouths. They were nectar from the sea.

155

RECIPES FROM THE PHILIPPINES

A bullock decorated for a Filipino festival.

All over the Philippines
VEGETABLE AND PRAWN (SHRIMP) FRITTERS
UKOY

At fiesta time, these fritters can be seen frying in hot oil, ready to be devoured the minute they emerge, with a dip of garlicky vinegar.

MAKES 8 FRITTERS, SERVING 4–8

For the batter:

130 g / 4½ oz / 1 cup plain (all purpose) white flour

115 g / 4 oz / 1 cup cornflour (cornstarch)

1½ teaspoons baking powder

1½ teaspoons salt

120 ml / 4 fl oz / ½ cup Chicken Stock, see p. 197

1 large egg, lightly beaten

You also need:

95 g / 3½ oz / 1 cup fresh bean sprouts

85 g / 3 oz / 1 cup peeled sweet potato that has been cut into very fine julienne strips

3 spring onions (scallions), quartered lengthways all the way up their green sections, then cut into 7.5 cm / 3 inch long shreds

8 medium-sized prawns (shrimp), peeled and deveined and cut crossways into 3 sections each

Vegetable oil for frying

Vinegar Dipping Sauce with Garlic, see p. 167

Combine all the ingredients for the batter and mix well.

Combine the bean sprouts, sweet potato and spring onions (scallions) in a bowl and toss together. Divide into 8 parts.

Heat about 2.5 cm / 1 inch oil in a large frying-pan over medium-low heat. Give it about 8–10 minutes to heat up. Put one lot of the vegetable mixture into a small saucer spreading it out to a diameter of about 9 cm / 4 inches. Lay 3 pieces of the prawns (shrimp) on top. Dribble about 2½–3 tablespoons batter on top of the vegetables and prawns (shrimp). Now slide this fritter into the hot oil. Make as many fritters this way as will fit easily in the frying-pan. Fry for 6–7 minutes on the first side. Turn the fritters over and fry for 4–5 minutes on the second side. Both sides should be golden-brown. Drain well on paper towels. Keep the first batch warm as you prepare the remainder in the same way. Serve hot, with the Vinegar Dipping Sauce with Garlic.

All over the Philippines
FISH AND VEGETABLE STEW
SINIGANG NA ISDA

Many Filipinos consider *sinigang* to be their national dish. It is mildly sour, as many dishes in this country are, and is made most frequently with fish, which for this nation of 7000 islands is not unnatural – though it could be made with pork and beef as well. It is a soupy stew, loaded with fish and vegetables and, eaten as it is with rice, can constitute a meal in itself. I often serve it as a light lunch or supper.

You may use almost any fish here: striped bass, sea bass, red snapper, pompano, pomfret, grey mullet, grouper, and even small salmon. Filleted cod, haddock and halibut may also be used but you will have to get fish bones and heads from your fishmonger to make the stock.

This soup is soured with *sampalok* (green tamarind) which is sold only by the Filipinos. Indeed, I cannot think of another nation in Asia that uses the green fruit in its cooking. As ripe tamarind is not a suitable alternative, I have used lime juice instead. If you can find green tamarinds, use 3–6. Throw them into the pan when preparing the stock. Make sure you mash them and strain out all their pulp when you strain the stock, pushing through a little pulp at a time and checking the sourness.

The thickening in this soup comes from rice-washing water. When rice is washed – and in Asia it could have dust on it – the first lot of water is thrown away as it is deemed to be too dirty. The water from the second washing is saved and used for cooking. It provides a faint aroma of rice, as well as a little thickening from the rice powder that still clings to the milled, polished grains. Rice in the West is now not only enriched but is so hygienically packed that it often requires no washing, so I have used a little rice flour as a thickener instead.

SERVES 4

675–800 g / 1½–1¾ lb fish (see above), filleted, the head and bones saved

Salt

Freshly ground black pepper

Vegetable and Prawn (Shrimp) Fritters (this page).

For the stock:

1.2 litres / 2 pints / 5 cups lightly salted Chicken Stock, see p. 197
Half a large onion (about 60 g / 2 oz), peeled and cut into large chunks
1 medium-sized carrot (85 g / 3 oz), peeled and cut into 3 parts
340 g / 12 oz large white radish, peeled and cut into chunky slices about 7.5 mm / ⅓ inch thick and 4 cm / 1½ inches long
2 bay leaves
½ teaspoon whole black peppercorns
1 celery stick

You also need:

1 tablespoon rice flour
2 tablespoons fresh lime juice, or to taste
4 teaspoons fish sauce, *patis* (or Chinese light soy sauce)
1 large onion (115 g / 4 oz), peeled and cut into 5 mm / ¼ inch thick half-rings
285 g / 10 oz fresh greens, such as mustard greens, swamp morning glory (*kang kung*), spinach, watercress, young spring greens (collard greens) or a combination thereof
4 plum tomatoes, peeled and quartered (or canned tomatoes)

Cut the fillets crossways into 5 cm / 2 inch pieces. Lightly salt and pepper them and set aside, refrigerating if necessary.

Combine the fish head and bones as well as all the ingredients for the stock in a good-sized pan. Add 300 ml / 10 fl oz / 1¼ cups water and bring to a boil. Cover partially, turn the heat to low and simmer for 45 minutes. Remove the radish pieces carefully with a slotted spoon and set aside. Strain the stock, pressing out as much liquid as you can. Pour the strained stock back into the pan. Mix the rice flour with 2 tablespoons water in a bowl. Add a ladleful of the stock to this mixture and stir. Pour the contents of the bowl into the stock pan and stir to mix. Add the lime juice, fish sauce, onion and reserved radish and bring to a simmer. Cover and simmer gently for 15 minutes. Put in the greens and bring to a simmer. Cover and simmer gently for 5 minutes. Now remove the

cover and add the tomatoes. Simmer uncovered for 2 minutes. Slide in the fish pieces and bring to a simmer. Simmer uncovered for 2–3 minutes or until the fish is firm and opaque.

Manila, Philippines

SALMON POACHED WITH TOMATOES AND SWISS CHARD
PIKADILYO

I have been to the Philippines several times but only once was this superb dish, or anything even resembling it, served to me. It was in the luxurious, modern home of Ruby Roa. In fact, she prepared it herself. It is easily one of the Philippines' most elegant dishes, part Spanish and part Malay. Ruby made it with mud fish, which we cannot get in Western markets, but if you make it with salmon, as I do, it is worthy of the grandest of dinners. Of course, you could use halibut or cod as well.

In the Philippines, this is served with rice. I like to put just the salmon and its sauce on individual plates and nothing else. Rice (or potatoes, if you prefer) may be put on small side plates. Ruby cooked the entire dish in thin coconut milk (see p. 212). I have used thick coconut milk from a well-stirred can (only because it is more convenient) and water to thin it out.

If there will be just four people for dinner, buy a little over 450 g / 1 lb salmon fillet. Do not change the rest of the recipe. You may have a little extra sauce but it is so delicious, I am sure it will all get eaten up.

In my local market, I can now get a red-stemmed Swiss chard. You may use that.

SERVES 5–6

675 g / 1½ lb salmon fillet (the thick centre section of a large salmon). Ask the fishmonger to remove the skin
Salt
Freshly ground black pepper
340 g / 12 oz Swiss chard
4 tablespoons olive oil

1 large onion (115 g / 4 oz), peeled and cut in half lengthways, then cut crossways into fine half-rings
4 cm / 1½ inch cube of fresh ginger, peeled and cut into very thin slices, then into very fine slivers
8 canned plum tomatoes, chopped
120 ml / 4 fl oz / ½ cup thick coconut milk straight from a well-stirred can

Cut the salmon fillet crossways into 5–6 portions (as many as there are people). Pull out bones, if any, with a pair of tweezers. Put some salt and pepper on both sides of the fish pieces and set aside for 20 minutes or longer.

Swiss chard leaves have a hard, central vein that eventually becomes the stem. Using a sharp, pointed knife, cut this out from all the leaves. Cut the green, leafy section crossways into 5 mm / ¼ inch wide strips. Set aside. Collect a few stems-veins at a time and cut them crossways into 3 mm / ⅛ inch strips.

Heat the oil in a very large frying-pan or a very wide sauté-pan over medium-high heat. When hot, put in the onion, ginger and chard stems-veins. Sauté for about 5 minutes. Add the tomatoes. Continue to sauté for another 4–5 minutes. Add the coconut milk and 450 ml / ¾ pint / 2 cups water, 1 teaspoon salt and some black pepper. Stir to mix, and bring to a simmer. Simmer on a low heat for 1 minute. This much of the recipe can be done ahead of time.

Just before you sit down to eat, bring the sauce to a simmer again. Put in the cut-up chard leaves and stir them in. Lay the fish pieces in a single layer over the top of the sauce. Spoon some of the thinner, more watery parts of the sauce over the fish. Cover. Simmer for 5 minutes or until the fish has just cooked through.

To serve, using a good-sized spatula lift a piece of fish with some of the greens and

Salmon Poached with Tomatoes and Swiss Chard (this page).

solids from the sauce and put it in the centre of a plate. Spoon some of the thinner part of the sauce over the top of the fish. The sauce will flow to the edge of the plate as it should. Make up all the plates this way and serve immediately.

Western Visayas, Philippines

GRILLED CHICKEN WITH A PINEAPPLE GLAZE
MANOKAN INASAL

At the El Ideal restaurant in the small town of Silay in Negros, chicken is left marinating for a day in a sour and salty mixture that includes coconut-water vinegar, ginger, lime juice and soy sauce. It is then grilled over charcoal and given a final glazing with a pineapple syrup (or ginger ale!). It is served with a dipping sauce of Spiced Vinegar (see p. 166) to which a touch of soy sauce and lime juice are added at the table.

Accompanied by salads and boiled corn, I cannot think of a more perfect meal for a summer day.

SERVES 4–6

For the marinade:

8 tablespoons Chinese light soy sauce

4 tablespoons distilled white vinegar

4 tablespoons fresh lime juice
(or lemon juice)

2 cloves garlic, peeled and crushed

5 cm / 2 inch cube of fresh ginger, peeled and grated to a pulp

4 teaspoons sugar

Freshly ground black pepper

You also need:

6 whole chicken legs (about 1.5 kg / 3¼ lb), with skin

For the pineapple glaze:

10 tablespoons pineapple juice

3 tablespoons sugar

Combine all the ingredients for the marinade in a very large bowl. Mix. Cut deep, diagonal gashes on the meatier sides of the chicken legs, about two on the thigh, and another

two on the drumstick, then prick holes on the opposite sides with a fork. Put the legs into the marinade and mix well. Cover and refrigerate for 24 hours, turning the chicken pieces around now and then so that they absorb the marinade evenly.

Make the pineapple glaze: Combine the pineapple juice and the sugar in a small, heavy pan. Stir and cook over medium heat until slightly syrupy.

The chicken may now be grilled outdoors over charcoal or in the kitchen.

To grill outdoors: Pre-heat your grill. If you do not have a covered grill, keep a wok cover at hand. When hot, place your chicken on a rack about 13 cm / 5 inches from the source of heat and cover. Grill for about 10 minutes on the first side and 8–10 minutes on the second side. The chicken should be three-quarters cooked. Now spoon the pineapple syrup generously over the first side and grill for 2 minutes, covered, or until that side is browned. Turn the pieces over and do the same on the opposite side, grilling for another 1½–2 minutes. Do not let the chicken burn. If necessary (and possible), increase its distance from the fire towards the end.

To grill (broil) indoors: Pre-heat your grill (broiler), and follow the same directions except for covering the meat.

Western Visayas, Philippines

CHICKEN WITH LEMON GRASS AND GINGER
BINACOL NA MANOK

Traditionally, this light, aromatic, soupy-stew is cooked in the hollow of a bamboo on the farms of the western Visayas. All the ingredients – and on the farms, they include the slithery-soft meat from young coconuts – are put inside the bamboo, which is then sealed and placed over embers to bake slowly. In the cities, this much-loved dish is prepared in sealed earthen pots. I have used a casserole dish and an oven.

Whatever method is used, the results are so

memorable that I have had very well-known chefs ask for the recipe. 'There is nothing to it,' I tell them. 'I just take chicken, potatoes, lemon grass, ginger, garlic, onion, a few tomatoes, some coconut milk, salt, pepper and water, put them all in a casserole dish and bake them.' The melding of the flavours creates a dish that is uncommon and uncommonly good.

If you cannot get fresh lemon grass, put 6 tablespoons dried, sliced lemon grass in a small pan with 400 ml / 14 fl oz / 1¾ cups water. Bring to a boil. Cover, turn the heat to low and simmer for 30 minutes. Strain and use this liquid (it will have reduced a bit) to cook the chicken.

Serve this stew in old-fashioned soup plates that can hold the wonderful juices or in shallow, wide bowls. Plain rice should be served on the side in separate bowls or on small plates.

SERVES 4

3 sticks of fresh lemon grass, just the lower 15 cm / 6 inches with the bulbous bottoms lightly crushed (or see above or 2 teaspoons grated lemon rind)

1.3 kg / 3 lb chicken (a whole bird cut into small serving pieces, or chicken pieces)

5 medium-sized potatoes (560 g / 1¼ lb), peeled and halved

2 tablespoons olive or other vegetable oil

1 clove garlic, peeled and finely chopped

2.5 cm / 1 inch piece of fresh ginger, cut into round, thickish slices

1 medium-sized onion (85 g / 3 oz), peeled and cut into 5 mm / ¼ inch thick half-rings

3 plum tomatoes, peeled and coarsely chopped (or canned tomatoes)

1½ teaspoons salt, or to taste

Lots of freshly ground black pepper

½ teaspoon sugar

250 ml / 8 fl oz / 1 cup coconut milk, fresh, see p. 212, or from a well-stirred can

Pre-heat the oven to gas mark 3 / 325°F / 160°C.

Use a large, casserole-type pan that can be used both on top of the cooker (stove) and in the oven. Put in all the ingredients in the order listed, except the coconut milk. Mix half the coconut milk (175 ml / 6 fl oz / ¾ cup) with 350 ml / 12 fl oz / 1½ cups water and pour it over the ingredients in the pan. Bring to a boil. Cover tightly and put in the oven. Bake for 30 minutes. Turn the chicken and potatoes over gently, cover again and bake for another 30 minutes.

Remove from the oven.

Put the remaining coconut milk in a bowl. Add about half a piece of potato and mash it in. Add a ladleful of liquid from the stew and mix. Pour this mixture back into the pan and mix it in gently. Boil the stew over medium-high heat, uncovered, for about 2–3 minutes and turn off the heat.

This stew may be made ahead of time and re-heated. Remove the sticks of lemon grass and, if you like, the ginger as well, before serving.

Northern Philippines

BONED, STUFFED CHICKEN
RELLENONG MANOK

Nothing could be more festive than this stuffed chicken from the central Luzon area. Indeed, it is at fiestas here that dozens of such birds appear on long tables lined with banana leaves. Being boneless, they are very easily sliced and served. They are somewhat time-consuming to prepare but well worth the effort for a dinner party. Or for a summer picnic.

This chicken combines the best of a roast chicken and a pork pie. Serve it at room temperature with salads, or warm, with Far Eastern or Western-style vegetables.

An ingredient note: Bottled mixed sweet pickles are available in most supermarkets. For those who cannot find them, it is best to take the same amount of chopped *cornichons* or pickled gherkins, rub about 1 tablespoon sugar into them and leave for 1 hour or longer. Drain and use.

SERVES 6

For marinating the chicken:

1.5 kg / 3½ lb chicken, boned, see p. 207
4 tablespoons Chinese dark soy sauce
3 tablespoons lime juice (or lemon juice)
Freshly ground black pepper

For the stuffing:

340 g / 12 oz lean, minced (ground) pork
115 g / 4 oz lean, minced (ground) veal
115 g / 4 oz minced (ground) cooked ham (preferably cooked Chinese or Smithfield ham)
1 Spanish or Filipino sausage, *chorizo de Bilbao* or *chorizo* (or a plain, Italian sausage, skinned and finely chopped)
2 slices white bread, crumbled and soaked in 4 tablespoons milk
3 large eggs, lightly beaten
6 large green olives, stoned and chopped
4 tablespoons drained, canned pimento, finely chopped
4 tablespoons drained, bottled, mixed sweet pickles, finely chopped (or see below left)
2 tablespoons sultanas (golden raisins)
2 tablespoons grated Parmesan cheese
¾ teaspoon salt, or to taste
Freshly ground black pepper
A little vegetable oil

Using a needle and thread, sew the tail area of the chicken closed. If there are any tears in the skin, sew them up as well. (Leave the neck area open for the stuffing.) Put the boned chicken into a bowl.

Add all the other ingredients for the marinade, mix well, cover and marinate overnight in the refrigerator.

Mix all the ingredients for the stuffing except the oil. Remove about 1 teaspoon of the stuffing and sauté it in a lightly oiled frying-pan.

Taste and check seasoning, adding more of anything you wish.

Pack the stuffing into the cavity of the chicken through the neck opening. Do not overstuff. Pat the chicken back into its original shape and sew up the neck opening. Keep the breast-side up. Arrange the chicken in the centre of a 90 cm / 3 ft long sheet of foil. Pat it once again into its chicken shape and wrap it tightly in the foil. Arrange the foil-wrapped chicken lengthways in the middle of a 60 cm / 2 ft long double thickness of cheesecloth. Fold the long sides over the chicken. Twist the ends and tie them closed with kitchen string.

Set up your steaming equipment (see p. 208) and bring the water in it to a boil. Keep extra boiling water ready in a kettle. Place the chicken, breast-side up, on a flat trivet in the steaming vessel. Cover, and steam for 1¼ hours, adding more water to the steamer as needed. Turn the chicken over and steam, breast-side down, for another hour, again adding more water to the steamer as needed.

Meanwhile, pre-heat the oven to gas mark 7 / 425 °F / 220 °C.

When the chicken has finished steaming, move it gently to a work surface and remove the cheesecloth and foil. Transfer the chicken, breast-side up, to a roasting pan and roast it in the pre-heated oven for 15–20 minutes or until it is golden-brown.

To serve, place the chicken on a cutting board or carving plate and let it come to room temperature or stay barely warm. Remove all threads. First cut off the wings and legs and arrange them in their places on a serving plate. Now cut the body of the bird in half lengthways. Cut the halves crossways into 1 cm / ½ inch thick slices. Arrange the slices, in slightly overlapping rows, in the centre of the plate, re-creating, in general, the shape of the chicken.

Batangas, Philippines

CHICKEN WITH VINEGAR, GARLIC AND COCONUT MILK
ADOBONG MANOK SA GATA

The classical Filipino dish, *adobo*, can take many forms and can be made with pork,

A village in Luzon. The recipe for chicken cooked in coconut milk, on this page, is very much in the style of this region.

chicken or squid, among other things. Here chicken is cooked with coconut milk in the Batangas style from southern Luzon. Since Batangas is also noted for the quality of its chickens, this is a felicitous combination. The one constant in all *adobos* is a souring agent – which happens to be vinegar here – and garlic.

The vegetable that goes into this stew-like dish is *sayote* or *chayote*, a pear-shaped, New World vegetable that travelled East with the Spaniards and Portuguese. If you can find it, buy one. Peel it and then quarter it lengthways. Remove the central stone. Now cut each section crossways into 5 mm / ¼ inch thick slices. *Sayote* takes about 25 minutes to get tender so put it in to cook nearer the beginning. I have used cucumber, which takes only 7–8 minutes to cook through.

Serve this stew-like dish with rice.

SERVES 4
For the marinade:

675 g / 1½ lb chicken drumsticks and thighs, skinned

4 tablespoons distilled white vinegar

8 cloves garlic, peeled and mashed to a paste

¾ teaspoon salt

Lots of freshly ground black pepper

For the simmering:

120 ml / 4 fl oz / ½ cup canned coconut milk, well-stirred and mixed with the same amount of water, or 250 ml / 8 fl oz / 1 cup fresh, thin coconut milk, see p. 212

340 g / 10 oz cucumber, peeled and cut crossways into 1 cm / ½ inch thick rounds

For the final cooking:

120 ml / 4 fl oz / ½ cup well-stirred canned coconut milk or fresh, thick coconut milk, see p. 212

Salt

Freshly ground black pepper

Combine the chicken and 120 ml / 4 fl oz / ½ cup water with all the remaining ingredients for its marinade. Mix well and set aside, covered, at room temperature for at least 2 hours. You may refrigerate it overnight, if you prefer.

In a large, wide pan, combine the chicken, its marinade and the coconut milk for simmering. Bring to a boil. Cover and turn the heat to low. Simmer for 20 minutes. Add the cucumber and bring to a boil again. Cover, turn the heat to low and simmer for another 7–8 minutes or until both chicken and cucumber are tender. Remove the cover. Add the coconut milk for the final cooking. Mix and taste. Add more salt and pepper as desired. Cook for another minute, uncovered, on medium heat, stirring gently as you do so.

All over the Philippines
SWEET AND SOUR PORK WITH CARROTS
PORK ESCABECHE

Just mildly sweet, sour and salty, this dish has its roots in the Chinese culinary world but, in its use of larger chunks of meat and carrots, it also has some of the qualities of a Spanish stew. It is quite wonderful in both taste and texture and is so easy to prepare that you may want to put it on your list of everyday or party dishes.

You may serve it the traditional way, with rice, or with boiled potatoes if you prefer. A salad, from the Philippines or otherwise, would complete the meal.

I used boneless meat from pork butt. You may substitute any relatively lean, boneless cut of your choice.

SERVES 3–4

2 tablespoons olive or other vegetable oil
3 cloves garlic, peeled and finely chopped
340 g / 12 oz boneless pork meat (see above), cut into 5 x 2.5 cm x 5 mm /
2 x 1 x ¼ inch slices
½ teaspoon whole black peppercorns
2 tablespoons Chinese dark soy sauce

Slowly add the remaining 250 ml / 8 fl oz / 1
cup stock to it, mixing well as you go. Add
this to the stock in the pan. Mix and bring to
a simmer. Simmer gently, stirring, for 3–4
minutes. Turn off the heat.

Just before you sit down to eat, bring a
large pan of water to a rolling boil and place
a colander in the sink. Heat up the sauce.
Drop the fresh noodles (or cooked noodles)
and the sprouts into the boiling water. Count
until 10 for fresh noodles and five for dried,
cooked noodles. Drain. Empty the noodles
and sprouts into a serving dish. Pour the
sauce over the top, straining it if it seems
lumpy. Scatter the pork, bean curd and
prawns (shrimp), etc. over the top of the
noodles. Finally, sprinkle the bacon, spring
onions (scallions) and Chinese celery on top
of the pork, etc. Arrange the wedges of hard-
boiled egg on the sides. Serve the lime
wedges and fish sauce separately. Each diner
should squeeze some lime juice and dribble
some fish sauce over the top of a serving, and
then mix everything up.

Most of the Philippines
TOMATO SALAD
SAWSAWANG KAMATIS

Here is a simple salad that is found in both
restaurants and homes. The tomatoes can be
chopped up, which turns this into a dipping
sauce-cum relish.

SERVES 4

2–3 large tomatoes (450 g / 1 lb), cut crossways
into 3 mm / ⅛ inch thick slices

1 spring onion (scallion), very finely chopped
all the way up its green section

1 tablespoon very finely chopped sour, green
mango (or fresh lime juice)

½ teaspoon peeled, finely chopped,
fresh ginger

¼ teaspoon salt

Freshly ground black pepper

Arrange the tomato slices on a plate in a
single layer. Sprinkle all the remaining
ingredients over the top.

Western Visayas, Philippines
SPICED VINEGAR
SINAMAK

This seasoning is found in the western
Visayas region of the Philippines. It sits in
bottles on most dining-tables and is used
frequently as a dip for grilled chicken and
grilled fish. It may be used as is, or it may be
put into small individual bowls and mixed
with a few drops of soy sauce. Some people
like to add a little fresh lime juice to their
portions. The spices seem to keep indefinitely
in the bottle. As the vinegar depletes, it is
just replenished. I often use this vinegar to
make spicy salad dressings.

MAKES 300 ML / 10 FL OZ / 1¼ CUPS

300 ml / 10 fl oz / 1¼ cups distilled white
vinegar

2.5 cm x 5 mm / 1 x 1¼ inch piece fresh
ginger, peeled and cut crossways into
3–4 pieces

3 cloves garlic, peeled

1 teaspoon whole black peppercorns

6 dried, hot red chillies

¼ teaspoon salt

166

Ancient and modern – a street scene that is typical of the Philippines, where Westernization merges with traditions inherited over the centuries from the Chinese, Malays and Spaniards who settled in the islands.

Combine all the ingredients in a clean bottle. Cover with a non-metallic lid and set aside for 3 days or longer to allow the flavours to merge.

The vinegar will last indefinitely.

All over the Philippines

VINEGAR DIPPING SAUCE WITH GARLIC
SUKA'T DINIKDIK NA BAWANG

This is a simple, all-purpose dipping sauce that is used all over the Philippines. It goes particularly well with fried foods such as the Vegetable and Prawn (Shrimp) Fritters on page 156.

SERVES 4

4 tablespoons distilled white vinegar

½ clove garlic, peeled and crushed

½ teaspoon salt

Freshly ground black pepper

Combine all the ingredients in a small bowl and set aside. Just before serving, spoon into 4 tiny saucers (less if there are fewer diners).

All over the Philippines

SWEET RICE PATTIES WITH COCONUT
PALITAO

Almost like candy, these are small patties of glutinous rice that are encrusted with fresh coconut, roasted sesame seeds and sugar. They are quite chewy.

SERVES 4–6

140 g / 5 oz / 1¼ cups glutinous rice powder plus a little extra for dusting

6 tablespoons grated fresh coconut, see p. 212, or dessicated, unsweetened coconut

3 tablespoons roasted sesame seeds, see p. 217

3 tablespoons sugar

Put the flour in a bowl. Slowly add about 75 ml / 2¼ fl oz / ⅓ cup water, just enough to gather the flour together to make a pliable ball. Work the ball until it is smooth and then break it off into 1 cm / ½ inch balls. Flatten the balls into 2.5 cm / 1 inch patties, elongating them slightly, and lay them down on a plate lightly dusted with some glutinous rice powder.

Spread out the coconut on a plate. Mix the sesame seeds and sugar and spread out on another plate.

Bring a large pan of water to a rolling boil. Drop in all the patties, one at a time, in quick succession. They will sink to the bottom and then rise up and float. As soon as one floats, remove it with a slotted spoon and put it on a clean plate. Remove all the patties this way and put beside each other in a single layer. Dip one patty at a time, first in the grated coconut and then in the sesame sugar.

When cool, cover the patties with cling film (plastic wrap) or put them in a closed plastic container. Do not refrigerate. The patties should keep for 24 hours.

Manila, Philippines

MRS IMELDA MARCOS' FRIED BANANAS
PRITONG SAGING

This happened more than 10 years ago. I had gone to the Philippines to do an article for *Gourmet* magazine and, through the help of various local friends, had managed to get an interview with the beautiful Mrs Marcos. Well, there she was in full regalia seated in her receiving-room in Malacanang Palace, and there I was, notebook in hand, trying to get her to talk about her culinary likes and dislikes, whereas all she wanted to talk about was how much the world misunderstood her and how much she really loved her people. When we finally did get to the subject of

food, Mrs Marcos said that she enjoyed cooking herself and that she had a private kitchenette just behind the room we were in where she whipped up her favourite dishes. Could she whip up something for me, I had the nerve to ask. Well, of course, she replied, she would show me how she made Bananas Flambé or Fried Bananas, whichever I liked. They could be made in just a few minutes.

I could not believe my good fortune. I had managed to get into the palace – no mean feat – and now the First Lady was about to demonstrate the preparation of one of her choice desserts.

Mrs Marcos conversed at length in Tagalog with the maids who were standing behind her. Then she turned to me and said, 'I can only make these dishes if I have Chiquita bananas and my maids tell me that there are no Chiquita bananas in the palace today.'

So much for that. But Mrs Marcos did give me her recipe. Here it is.

The results are exceedingly good. The amounts can easily be doubled or tripled.

SERVES 2–4

2 bananas, firm but ripe

4 tablespoons unsalted butter

4 teaspoons fresh lime juice

2 tablespoons honey

2–4 generous dollops of lightly whipped cream (optional), as many dollops as there are diners

Cut each banana into half lengthways, and then cut each piece in half crossways.

Melt the butter over medium heat in a non-stick frying-pan. As soon as it has melted, turn the heat to high and put in the banana pieces. Fry quickly on both sides. The banana pieces should get lightly browned. This should take no more than 1–2 minutes. Remove with a slotted spoon and divide among warmed, individual plates. Spoon the lime juice over the top and then the honey. Put a dollop of cream over each serving and take to the table immediately.

INDONESIA

Tom-toms, like alarms, sound in the middle of the night to awaken the sleeping. While the moist, teeming earth gives off the sweet smell of frangipani, the gods that inhabit the misty upper reaches of Bali's volcanic peaks look down with approval. A feast is about to be prepared.

The pigs, dangling by their feet from poles set on the shoulders of small, wiry, betel-chewing men, have already been carried to the site. Perhaps they were promised to a god in some dire, anxious moment. Here, on this Indonesian island, they are ceremoniously slaughtered, their skins rubbed with pounded turmeric (not the dry, powdered variety but the fresh rhizome that resembles ginger), lime juice and salt. Then the abdominal cavities are filled with spring onions (scallions), Asian celery, lemon grass, aromatic kaffir lime leaves and a mixture of sautéd red chillies, shallots, garlic, coriander and that intense, dryish, shrimp paste known as *terasi*. The pigs are skewered and set to roast over an open wood fire. As they are slowly turned, the skins become cracklingly crisp while the flesh becomes meltingly tender, juicy and spicy.

All the cutting and chopping must be done in the dead of night. Coconuts must be scraped, two pieces at a time (why grate one when you can grate two?) on wooden graters that have fine pins sticking out of them. Mounds of shallots – they are used like onions here and are sold for about one-third the price of garlic – red chillies, plump candle nuts (the nuts can actually be lit), and garlic cloves need to be crushed in stone mortars under the weight of pounding pestles. Stiff stalks of lemon grass must be bruised before they can release their citrus

Opposite: A buddha at Borobudur's 9th-century shrine on Java.

169

Piglets are carried to a morning market. Although pork is taboo to Indonesia's Muslims it is festive food for many Hindus and Christians.

perfume. All the food must be fresh when served, for the gods will sample the dishes first and draw off their essence. Only then may mortals sit in long, silent rows – the Balinese do not like to converse when they eat – to enjoy what the gods have blessed.

Besides the roasted pig (*babi guling*) there may be *satay babi*, small pork cubes marinated with a paste of red chillies, shallots, sweet soy sauce (*kecap manis*) and lime juice, then skewered and grilled. There may also be fresh turtle soup (*sop penyu*), vegetables in a coconut sauce, chicken baked in a banana leaf, rice, and mounds of tropical fruit:

rambutans and mangosteens, bananas and snake-skinned *salak*.

Is this then a typical Indonesian meal? It is typical only for the island of Bali on a feast day. Indonesia is the world's largest archipelago, a necklace of 13 667 disparate islands stretching 5152 kilometres from Malaysia to Australia. Some islands are blessed with nourishing rain for half the year, others, closer to Australia, are dry. The islands' inhabitants are chiefly of Malay ancestry but many have Chinese, Indian, Dutch, Portuguese, Spanish, Arab and local tribal blood.

Some of the outsiders came to trade and some to colonise. Some also came to spread religion, with the result that the most populated islands, Sumatra and Java, are mainly Muslim, North Sulawesi is basically

Protestant Christian, Flores has Catholic pockets and Bali is Hindu – with all of the islanders sharing deep-seated animist beliefs that seem to ooze from the soil.

The foods, in the natural course of things, reflect this happy diversity. But there is a common umbrella under which all Indonesian foods may be placed, a common pattern to the dining – with many exceptions.

Rice is the staple and its patron goddess, Dewi Sri, is deeply revered. Shrines to her, little graceful pagodas, stand in the midst of shimmering paddy fields, encouraging the general fecundity. A carefully evolved social and ecological system keeps the rice fields in full gear. The fields need to be flooded so villagers have worked out elaborate communal systems of sharing water, and therefore sharing their lives. Ducks and fish are let loose in the paddies. They eat the insects, their droppings fertilise the fields and they themselves may be snatched up and thrown into a pot when hunger strikes.

Whether rice is grown by the wet cultivation method, as in Bali, or the dry one, as in the hilly tracts of eastern Sumbawa, numerous varieties are produced: long-grain, glutinous, red and black. The quality, too, is different from region to region. The Balinese claim that their fat-grained rice, grown with the aid of frequent ritual offerings, is the best in the world. They offer it to the gods in the form of tall cookie sculptures, and as appeasement to demons in the form of scattered grain. But most importantly, through much of Indonesia, rice serves as daily bread. Generally, this is white rice – the milling being a symbol of doing well – that is parboiled first and then steamed in a basket until every grain is separate and fluffy.

A meal without rice is not a meal. A modern working woman in Jakarta explained to me once that even if she and her husband eat a hamburger in town, which they sometimes do before they return home in the evening, they will not feel that they have dined until they still sit down to a 'proper' meal with rice at its centre.

170

Rambutans for sale in a market. These tropical fruits are like large, red litchis.

I have watched the humblest of farmers make a meal out of a big bowl of rice and just a dollop of *sambal*, in this case red chillies pounded in a mortar with salt, to perk it up. It was eaten with the same relish that an Italian peasant may show to pasta dressed with garlic and olive oil. The daily ration for a soldier is about 450 g (1 lb) rice which he eats for breakfast, lunch and dinner. In a small fishing village near Padang, in West Sumatra, I once caught a little boy looking wistfully at the *satay*-man who was selling his *satays*, or skewered kebabs, from a push-cart. He could not afford the kebabs. What he could – and did – buy was some rice in the form of a firm cake (*ketupat*) and some spicy *satay* sauce to put over it. In wealthy homes, the rice would be accompanied by meats and vegetables that have been made into soups (*soto*), curries (*gulai*), roasts (*panggang*), stir-fries (*tumis*), soupy vegetable stews (*sayur*) or have been fried (*goreng*) or grilled (*bakar*).

171

Offerings of rice cakes. Rice is Indonesia's staple food and has its own patron goddess whose shrines stand in paddy fields.

For special occasions, such as the falling off of a baby's umbilical cord, the baroque confection *nasi kuning* is prepared. Coconut milk, tinged with the yellow of freshly grated turmeric root, is first brought to a boil. Rice, both plain and glutinous, is folded in and left to absorb the liquid. A final steaming, with the addition of fragrant pandanus leaves, finishes off the preparation. It is mounded on a platter – the glutinous rice holds the mound together – and festooned with egg strips, cucumber slices, potato croquettes and red chilli flowers. Banana-leaf bowls, filled with spicy matchstick potatoes and *opor ayam*, chicken cooked with coconut milk, are served on the side.

Not all of Indonesia's islands grow rice. Ternate, in the northern Moluccas is an example. In ancient times, Ternate did have a very precious commodity, much desired by the world – cloves – which it traded for rice. Throughout the Middle Ages, every roast, every mulled wine or cider served in Europe used cloves that came from just two little neighbouring islands: Ternate and Tidore.

All went well until the arrival of the Europeans who insisted that they be granted a clove monopoly. When the people of Ternate resisted, all their clove trees, their sole livelihood, were destroyed by the Dutch who calmly transported saplings to an island that they could control: Ambon in the central Moluccas. But the habit of eating rice still remained.

The staple in Ambon is not rice but sago. I certainly knew sago only as white pearls which my mother in India cooked with milk, sugar and cardamom into a soothing pudding. Here sago, in the form of fresh, rough meal or smooth flour, is made into everything from the most deliciously toasted waffles (*sagu gula*) which are served, all hot and crisp, for breakfast, to a viscous paste (*papeda*) which is

made on the spot with sago flour and hot water and served with lunch and dinner as rice might be.

Where does sago come from? I was somewhat confused myself until I watched the entire process in an Ambonese plantation. Sago comes out of the stocky and sturdy sago palm. It is the pith of the trunk. A tree, about 16 years old, is felled and its trunk halved lengthways. Then a man sits astride it on a bamboo seat and scrapes out the pulp, all flecked with reds and browns and white. It is these fresh scrapings, when mixed with freshly grated coconut, that go to make the waffles that I, even now, yearn for. To make the white flour, the scraped pulp is mixed with water and sent down a shute made out of a hollowed trunk. White sago particles settle at the bottom. These are dried and sifted into flour. This flour is also made into sago pearls.

Where there is neither rice nor sago, there is corn, courtesy of the Spaniards and Portuguese, who brought nutritious offerings to the East from the New World in the sixteenth century. A group of us once visited a small, tribal village in the volcanic Iliape district of Lomblen Island. We sensed a general disapproval of foreigners but, after many chants to ward off any evil that might attach to us, we were allowed to see some 'ancient', traditional dances performed under the shade of a banyan tree. Women, dressed in mannish hats, moved sinuously through imaginary fields reaping corn, removing the kernels, roasting them until they burst – as they danced they sang 'pop, pop, pop' – and then crushing them. Indeed, it is the crushed – perhaps flattened describes it better – roasted corn kernel, so well-mimed in the dance, that is the staple here, eaten with all meals.

What do Indonesian meals consist of? They vary, of course, from island to island, often from town to town, but after the staple, fish is paramount. With their enormous coastline and their equatorial waters teeming with aquatic life, the Indonesians get their

protein the easiest way they can. Those who do not live by the sea raise their fish in the wet paddy fields, and those who do not have access to paddies get them from rivers and lakes or, in some areas like the hills of West Sumatra, from large tanks that are built next to homes, as kitchen gardens might be, specifically for the breeding of fish.

Fish at a meal could make its presence felt very subtly in the form of dishes cooked with *terasi*. *Terasi* is a paste, fairly dry and cake-like, made out of processed shrimps. Not all islands use it but where they do, as in Java, it is put into *sambals* and sauces. The closest equivalent in European cooking is, perhaps, the French meat glaze, *glace de viande*, whose concentrated intensity immediately enriches a sauce. *Terasi* does have a strong smell but it is hardly 'fishy'. In fact, I find that once I have fried, grilled or sautéd the *terasi* and used it in a dish, the smell of the paste is more in my kitchen than in the food itself. (The kitchen can be easily aired.) Whenever it is used, the dish gains dramatically in depth and character. I have suggested the use of anchovy paste as an alternative to *terasi*. But do give the real thing a chance.

Sometimes, as in West Sumatra, I have seen a piece of dried fish first fried and then cooked along with, say cabbage, to give the vegetable the same depth of flavour that *terasi* would in Java. In Manado (North Sulawesi), where they specialise in the most exquisitely smoked bonito (a small tuna, locally called *cakalang*), I have partaken of a corn soup that is cooked with the head of this smoked fish in the same way that a dried pea soup may be cooked with a ham bone in the West.

Other than fish used as flavouring, fish can be used as stuffing – I have had bitter gourd stuffed with ground fish – it can be rubbed with salt and lime juice and fried, it can be grilled with lavish bastings of a chilli-ginger-shallot sauce, it can be smothered with a hot sauce of pounded spices and wrapped in banana leaves and then grilled, it can be 'curried' and, in perhaps the most complex of preparations, *Satay Bandeng*, it can be deboned and defleshed, while still keeping its full shape, stuffed with its own meat that has been nicely mixed with spices, wrapped in banana leaves and first steamed and then grilled.

In a land where most of the population is Muslim, everyone can eat fish. It has no taboos attached to it and it is plentiful and often cheap. But people here do yearn for meat which, because of its expense, becomes the treat for Fridays and for all celebrations. In West Sumatra no wedding takes place without the magnificent *rendang*, beef chunks simmered with lemon grass and coconut milk until they are dry and encrusted with spices. This is also taken long distances – even to Mecca – as it travels well and can last a good month. In Ternate, in the north Moluccas, a much-loved dish for the Lebaran celebrations that follow the fasting of Ramadan, is *garu kecap*, a stunningly simple stew of beef (or lamb) with cinnamon, ginger and sweet soy sauce.

Pork, frowned upon by the Muslims, is not only party food for the Hindu Balinese, as I have already described, but for the Christians of North Sulawesi as well. I remember once going into raptures over a *kinetor* I had just sampled in an open market outside Manado. I was desperate for the recipe. My hostess wished to oblige but she had only eaten it in restaurants and never cooked it herself. All this time our chauffeur had been listening to the conversation with some frustration. Unable to restrain himself, he broke in. 'It is so easy,' he said, 'so very easy. I make it all the time myself. All you have to do is put some cubed pork in a pot, throw in some seasonings – chives, lemon grass, turmeric leaves, ginger, chillies, shallots, spring onions (scallions) and kaffir lime leaves, mix it all well – add a little water and then let it cook. When it is done, you get a jug of *saguer* (a local beer-like palm toddy), sit under a shady tree and enjoy.'

The larger animals are not only eaten in Indonesia with gusto, they are eaten in their entirety. No part of the animal is wasted,

Sunrise in a fishing village. Unlike pork, fish has no taboos and can be eaten by everyone.

heart, lungs and skin included. In fact, hearts are much prized and are very expensive. I have had fried lungs in Padang in West Sumatra, beef skin crackings in Yogyakarta and, in Jakarta's Pasar Senem market, an unforgettable soup, *soto Betawi*, made entirely with innards: lungs, tongue, tripe, skin, intestines, kidneys, etc.

This is no fancy dining. You make your way through the crowded bazaar and find a seat on a bench at the soup stall. Steam rises from stock pots; innards are propped up in glass-fronted display cases. As soon as you give your order, the soup man, with devilish speed, chops up the innards of your choice and puts them into a bowl. Over them go Chinese celery leaves, crisply fried shallots, sliced tomatoes, some crushed *emping* (a crisp wafer made from the *melinjo* nut), some salt, pepper, sweet soy sauce (*kecap manis*) and a little vinegar. Then a ladle is dipped into the stock pot and a light broth made with the innards and lemon-grass-flavoured coconut milk is poured over the top. The soup man has now done his job. The rest is up to you. You have to add your own dollop of chilli *sambal* and finish off by squeezing some lime juice over the top. A big soup plate of rice comes with the *soto* and you wet the rice with the soup and eat. Do you want a drink? Just tell your soup man. He does not sell it himself but he can yell to his neighbour or send a boy around to pick it up . . . What will it be? *Es teler*, made with avocado, jackfruit, young coconut, coconut milk and crushed ice or *es timun*, an icy limeade flavoured with cucumber?

Chickens, ducks and little animals from the fields are cooked in pretty much the same manner as the fish and meats. There is one Yogyakarta speciality, however, that is made only with chicken. It is *ayam goreng*, the crispest and tastiest fried chicken I have ever eaten. Its recipe is hard to come by. What *is*

175

known is that a free-range chicken is thrown into a pot with garlic, salt and the sweet water found in young coconuts. It is boiled first until all the liquid evaporates and then deep-fried. But what makes the breast bones as crisp and edible as matchstick potatoes? Some say that it is the judicious use of soda bicarbonate (baking soda) that does it. This fried chicken is served with rice, a spicy *sambal* made with chillies, shallots and tomatoes, and some raw vegetables – long beans, cabbage and cucumber – that are dipped into the *sambal* and eaten as an accompaniment.

Indonesians eat a lot of vegetables – everything from fiddle-head ferns, young papaya buds and the leaves of a swamp-growing morning glory (*kang kung*) to vegetables that we are more familiar with:

Street vendors at a market. Fruit and vegetables grow quickly in Indonesia's tropical climate.

---

cauliflower, cabbage, cucumbers, beans and carrots. Many are eaten raw, with dipping sauces. Some, in salads such as *ulang ulang*, *gago gado* or *karedok* are blanched and then doused with a nutty dressing that could include *kenari* nuts or peanuts. Sometimes the vegetables are stewed – it could be with coconut milk or with tomatoes – to make what I find I eat the most of at an Indonesian meal: the *sayurs*. A few of the greens that we associate with Chinese food, such as mustard greens, may be cooked this way.

Besides the vegetables themselves, there might be vegetarian dishes made with soy bean products, such as the more familiar bean curd and the almost unknown *tempeh*. *Tempeh* originated in Java and consists of a flat cake of halved soy beans that hold together with the help of a white cotton-candy-like mould. It is exceedingly rich in protein – it is said to contain as much as chicken – and in the B_{12} vitamins, besides having a lot of natural roughage. In its raw form it is disgustingly

inedible but fried in thin matchsticks with peanuts, chillies, onions and tamarind, it adds an exquisite crunchiness to a meal.

An Indonesian meal then, in a well-to-do home, will have the staple, which is usually rice, it will have fish in some form, a soup which might be eaten *with* the meal and chicken or meat if it is a party. There will surely be some *sayur* or other vegetable dish, and a *sambal* as well as some crisp, fried accompaniments such as prawn (shrimp) wafers (*krupuk*) or fried *tempeh*. All the food will be laid out on the table or floor cloth at the same time. It will be at room temperature, which here hovers around 27°C (80°F), except for the soup and maybe the rice which will be hot. A few candles may be lit, even in daytime, not for their romantic glow but to ward off flies. If seated on the floor, the men will sit crosslegged, the women with their legs swung to one side. People will eat with their hands or with the help of a spoon and fork, taking food from the common serving plates and putting it on their own. The accompanying drink may be sweetened tea, poured hot from a thermos flask. In Ambon, this tea would have ginger and *kenari* nuts in it.

Not all the food will necessarily be prepared at home. In Java, it is quite customary to buy ready-made foods from professional people who specialise in them, and to bring them home to eat with dinner. A member of the family may be told, 'On your way back from work, please collect the fried chicken from Nonya Suharta, the sweet cakes (*kuey*) from Nonya Ali and, yes, do get some *satay* – six sticks of beef and maybe eight of chicken from the *satay* man who sits in the square on the right of the palace gate.'

Perhaps more than anything else, what makes Indonesian food so intriguingly different are the hot and aromatic seasonings. The whole world may have once come to this nation for the cloves, nutmeg and mace that grow on its volcanic soil, but it is not these that dominate the local cuisine. There is indeed a clove aroma that hangs like a

Tea pickers. Hot, sweet tea is served with most Indonesian meals. On some islands it is flavoured with ginger and kehari nuts.

cloud above the nation but that comes from the manic consumption of clove-flavoured cigarettes! What is so unique about the food is the use of *fresh*, highly aromatic seasonings: fresh red chillies, fresh galangal, fresh turmeric root, fresh turmeric leaves, fresh kaffir lime leaves, fresh basil and mint leaves, fresh curry leaves and fresh lemon grass.

Most of the country is like an over-productive hot house. Why buy dried seasonings when fresh aromatic ones are sprouting at your doorstep? A young German woman, travelling with me to Banda, the nutmeg islands, looked down at the lushness as we were landing and said, 'I am sure that if I planted an umbrella here it would grow!' Chillies, of course, came from the New World, but many of the other seasonings originated in the damp and teeming jungles.

To these seasonings, add the sweetness of coconuts and sweet soy sauce, the sourness of aromatic limes and tamarinds and the nuttiness of candle nuts, peanuts and *kenari* nuts and you get dishes that can be sweet, sour, hot and nutty, sometimes all at the same time. This is Indonesian food.

Exquisite examples can be found all over the country. In North Sulawesi, I was once invited to a picnic lunch at a coconut plantation. Nature abundantly proferred, apart from the coconuts, vanilla beans, pomelos, guavas, mangoes, jackfruit, nutmeg and cloves. Man had added his own creature comforts: a tennis court and an airy, double-storied pavilion set beside a pond.

The older ladies, all church-going Protestants of mostly Chinese lineage, drifted about gently, speaking to each other in Dutch of old times when vinegars and coconut oils were made at home ('Now it's all chemicals, isn't it?') and what they should do with inherited farmland ('We could try growing cassava but who wants all the

headaches that come with hired hands?'). The
younger generation, in jeans and Nikes,
babbled away in Bahasa Indonesia and
English. The little children, guided by a
servant, were taken off to fish.

The cook, a wizened creature with a few
betel-stained teeth, went straight to her task,
which was to get the outdoor kitchen stove
going with coconut husks. This she did, with
much blowing and puffing, and then set
about making a feast: fried chicken (*ayam
goreng*), a stir-fried dish of hard-boiled eggs
(*blado telor*), papaya salad (*gohu*), a *sambal* of
fried chillies, fried shallots and fried tomato
(*dabu dabu lilang*), rice, a *sayur* of fiddle-head
ferns and papaya buds (*sayur paku*), fried
cakalang and, a dish that I had been hearing
about when I was as far away as Jakarta, *bubur
Manado* – the Manadonese porridge.

To make the last, she set a large pot of
water to boil. Into it went corn kernels
(maize really), chunks of pumpkin, aromatic
turmeric leaves and lemon grass. Once they
had cooked for a bit, rice and chunks of
cassava root (tapioca) were stirred in to add
thickness and body. Sliced spring onions
(scallions) and basil leaves followed soon
after. The *bubur* was almost ready now, thick
as a stew with bits of white and orange
bobbing up and down. Just one more step
was required. The cook picked up a basket
filled with red spinach and swamp morning
glory leaves and emptied them into the pot.

As we moved to the dining-table set by the
water, we were offered a refreshing cup of
coconut punch – iced and sweetened strips
of creamy young coconut in their water,
flavoured with fresh vanilla beans. Dragon-
flies flitted about and a cool breeze swept
over the pond and fanned our faces. It was a
perfect day in Indonesia.

Note: All 'c's' in this country seem to be
pronounced as 'ch' – hence *kecap* is 'kechap'
and *cakalang* is 'chakalang'.

RECIPES FROM INDONESIA

A street vendor prepares a pineapple for sale.

Pandai Sikat, West Sumatra, Indonesia

FRIED PEANUTS WITH GARLIC AND CELERY
KACANG TOJIN

On several occasions I have managed to arrive in Indonesia just as Ramadan, a long month of fasting and prayers, has ended and Lebaran, the 2-day celebration that starts off the New Year, just begun. This holiday is a time for feasting and much visiting between family and friends. Every Muslim family keeps open house: brothers visit sisters, nephews visit aunts and cousins visit cousins. Employees in big cities go back to ancestral towns and villages, so all buses and trains are packed to capacity. Every home offers some food to incoming guests – not whole meals necessarily, but something sweet and something savoury to leave a good feeling in the mouth.

To this end, most living-rooms have on their coffee-tables, or nearby, large, covered jars of clear glass – all the better to see through, my dear – containing everything from tiny pineapple cookies to miniature turnovers filled with spicy shredded beef. Among the good things found in such jars in the region of West Sumatra are these peanuts.

In some ways, they are just, well, fried peanuts. But as you eat them – and I can assure you that it is very hard to stop eating them – you begin to sense that they are wonderfully, delicately, different. First, there is the texture. Because they are soaked before frying, their outsides turn harder and crisper. Then, there is their taste: peanuttiness, if one may coin the word, combined with gentle hints of garlic, shallots and *seledri*.

A word about *seledri*. This is what is sold as Chinese celery in Chinese markets across the West. Most of the time just the leaves are used. They look and taste like a cross between the leaves of flat-leaf parsley and those sprouting on top of our sticks of regular celery. You may use either of the two, though I have a preference for the celery leaves which are normally just wasted. A head of celery will supply enough leaves for this recipe. Just make sure that they are quite dry.

ENOUGH TO FILL A 750 ML / 1¼ PINT / 3 CUP JAR

450 g / 1 lb / 3 cups raw, shelled peanuts (preferably without their red skins)
6 cloves garlic, peeled
¾ teaspoon salt
6 large shallots or 1 good-sized onion (about 90 g / 3½ oz), peeled
25 g / 1 oz / ¾ loosely packed cup Chinese celery, *seledri*, leaves (or ordinary celery leaves), coarsely chopped
Vegetable oil for deep-frying

Soak the peanuts for 1 hour in enough very hot water to cover them generously.

Meanwhile, either pound the garlic and salt to a paste in a mortar or else put the garlic through a garlic press and mix with the salt. Set aside.

Cut the shallots into very, very fine, slices.

If the peanuts have red skins on them, remove them by rubbing the nuts between your hands. A few obstinate peanuts may have to be peeled individually. Drain the peanuts thoroughly, making sure all the skins are washed away. Rub the garlic-salt mixture on the peanuts and set aside for 10 minutes.

Meanwhile, balance a sieve over a large bowl and line 2 large trays or plates with paper towels.

In a large wok, heat the oil for deep-frying (enough to have at least 7.5 cm / 3 inches in the centre of the wok) to a medium temperature (350°F / 180°C). When hot, put in all the peanuts. Stir and fry for 8–10 minutes or until they are light golden-brown. Empty the contents of the wok, oil and nuts, into the strainer sitting over the bowl. Lift up the strainer carefully and let as much oil drip out as possible. Now scatter the hot nuts over the paper towels.

Put the oil back into the wok and let it heat up again. Put the strainer back over the bowl. Now, put the shallots into the oil. Stir and fry them for 2–3 minutes or until they are reddish-brown and *crisp*. Again, empty the oil into the strainer, lift up the strainer and spread the fried shallots over part of the second tray. Fry the celery leaves in the same way, making sure that they get quite crisp. Spread them out near the shallots.

Let everything cool. Mix the peanuts, shallots and celery and store in tightly lidded jars or tins.

Madura, Java, Bali, Indonesia

CHICKEN VERMICELLI SOUP
SOTO MADURA

This soup, though technically from the island of Madura, just north-east of Java, can now be found in most of the neighbouring islands. In Jakarta it is sold from tiny stalls in all the

Fishing with a harpoon. Fish is used for flavourings and stuffings as well as in a wide variety of spicy – often hot – dishes.

Heat the oil in a small frying-pan over medium-high heat. When hot, put in the shallots and garlic. Stir and fry until they brown on the outside. Put in the lump of shrimp paste and let it brown too. Remove the shallots, garlic and shrimp paste with a slotted spoon and put into the container of an electric blender. Add 8 tablespoons hot water and blend thoroughly.

Empty the contents of the blender into the bowl with the cumin and coriander. Add another tablespoon or so of hot water to the blender to remove the last of the lurking paste and empty that into the bowl as well. Now add the sweet soy sauce, the lime juice and the chilli powder (cayenne pepper). Mix thoroughly and taste for the blend of seasonings, adding a bit more of this or that if you need it. Set aside.

Pre-heat the grill (broiler). Lay the fish on a grilling tray (broiling pan) skin-side down, and lightly salt and pepper it. Grill (broil) for 5–10 minutes, according to its thickness, letting it brown and just cook through. Heat the sauce. When hot, take it off the heat and beat in the pieces of butter. Pour some sauce over the fish and serve. Put the rest of the sauce in a sauce boat and pass at the table.

Suwaan, North Sulawesi, Indonesia

WHOLE GRILLED FISH WITH A CHILLI-GINGER SAUCE
IKAN BAKAR RICA

Ikan means 'fish', *bakar* means 'grill' and *rica* (pronounced 'reachah') is the local word for hot chillies. The three words add up to one of the most mouthwatering fish dishes in Indonesia.

Deep slits are cut into both sides of a whole fish – in this region it is often a good-sized goldfish, as fresh as can be managed. The fish is then left in a marinade of lime juice and water for 15 minutes. The lime is quite special. Known as *limau jeruk*, it is small, greenish on the outside, yellowish-orange on the inside and highly aromatic – not unlike our ornamental mandarin orange. Both the skin and juice are used for the marinade. While the fish marinates, a sauce of shallots, ginger, hot red chillies and salt is pounded in a mortar. Lime juice is added to it as well. Some of this sauce is later served with the cooked fish. The rest is mixed with oil and used to baste the fish as it grills over a fire of coconut husks.

This fish should, ideally, be grilled outdoors. If you happen to have some coconut husks lying around, you could add them to the charcoal. In North Sulawesi, a rod is pushed right through the fish. It goes in through the mouth and comes out near the tail. The fish can then be turned around with the help of the rod. I find it much easier to use a two-sided hinged grill that allows the fish to be ensconced within it.

You can also cook the fish indoors under a kitchen grill (broiler).

This fish is generally served with lots of plain rice and a green vegetable.

SERVES 3–4

Whole 900 g / 2 lb fish, such as grey mullet, red snapper, trout, salmon trout, small salmon, pompano or goldfish, scaled and cleaned

Salt

5 tablespoons lime juice
(or lemon juice)

Half a large red pepper

6 fresh, hot red or green chillies

4 large shallots or 1 small onion
(75 g / 2½ oz)

4 cm / 1½ inch piece of peeled
fresh ginger

2 tablespoons vegetable oil

Pre-heat the outdoor charcoal grill or indoor kitchen grill (broiler), setting a rack 15–18 cm / 6–7 inches away from the heat source. If you can adjust the heat, keep it at medium high.

Cut deep, diagonal slits, about 4 cm / 1½ inches apart, on both sides of the fish, starting near the gills and going all the way down to the tail. Put the fish on a large plate. Rub 1 teaspoon salt all over the fish, going well into the slits and the abdominal cavity. Then spread 2½ tablespoons of the lime juice all over the fish, again making sure to go into all the slits and cavities. Set the fish aside for 15 minutes.

Chop the red pepper and chillies coarsely. Peel the shallots and ginger and then chop them coarsely. In the container of an electric blender, combine the red pepper, chillies, shallots, ginger, ¾ teaspoon salt and the remaining 2½ tablespoons lime juice. Blend until you have a very coarse paste. Put half of the paste in a serving bowl and set the bowl on your dining-table. This is to be eaten with the fish, as a kind of dipping sauce. Put the remaining sauce in a work bowl. Add the oil to the sauce in the work bowl and mix well. This is the basting sauce.

Rub half of the basting sauce all over the fish, making sure you go into all the slits and cavities. Arrange the fish on a grilling rack. Control your heat so that it takes 8–10 minutes to brown one side. Baste once during the middle of this period.

Turn the fish over carefully and grill the second side, again basting with the sauce after 3–4 minutes. The fish should get nicely browned, remain moist inside and be cooked all the way through.

Serve hot with the dipping sauce.

West Sumatra, Indonesia

CHICKEN WITH GREEN SEASONINGS
AYAM MASAK

I do believe I could eat this hot and aromatic chicken every day. Serve it with rice – plain or with ginger and coconut milk (see p. 190) – and at least one vegetable and salad.

Normally, this dish is made with a lot of fresh, hot green chillies. I have combined a green pepper with the chillies in order to keep the bulk but lessen the fire. Also, in Indonesia, a green tomato is used. If you can find one, do use it.

SERVES 4

1.5 kg / 3½ lb chicken, cut into 10 pieces
(breasts should be quartered and legs halved)

2 teaspoons tamarind paste, see p. 218
(or lemon juice)

Salt

1 small green pepper (about 150 g / 5 oz),
de-seeded and coarsely chopped

12 fresh, very hot green chillies, coarsely sliced

8 large shallots or 2 small onions (175 g / 6 oz),
peeled and coarsely chopped

4–5 cloves garlic, peeled

1 medium-sized tomato (150 g / 5 oz),
coarsely chopped

1 stick of fresh lemon grass (or ¾ teaspoon
powdered lemon grass)

10 tablespoons vegetable oil

4 fresh or dried kaffir lime leaves (or 4 strips of
lime or lemon rind)

Put the chicken in a bowl. Combine the tamarind paste with 1 teaspoon salt and 2 tablespoons water in a cup. Mix and pour over the chicken. Rub the seasonings in and leave for 30 minutes.

Put the green pepper, chillies, shallots, garlic and tomato into the container of an electric blender. Blend until you have a paste.

Cut off and discard the top of the lemon grass, leaving the bottom 15 cm / 6 inches. Crush the bulbous bottom lightly with a heavy object.

Heat the oil in a large, non-stick frying-pan over a high heat. When hot, put in the chicken and its marinade. Brown the chicken pieces on both sides. Remove with a slotted spoon and save in a bowl.

Remove 5 tablespoons of the oil. Now put in the paste from the blender, the lemon grass and the kaffir lime leaves. Stir and fry for 6–7 minutes or until the paste is nicely browned. Now put in the chicken, 300 ml / 10 fl oz / 1¼ cups water and ½ teaspoon salt. Bring to a boil.

Cover, turn the heat to low and simmer gently for 25 minutes, turning the pieces over every now and then.

Lombok, Nusa Tenggara, Indonesia
CHICKEN CURRY, LOMBOK STYLE
OPOR MANUK

The island of Lombok was once an important link in the spice trade chain and it is not too surprising that its name actually means peppers. The dishes here tend to be fiery. In Indonesia, the sauce for this dish is made with fresh, hot red chillies, the kind that are slim and long. I have used a combination of sweet red pepper and chillies to calm the heat a bit but retain the bulk.

If you can get fresh galangal, you should add a 2.5 cm / 1 inch piece, peeled and chopped, to the ingredients in the electric blender, instead of grinding it with the dry spices.

I like to use just chicken thighs for this dish though you could use a cut-up chicken.

Even though there are a fair number of ingredients in this recipe, it is quite easy to put this mouthwatering dish together. It may be made ahead of time and refrigerated, so it is ideal for parties. Serve it with plain rice.

SERVES 4–6

1 red pepper (175 g / 6 oz), de-seeded and coarsely chopped

3 fresh, long, hot red chillies, coarsely chopped (or 1 teaspoon chilli powder / cayenne pepper)

2.5 cm / 1 inch piece of fresh ginger, peeled and coarsely chopped

3 candle nuts or 6 raw cashew nuts

8 shallots or 1 large onion (135 g / 4½ oz), peeled and coarsely chopped

4–5 cloves garlic, peeled

½ teaspoon shrimp paste, *terasi*, see p. 217 (or anchovy paste)

½ teaspoon cumin seeds

1 teaspoon whole black peppercorns

4 good-sized slices of dry, sliced galangal (or see below left)

4 whole cloves

2.5 cm / 1 inch cinnamon stick

One 400 g / 14 oz can of coconut milk

8 tablespoons vegetable oil

1.5 kg / 3½ lb chicken thighs (see below left)

1½ teaspoons salt

Garnish (optional):

1–2 fresh, hot red and / or green chillies, plain or cut into flowers, see p. 211

Put the red pepper, the 3 chillies, ginger, candle nuts, shallots, garlic and shrimp paste into the container of an electric blender. Blend until you have a smooth paste, adding a little water only if it is needed. Leave it in the blender container.

Put the cumin seeds, peppercorns, galangal, cloves and cinnamon into the container of a clean coffee-grinder or other spice-grinder and grind until fine. Put this powder into the blender and whir for a few seconds to mix. (This paste may be made ahead of time and frozen. Defrost thoroughly before using.)

Open the can of coconut milk without shaking it. Spoon off the cream at the top and set aside. Pour the remaining milk into a measuring jug. Add water to make 350 ml / 12 fl oz / 1½ cups.

Heat the oil in a well-seasoned wok or a wide, non-stick pan over medium-high heat. When hot, put in the curry paste from the blender. Stir and fry for 6–8 minutes or until the paste is dark red and quite reduced. Add the chicken pieces and salt. Stir and fry for another 2 minutes. Now put in the thinned coconut milk and bring to a boil. Cover, lower the heat and simmer gently for 30 minutes. Uncover and cook on medium heat for 5 minutes. Turn the heat off.

Spoon off most of the oil that will have risen to the top. Stir in the coconut cream and mix well. Heat through gently. Serve, garnished with the additional chillies.

Jakarta, Java, Indonesia
CHICKEN LIVERS WITH MUSHROOMS
HATI AYAM MASAK JAMUR

This may be one of the best ways to cook chicken livers. Spicy and luscious, this dish may be served for breakfast, lunch or dinner, on toast or, the Indonesian way, with rice. I often serve it for brunch when I have guests.

The red and green chillies used here are the long, slim kind that are of medium heat. They are sold by all oriental grocers.

SERVES 4

225 g / 8 oz chicken livers, separated into 2 lobes and with the fat removed

1 teaspoon sweet soy sauce, *kecap manis*, (p. 214) (see p. 214)

Lots of freshly ground black pepper

Salt

5 mm / ¼ inch slice of peeled fresh ginger, very finely chopped

4–5 cloves garlic, peeled and very finely chopped

7 tablespoons vegetable oil

1 small onion (75 g / 2½ oz), peeled, halved lengthways and cut into 5 mm / ¼ inch wide half-rings

275 g / 10 oz mushrooms, trimmed, wiped with a damp cloth and halved lengthways

2 fresh, hot red chillies, cut crossways into 1 cm / ½ inch thick rounds

2 fresh, hot green chillies, cut crossways into 1 cm / ½ inch thick rounds

1 medium-sized tomato (150 g / 5 oz), cored and cut into 6–8 wedges

Combine the chicken livers and sweet soy sauce in a small bowl. Mix. Add lots of black

Chicken Curry, Lombok Style (this page) and Iced Cucumber Limeade (page 194).

use your outdoor grill, make sure that the fire is gentle so that you do not scorch the kebabs.

SERVES 4

12 fresh, hot red chillies for a very hot dish or half that quantity of chillies mixed with half a sweet red pepper for a milder version, all de-seeded and chopped (or see p. 187)

2–3 shallots or 1 small onion (30 g / 1 oz), peeled and chopped

2 cloves garlic, peeled

1 teaspoon salt

6 tablespoons sweet soy sauce, *kecap manis*, see p. 214

2 tablespoons lime juice (or lemon juice)

340 g / 12 oz boneless pork from the loin, cut into 2.5 x 2.5 x 1.25 cm / 1 x 1 x ½ inch pieces

Vegetable oil for brushing on meat

Put the chillies, shallots, garlic and salt into the container of an electric blender and blend, pushing down as needed, until you have a coarse purée. Add the sweet soy sauce and lime juice and blend again. Pour half the paste into a bowl. Add the pork to this bowl. Toss to mix, and set aside for 2 hours or longer.

Pre-heat the grill (broiler).

Remove the pork from the marinade. (Reserve the marinade.) Thread the meat closely on to the 4 skewers. If using bamboo skewers, cover any exposed end with foil. Arrange the skewers on a grilling tray (broiling pan).

Pour the reserved marinade from the bowl into a small pan. Add to it the paste from the blender. Stir and bring to a simmer over medium heat. Cook, stirring, for 5 minutes. Keep this dipping sauce warm.

Grill (broil) the kebabs 10–13 cm / 4–5 inches from the source of the heat for about 3 minutes on each side, or until done. Put the dipping sauce in a bowl or sauce boat and pass on the side. It may be ladled over the kebabs or dipped into.

Manado, North Sulawesi, Indonesia

SPICY, AROMATIC PORK
BABI KINETOR

Pork is eaten only by the non-Muslim cultures of Indonesia such as the Christians and the Hindus. This dish comes from the hilly, Minhasa region of North Sulawesi where a good 80 per cent of the people are Christians, having been converted to Catholicism by the Spaniards – and then re-converted to Protestantism by the Dutch.

This dish, as with many of the meats here, tends to be very hot; the meat chunks are just smothered with a hot spice paste. To make it, I used 10 fresh hot red chillies weighing about 140 g / 5 oz. I would describe their heat as medium. If you wish to lessen the heat, use a similar weight of sweet red pepper and then put in as much chilli powder (cayenne pepper) as you can handle – anywhere from ¼ teaspoon up. You could also use a mixture of red pepper and hot red chillies that adds up to the required weight.

In North Sulawesi, this dish calls for a fresh turmeric leaf (see p. 218). Since I can never find one, I have left it out. If you have access to one, shred it finely and mix it with the pork cubes just before cooking.

SERVES 4–6

1 kg / 2¼ lb boneless pork from the loin or shoulder, cut into 4 cm / 1½ inch cubes

5 tablespoons finely chopped fresh Chinese chives or ordinary chives

3 spring onions (scallions), cut into fine rounds all the way up their green sections

10 shallots (180 g / 6 oz), peeled and cut into thin slices, or 2 medium-sized onions, peeled and sliced into fine half-rings

4 fresh, dried or frozen kaffir lime leaves (or 4 strips of lime or lemon peel)

5 cm / 2 inch piece of fresh ginger, peeled and finely sliced

8–10 fresh, hot red chillies, coarsely sliced (or see above)

1 stick of fresh lemon grass (or 1 teaspoon powdered lemon grass)

1 teaspoon salt

Put the pork, chives, spring onions (scallions), shallots and lime leaves into a wide, preferably non-stick, pan or in a wok.

Put the ginger and red chillies into the container of an electric blender. Cut off the spindly top of the lemon grass, leaving about 15 cm / 6 inches. Also cut off the knot at the very bottom of the bulbous section. Now cut the stick crossways into fine rounds. Put these into the blender, along with 4 tablespoons water. Blend thoroughly, pushing down with a rubber spatula as many times as is necessary. Empty this paste into the pan with the pork. Put another 3 tablespoons water into the blender and blend for 1 second to pick up the last, lurking remnants of the paste. Pour this into the pan as well. Add the salt and mix well, making sure that each piece of pork is covered with the seasonings.

Put the pan over medium heat and bring to a simmer. Cover, turn the heat to low and cook for about 55 minutes or until the pork is tender. Uncover and turn the heat to high. Stir and fry for about 10 minutes, or until all the liquid is gone and the spice paste is not only lightly browned but also encrusts the pork.

Manado, North Sulawesi, Indonesia

GREEN BEANS IN A COCONUT SAUCE
SAYUR BUNCHIS MANADO

This recipe was given to me by the grandmother of my Manadonese friend, Lingkan Pua. It is an aromatic, everyday dish with a little sauce – just perfect for eating with rice.

If you cannot get fresh lemon grass, use ½ teaspoon powdered lemon grass, putting it into the frying-pan at the same time as the green beans. If no lemon grass is available, put in 2 teaspoons grated lemon rind at this time.

SERVES 4–6

675 g / 1½ lb green beans

1 fresh, long, hot red chilli

1 fresh, long, hot green chilli

1 spring onion (scallion)

1 stick of fresh lemon grass
(or see below left)

6 shallots or 2 medium-sized onions
(100 g / 4 oz), peeled and coarsely
chopped

4 cm / 1½ inch piece of fresh ginger, peeled and
coarsely chopped

5 tablespoons vegetable oil

2 fresh or dried kaffir lime leaves (or 2 strips of
lime or lemon rind)

250 ml / 8 fl oz / 1 cup canned coconut milk, well
stirred and combined with an equal quantity of
water, or 450 ml / 15 fl oz / 2 cups fresh coconut
milk, see p. 212

1¼ teaspoons salt

Keeping each well-separated, cut the green
beans, red and green chillies and spring
onion (scallion) into 4 cm / 1½ inch lengths,
preferably at a slight diagonal.

Discard the top part of the lemon grass,
leaving just about 15 cm / 6 inches. Crush the
bulbous bottom lightly with a heavy object.
Cut the stick into 2 pieces.

Put the shallots and ginger into the container of an electric blender along with about
2 tablespoons water. Blend to a paste.

Heat the oil in a large, non-stick frying-
pan over medium-high heat. When hot, put
in the paste from the blender, the lemon
grass and the lime leaves. Stir and fry for
about 5 minutes or until the paste is lightly
browned. Put in the red and green chillies
and the spring onion (scallion). Stir and fry
for another minute. Now put in the green
beans, the blended canned coconut milk or
the fresh milk, and the salt. Mix and bring to
a simmer.

Cover and cook gently about 20 minutes
or until the beans are tender.

Long green beans (petai) for sale in a morning
vegetable market. These are peeled to reveal broad
beans which can be stir-fried with a hot chilli
sambal sauce.

Manado, North Sulawesi, Indonesia

QUICK STIR-FRIED CABBAGE
TUMIS KOL

Here is a simple and fast way to prepare green cabbage. The seasonings are just shallots, garlic and celery leaves but when properly used, how marvellous they can be. You could serve this with any Indonesian meal or, for that matter, with roast beef!

SERVES 4

6 good-sized shallots or 1 large onion (100 g / 4 oz), peeled and coarsely chopped

4 cloves garlic, peeled and coarsely chopped

5 tablespoons vegetable oil

675 g / 1½ lb green cabbage, cored and cut lengthways into very fine, long strips

2 spring onions (scallions), cut into 7.5 cm / 3 inch lengths all the way up their green sections, then cut lengthways into fine, long strips

A good handful of Chinese celery, *seledri*, leaves or ordinary celery leaves, finely chopped

¾ teaspoon salt, or to taste

Put the shallots and garlic into the container of an electric blender along with 3 tablespoons water and blend until smooth.

Heat the oil in a wide, non-stick pan or in a wok over medium-high heat. When hot, put in the paste from the blender. Stir and fry for 5–6 minutes or until it has browned. Now put in the cabbage, spring onions (scallions), celery leaves and salt. Stir for 1 minute. Add about 3 tablespoons water and cover. Turn the heat to low and simmer for 5 minutes. Uncover, turn the heat to high and boil off any liquid in the pan, stir-frying gently.

Manado, North Sulawesi, Indonesia

A DELIGHTFUL STEW OF RICE AND VEGETABLES
TINUTUAN or BUBUR MANADO

As we in the West start looking back towards old-fashioned, hearty and nourishing meals, we often find ourselves resurrecting slow-cooked porridges and stews. This dish is both a porridge *and* a stew. It comes from Manado in North Sulawesi, where it is known as *tinutuan*. However, since it is now enthusiastically eaten in many other parts of Indonesia as well, it is more widely known as *bubur Manado* or 'the porridge of Manado'.

Buburs (the two 'u's here are pronounced as the u in 'bull') are wholesome porridges made from grains or beans. Though generally eaten as a late breakfast, they seem flexible enough to be served also as light lunches and suppers. This particular *bubur* is somewhat special as it is delicately flavoured with lemon grass, basil leaves (*daun kemangi*) and turmeric leaves (so aromatic and, alas, so hard to find in the West). Apart from its basic grain – rice in this case – it has, added to it, a medley of vegetables from orange pumpkin and golden corn to local greens and root vegetables. To give it extra pep, it is eaten with dollops of a spicy sauce, a *sambal*, made with roasted ingredients – tomatoes, red chillies and shallots – and known as *dabu dabu*. It is quite wonderful.

I find that this *bubur* makes an ideal brunch dish. The people of North Sulawesi serve slices of a delicious smoked and fried tuna-like fish – *cakalang* – on the side. You may serve smoked and grilled mackerel or, as I often do, Indian poppadom or Indonesian Prawn (Shrimp) Wafers (*krupuk*), p. 202.

Because we cannot easily find all the flavourful herbs and greens used in Indonesia, I find that the stew tastes richer if I start with chicken stock instead of water. If the stock is salted, omit the salt in the recipe.

If an oriental market is accessible, use the leaves and tender stalks of *kang kung* (swamp morning glory), instead of the spinach. You may also throw in peeled chunks of the tapioca root, known sometimes as cassava, about the same time as you add the pumpkin.

SERVES 6

2 litres / 3½ pints / 8¾ cups Chicken Stock, see p. 197

Long-grain rice measured to the 150 ml / 5 fl oz / ½ cup plus 2 tablespoons level in a measuring jug

2 sticks of fresh lemon grass, just the lower 15 cm / 6 inches with the bulbous bottom lightly crushed (or 4 tablespoons dried, sliced lemon grass tied loosely in a cheesecloth bundle, or 2–3 strips lemon rind)

115 g / 4 oz / 4 cups coarsely chopped spring greens (collard greens) or kale

225 g / 8 oz / 2 cups orange pumpkin flesh, cut into 4 cm / 1½ inch chunks

225 g / 8 oz / 1⅔ cup corn kernels, fresh from the cob or, if frozen, lightly defrosted

About 2 teaspoons salt (see below left)

50 g / 2 oz / 1 cup trimmed spinach leaves

About 40 fresh basil leaves (or *daun kemangi* if available)

2 spring onions (scallions), cut crossways into very fine rounds all the way up their green sections

Roasted Tomato Chilli Sambal, see p. 193

Combine the stock, rice and lemon grass in a large, heavy pan and bring to a boil. Lower the heat and simmer gently for 30 minutes. Put in the spring greens (collard greens), pumpkin, corn, and salt if needed. Bring to a boil. Lower the heat and simmer gently for 45 minutes, stirring now and then to prevent sticking. Check the salt, adding more if required. Remove the lemon grass. Put in the spinach, basil leaves and spring onions (scallions).

Cook gently for another 5 minutes, stirring every now and then. Serve with the Roasted Tomato Chilli Sambal.

Airmadidi, North Sulawesi, Indonesia

RICE WITH GINGER AND COCONUT MILK
NASI JAHE

The small town of Airmadidi in North Sulawesi has an open-air market that seems to specialise in rice-based confections, both sweet and savoury, displayed on long tables lined with banana leaves. *Nasi jaha* hides inside its own very special cooking container: a hollow, green bamboo section. To make the dish, a length of 7.5 cm / 3 inch thick bamboo

Banana trees. Their leaves are used as 'baking dishes' and bowls for food, and to cover tables or stalls in outdoor markets.

is first lined with a banana leaf, God's very own non-stick creation. Then a little glutinous rice is poured in, to be alternated with ginger-flavoured coconut milk until the bamboo hollow is two-thirds full. It is then

sealed, stood before an open fire and rotated at intervals. When the rice is ready to be served, the banana leaf is pulled out and the rice 'log' cut into neat sections.

Needless to say, it is hard to come by green bamboos in most Western markets! I think I have still managed to capture the spirit – and taste – of the dish, even though I have used an ordinary pan to cook in and have used jasmine rice, sold by all East

Asian grocers, instead of the glutinous rice.

This rice may be served with all Indonesian meals. It may also be served with Thai, Malaysian and Filipino ones.

SERVES 4–6

5 cm / 2 inch piece of fresh ginger, peeled and coarsely chopped

3 large shallots or 1 small onion (50 g / 2 oz), peeled and coarsely chopped

191

Rice terraces on the island of Bali. Indonesian rice comes in a variety of forms: long-grain, glutinous, red and black.

One 400 ml / 14 fl oz can of coconut milk or about 900 ml / 1½ pints / 3¾ cups fresh coconut milk, see p. 212

1 teaspoon salt

Jasmine rice measured to the 450 ml / 15 fl oz / 2 cup level in a measuring jug (or any plain long-grain rice)

Put the ginger and shallots into the container of an electric blender along with 3 tablespoons water and blend thoroughly.

Mix the contents of the can of coconut milk well and put it into a large measuring jug. Add the paste from the blender, the salt and enough water to make 1 litre / 1¾ pints / 4 cups. If you are using fresh coconut milk, put the paste from the blender and the salt into a large measuring jug and then add enough coconut milk to make up 1 litre / 1¾ pints / 4 cups. Mix well.

Put the rice in a heavy-bottomed pan along with the coconut milk mixture and bring to a boil. Turn the heat to medium and cook, uncovered, until the liquid is at the same level as the rice. You may need to turn the heat to medium low towards the end. Stir gently a few times during this period, bringing the rice from the bottom of the pot to the top. Now cover very tightly, turn the heat to very, very low and cook for 25 minutes. Stir gently before serving.

All over Indonesia

NOODLES WITH CHICKEN AND PRAWNS (SHRIMP)
BAKMIE GORENG

The Chinese have not only traded with Indonesia since ancient times but have, over the centuries, settled on most of the islands. Many of the families have intermarried with the locals. The foods of this nation are among the most noteworthy benefactors of this happy miscegenation. This noodle dish is one such example. The use of the noodles and soy sauce is quite obviously Chinese. But shallots and sliced green chillies give the dish a decidedly Indonesian cast.

The ideal noodles to use here are the fresh egg noodles, *lo mein* noodles, found in the refrigerated compartments at Chinese grocer shops. The second best choice is dried Chinese noodles. If all else fails, use Italian *linguini*, cooking them first according to the directions on the package.

In Indonesia, this dish is always accompanied by a *sambal* such as Chilli Sauce with Shrimp Paste, see p. 200, Chilli Sauce with Tomatoes, see right, or Chilli Sambal, see far right. Prawn (Shrimp) Wafers, see p. 202, may also be served with it.

SERVES 4

300–350 g / 11–12 oz boned, skinned chicken breast

Salt

Freshly ground black pepper

About 5½ teaspoons vegetable oil

100 g / 4 oz unpeeled medium-sized prawns (shrimp), peeled and deveined, or 60 g / 2 oz peeled and deveined prawns (shrimp)

A quarter of a medium-sized green cabbage (275 g / 10 oz), cored

225 g / 8 oz fresh *lo mein* noodles (or see above)

1 fresh, hot red or green chilli (more, if desired), cut into very fine rounds

3 medium-sized shallots or 1 small onion (30 g / 1 oz), peeled and cut into very fine slivers

2.5 cm / 1 inch piece of fresh ginger, peeled and cut into minute dice

2–3 cloves garlic, peeled and very finely chopped

2 tablespoons Chinese dark soy sauce

2 tablespoons Chicken Stock, see p. 197

2 spring onions (scallions), cut into very fine rounds all the way up their green sections

Cut the chicken breasts into 1 cm / ½ inch cubes and put them in a bowl. Now add ¼ teaspoon salt, some black pepper and 1 teaspoon oil. Mix well. Cover and set aside, refrigerating if necessary.

Cut each prawn (shrimp) into half. Cover and set aside, refrigerating if necessary.

Cut the cabbage into very thin, long shreds.

Bring a very large pan of water to a rolling boil. Drop in the noodles, separating them with a fork. Boil rapidly for 3–5 minutes or until they are just tender. Drain immediately and rinse under cold water. Drain again and put back in the pan. Add 1 tablespoon of the vegetable oil, toss and set aside.

Just before you sit down to eat, heat 4 tablespoons oil in a large wok or large frying-pan over medium-high heat. When hot, put in the chilli, shallots, ginger and garlic. Stir and fry until the shallots turn golden. Add the chicken and prawns (shrimp). Stir and fry until they just turn colour. Add the cabbage and about ¼ teaspoon salt. Stir and fry for 1 minute. Add the cooked noodles, the soy sauce and the stock. Stir and fry until the noodles are heated through.

Scatter the spring onions (scallions) over the top and serve.

Padang, West Sumatra, Indonesia
CHILLI SAUCE WITH TOMATOES
BALADO

Balado is a piquant relish which may be served with all Indonesian meals. At Western meals, it could be served with sausages instead of mustard, it could be layered on to a hamburger before the top of the bun is put on and a dollop of it would work wonders for a potato patty.

If covered and refrigerated, this sauce will last for several days.

SERVES 4–6

7–8 fresh, hot red chillies, coarsely chopped (or half a large, sweet red pepper, de-seeded and chopped, combined with 1 teaspoon chilli powder / cayenne pepper)

2–3 shallots or half a small onion (30 g / 1 oz), peeled and coarsely chopped

¼ teaspoon salt, or to taste

3 cherry tomatoes, very finely chopped

Combine the chillies, shallots and salt either in a mortar or in the container of an electric blender and make a somewhat coarse paste. If using a blender, you might need to add a tiny bit of water. Empty the paste into a small bowl. Add the tomatoes and mix. Check the salt and add more if you need it.

All over Indonesia
CHILLI SAMBAL
SAMBAL ULEK

Versions of this *sambal* – red chillies crushed in a mortar with salt – are to be found all over Indonesia. It is a condiment used in both homes and restaurants. Sometimes there is Indonesian shrimp paste (*terasi*) in it (it has to be fried or roasted first). In that event it is called *sambal terasi*. Its other variations could include shallots or garlic or tomato or vinegar.

If you cannot get fresh, hot red chillies, combine a large, sweet red pepper with about 1 teaspoon chilli powder (cayenne pepper).

MAKES 150 ML / ¼ PINT / ⅔ CUP

12 fresh, hot red chillies, coarsely sliced (or see above)

1½ teaspoons salt

2 tablespoons lime juice (or lemon juice)

Combine all the ingredients in the container of an electric blender and blend until you have a coarse paste. A little roughness gives a better texture.

If put in a lidded jar, this may be stored in the refrigerator for a few weeks.

Manado, North Sulawesi, Indonesia
ROASTED TOMATO CHILLI SAMBAL
DABU DABU LILANG

This fiery, chutney-like *sambal* is served with the Delightful Stew of Rice and Vegetables on p. 190. You may, if you like, add 2 tablespoons smoked mackerel or canned tuna or else a 2.5 cm / 1 inch cube of roasted shrimp paste (*terasi*) to it when you are blending the mixture – in which case the dish would be called just plain *dabu dabu*.

This *sambal* may be served with almost any meal. It is quite good on fried and hard-boiled eggs too!

SERVES 6

2 medium-sized, ripe tomatoes (about 340 g / 12 oz)

3–6 fresh, hot red or green chillies

3 good-sized shallots or a piece of onion (40 g / 1½ oz), peeled

2 tablespoons lime juice (or lemon juice)

1 teaspoon salt, or to taste

Using a set of tongs, hold the tomatoes, one at a time, over an open flame and let them brown on the outside. Put into the container of an electric blender. Brown the chillies and shallots in the same way. Do not worry about slight charring. (If you have an all-electric kitchen, use your grill / broiler to achieve the same result.) Add the lime juice and salt to the blender and blend until you have a coarse paste. Taste for seasoning and adjust if needed.

This *sambal* may be made ahead of time, covered and refrigerated.

Jakarta, Java, Indonesia

ICED CUCUMBER LIMEADE
ES TIMUN

The Pondok Laguna restaurant in Jakarta has a section of its kitchen devoted just to iced drinks. Many of these are so thick with finely crushed ice that spoons as well as straws are offered. On a steamy hot day, such drinks are most welcome. Here is one of them, an unusual limeade flavoured with cucumber. It is invitingly pale green and very refreshing. You could stick sprigs of fresh mint in the glasses before serving.

Variation: Instead of cucumber, grate some sweet melon into the limeades. This is a thirst-quencher often served during the fast days of Ramadan.

SERVES 2

120 ml / 4 fl oz / ½ cup freshly squeezed lime juice. (I used 2½ large, juicy limes)

4½ tablespoons sugar, or to taste

1 good-sized cucumber (275 g / 10 oz)

10 ice cubes

Mix the lime juice and sugar thoroughly and pour equal quantities into 2 glasses.

Peel the cucumber and cut it in half lengthways. Remove the seeds. Chop the rest coarsely and put it into the container of an electric blender. Blend until smooth. Put in the ice cubes and blend until fairly mushy. Pour equal quantities into the 2 glasses with the lime juice and mix thoroughly. Serve.

Yogyakarta, Java, Indonesia

SWEET TAPIOCA DROPLETS AND FRUIT IN COCONUT MILK
ES CENDOL

Much of South-East Asia serves an array of what may be classifed as dessert-soups or dessert-drinks. *Es cendol* is a refreshing, cooling dessert-drink which has enough floating solids in it to require the use of a spoon. The '*es*' in the name refers to crushed ice and the '*cendol*' (pronounced 'chendol') to the long, slithery droplets of tapioca – you could call them tapioca noodles – which are coloured green with the juice of fresh pandanus leaves.

Most Indonesians buy their tapioca droplets ready-made from the market. We in the West cannot do that. I find that tapioca pearls make a very good substitute. Just get the largest ones that you can find.

In addition to the tapioca pearls and ice, the dessert is blessed with a selection of fruit, fruit syrup and a topping of coconut milk. You may use whatever fruit you fancy. Canned ripe jackfruit in syrup, available from most East Asian grocers, would probably be the most authentic but a mixture of sliced bananas, ripe pineapple, mango, halved grapes and litchis works very well. This dessert is best served in individual bowls.

SERVES 6

70 g / 2¾ oz / ½ cup large tapioca pearls

175 ml / 6 fl oz / ¾ cup golden syrup (corn syrup) or treacle, molasses or maple syrup

4 tablespoons caster sugar (extra fine sugar)

About 3 ripe but not mushy bananas

1 ripe, sweet mango

3 slices ripe, sweet pineapple

12 large seedless grapes of any colour

175 ml / 6 fl oz / ¾ cup fresh or canned coconut milk, see p. 212, well stirred

1 tablespoon rose water or orange blossom water (optional)

10–20 ice cubes

As tapioca pearls come in so many sizes, it is best to follow packet directions about cooking them. Mine call for an overnight soak and then need boiling. Here is what you do with my kind of pearls. Put the pearls in a bowl. Cover with water by about 5 cm / 2 inches and leave to soak overnight. Drain and put in a small pan. Cover with fresh water by 5 cm / 2 inches and bring to a boil. Turn the heat to low and simmer gently for 10–15 minutes or until the pearls are soft and translucent all the way through. Drain and rinse under cold water. Put in a bowl and cover with fresh water. Set aside.

To assemble the dessert for 6 individual servings, drain the pearls and divide among 6 bowls. Top with 2 tablespoons each of the syrup and 2 teaspoons of the sugar. Stir to mix. Slice half a banana into each bowl.

Peel the mango and dice its flesh. Cut the pineapple into pieces about the same size as the mango bits. Cut the grapes in half lengthways. Divide this fruit among the bowls. Add about ½ teaspoon rose water or orange blossom water and 1 fl oz coconut milk to each bowl. Crush the ice and divide among the servings.

Each person should stir the contents of their own bowls before eating.

Prawns Encrusted with Spices (page 180) and Chilli Sambal (page 193).

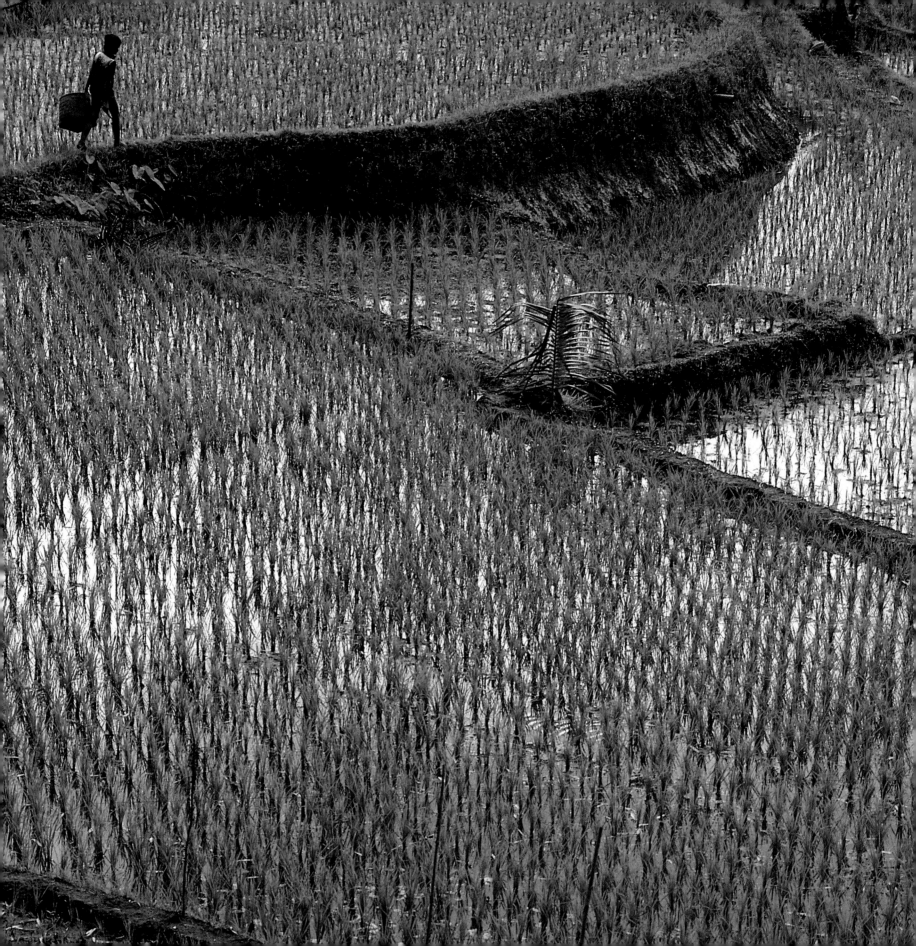

BASIC RECIPES

CHICKEN STOCK

•

Good chicken stock is needed for many recipes in this book, so it is useful to keep a supply in your refrigerator or freezer. Here are a few tips:

1 Whenever you poach a chicken breast, strain the liquid and save it. Use it when small amounts are called for.

2 Store chicken bones and carcasses in the freezer; they can be used for stock.

3 When cooking stock, maintain it at a low simmer or it will turn cloudy. It should bubble only very slightly. Skim the stock frequently as it cooks, especially in the first 30 minutes.

4 Sometimes just a little salt can be added to the stock at the end of the cooking time to bring out its flavour. You should leave the salt out when making stock for use in Japanese cooking.

5 Before freezing stock you can boil it down to half its original quantity so that it occupies less space. It can easily be reconstituted later.

6 Pour cooled, de-greased stock into ice-cube trays and freeze. When frozen, the cubes can be transferred to freezer bags. You will then be able to use small quantities of stock as you need them.

7 Frozen stock can be defrosted very quickly in a microwave oven.

MAKES ABOUT 2.75 LITRES / 5 PINTS / 12 CUPS

1.5 kg / 3 lb chicken necks, wings, backs and bones
1 kg / 2 lb chicken pieces, such as legs
2 thin slices of fresh ginger
2 spring onions (scallions)
Salt (optional)

Wash the chicken pieces and put them into a large pan. Add 3.4 litres / 6 pints / 3¾ quarts water and bring it to a simmer. Maintain the simmer and do not let the stock boil. Over the next 30 minutes, keep removing the scum that rises to the top. Now put in the ginger slices. Trim the spring onions (scallions), discarding the green sections, and add the white part to the stock. Cook partially covered, maintaining the heat at a bare simmer for 3–4 hours. Strain into a bowl through a triple layer of dampened muslin, cheesecloth or a large clean handkerchief and add a little salt if required. Stand the bowl in a large basin or sink of cold water to cool it off quickly. Pour the stock into containers. Cover and refrigerate. Remove the fat when it has solidified.

You can now freeze the stock.

BEEF STOCK

•

MAKES ABOUT 2.25 LITRES / 4 PINTS / 10 CUPS

1.75 kg / 4 lb beef marrow bones or oxtails, sawed into smaller pieces
1.5 kg / 3 lb stewing beef
1 large onion (100 g / 4 oz)
7.5 cm / 3 inch piece of fresh ginger
1 medium-sized carrot (85 g / 3 oz), peeled
About 1 teaspoon salt

Put the marrow bones and stewing beef into a very large pan. Add 5 litres / 9 pints / 6¼ quarts water and slowly bring it to a simmer. Over the next 15 minutes, keep removing the scum that rises to the top. Then put in the onions, ginger, carrot and salt. Cover partially and cook very gently for about 4–5 hours. Add more salt as needed, a little at a time, tasting the stock until it is of the desired saltiness. It should remain slightly under-salted.

Strain the stock into a large bowl through a double thickness of dampened muslin, cheesecloth or a large clean handkerchief. Cool it quickly by standing the bowl in a large basin or sink of cold water.

Pour the stock into containers, cover and refrigerate. When the stock is cold, remove the fat – if you are in a hurry, you will have to do this with a spoon before the fat has solidified. The stock may now be frozen. See Chicken Stock, points 5–7 (opposite), for instructions.

Much of the Far East

PORK AND CHICKEN STOCK

•

Here is a stock that you may use for many Chinese, Vietnamese, Korean and Chinese-Malay dishes. In Hong Kong, it is known as Superior Stock and is the one most commonly used.

MAKES ABOUT 2 LITRES / 3½ PINTS / 8¾ CUPS

2 kg / 4½ lb pork bones with meat
2 kg / 4½ lb chicken wings, necks and assorted parts (no liver)
4 spring onions (scallions)
1 medium-sized carrot (85 g / 3 oz), peeled
Two 2.5 cm / 1 inch chunks of fresh ginger, lightly crushed
4 cloves garlic, peeled
About 2 teaspoons salt

Put the chicken and pork into a large pan with water to cover – about 4.25 litres / 7 pints / 4½ quarts. Bring to a boil. As the water boils, keep removing the scum for about 10–15 minutes. Add the spring onions (scallions), carrot, ginger, garlic and salt. Turn the heat down to a simmer, cover partially and cook for 3½–4 hours. Strain the soup through several layers of cheese-cloth, dampened muslin or a large clean handkerchief. Cool and refrigerate. Remove most of the fat at the top before using.

This stock may be frozen. See Chicken Stock, points 5–7 (p. 197) for instructions.

Japan

JAPANESE SOUP STOCK
DASHI

Unlike much of the world, the Japanese make their basic stock out of fish and sea kelp. The most commonly used fish is bonito, a member of the tuna family. It is sold in Japan in a dried, filleted form that looks rather like a piece of smooth, hard, petrified wood, and in fact needs to be shaved with a plane. The delicate, curled shavings are at their best when they are freshly done and when they are a pale pinkish-brown colour. The finest of Japanese food establishments would consider using no other, just as the best French restaurant would always make its stock from scratch. The discriminating Japanese housewife does not shave her own bonito, but she can go to any good market and get it shaved for her on the spot. The average Japanese, on the other hand, either buys packaged bonito shavings, which come in plastic bags or in cornflakes-like boxes, or uses instant soup stock (dashi-no-moto) which is available in granular form.

The other ingredients used in good dashi – and for vegetarians it is often the only ingredient – is konbu, a special kelp sold in the form of large, dried leaves. Only sections of it are used at a time. The kelp needs to be of good quality. Its flavour is said to reside on its surface, so it is never washed, just wiped

lightly with a damp cloth. This kelp should never be boiled vigorously; it is either soaked overnight or allowed to simmer very gently.

Whether you will be able to get shaved bonito (hana-katsuo) and the right kelp (dashi-konbu) is another matter. You should make an effort, as their flavours are the purest. If you cannot, use instant dashi-no-moto, which is sold by all Japanese grocers and is a useful item to have in your kitchen cupboard. As a last resort, you may use very light, unsalted chicken stock.

Let me, here and now, tell you how to prepare instant dashi from the granules as the packages one buys tend to have instructions only in Japanese. Put about 2 teaspoons of the granules in a bowl. Over them, pour about 450 ml / ¾ pint / 2 cups boiling or very hot water. Stir to mix and, if you like, strain through a dampened cloth to get rid of dark grounds. For extra flavour, you could add 1 teaspoon mirin, 1 tablespoon Japanese light soy sauce and a pinch of salt. Instant dashi is salted, so taste it before adding that pinch of salt. This recipe may be doubled or halved.

The correct way to make authentic dashi was demonstrated to me by Mr Saito at the École Technique Hôtelière Tsuji, the largest school training professional chefs in Japan. First, a hunk of wood-like bonito was quickly rinsed and dried. Odd bits of dried skin and dried blood were scraped off. Just before the stock was made, the bonito was shaved with a plane that was affixed to a box. The shavings fell neatly into a drawer!

MAKES 1 LITRE / 1¾ PINTS / 4⅓ CUPS
20–25 cm / 8–10 inch (about 30 g / 1 oz) piece of kelp, konbu
Dried bonito shavings, hana-katsuo, measured to the 450 ml / ¾ pint / 2 cup level in a measuring jug

Wipe the kelp lightly with a damp cloth and put it into a medium-sized pan. Pour in 1 litre / 1¾ pints / 4⅓ cups of water and very slowly bring it to a simmer over medium-low heat. If you are using the stock to make clear soup, remove the kelp just before the water

comes to the boil. If you are using the stock for anything else – such as noodles, sauces or for cooking vegetables – let the kelp simmer gently for 10 minutes without ever letting the water come to the boil. Remove the kelp and then add the bonito shavings. Immediately take the pan off the heat. Do not stir. Within the next minute or so, the shavings will sink to the bottom. Strain the soup through a piece of dampened cloth.

While stock for clear soups is best when freshly made, all other Japanese Soup Stock may be made ahead of time and refrigerated. It could keep thus for 3 days and may be re-heated by being brought to a bare simmer. It is generally seasoned with a little salt and/or soy sauce when it is used for clear soups.

PLAIN LONG-GRAIN RICE
•

SERVES 4–6
Long-grain rice, measured to the
450 ml / 15 fl oz / 2 cup level in a measuring jug

Put the rice in a bowl and fill the bowl with water. Rub the rice gently with your hands and then pour off all the milky water. Do this several times until the water runs clear. Now fill the bowl with fresh water and let the rice soak for 30 minutes. Drain.

Put the drained rice in a heavy, medium-sized pan. Add 600 ml / 1 pint / 2⅔ cups water and bring to a boil. Cover with a tight-fitting lid. (If your lid is not the tight-fitting kind, cover first with foil, crimping the edges, and then cover with the lid.) Turn the heat to very low and cook for 25 minutes.

If left uncovered in a warm place, this rice will retain its heat for a good hour.

Japan, Korea

PLAIN JAPANESE AND KOREAN RICE
GOHAN, BAB

The rice in Japan and Korea is a fat, short-grained variety which develops a most pleasing stickiness when it is cooked. The grains not only adhere to each other, thus allowing them to be picked up easily with chopsticks in small lumps, but they can also be rolled into ovals and rounds, all the better to be devoured with neat slivers of fish or roasted sesame seeds.

One brand to look for in Asian grocery shops is *Kokuho Rose*. This recipe makes about 6 cups of rice. If you wish to cook more or less rice, remember that the proportion of raw rice to water, in volume, is 1:1¼. The cooking time remains exactly the same.

SERVES 4–6

Japanese rice, measured to the
475 ml / 16 fl oz / 2 cup level in a measuring jug

Put the rice in a bowl and add water to cover it generously. Swish the rice around gently with your hand, kneading it lightly as you do so. Pour off the water when it turns milky. Do this several times in quick succession, until the water remains almost clear. Drain the rice through a sieve. Leave the rice in the sieve for 30 minutes to 1 hour, allowing it to absorb the moisture that clings to it.

Put the rice into a heavy-bottomed pan. Add 600 ml / 1 pint / 2½ cups water and bring to the boil. Cover, turn the heat to very low and cook for 20 minutes. Turn the heat to high for 30 seconds and then turn it off. Let the pan sit, covered and undisturbed, for another 10–15 minutes.

All over East Asia
GLUTINOUS RICE
•

Glutinous rice is also known as sticky rice and sweet rice. These days, in fact, the label often reads 'Sweet Rice'. The grains are short and white and turn translucent and slightly glutinous when cooked. Through much of East Asia this rice is used for both sweets and stuffings. In the region around northern Thailand, however, it is a staple grain. At each meal it is served from a large basket. Each diner forms a little ball, combines that ball with a bit of meat and a bit of vegetable

and then pops the morsel into his or her mouth. The two easiest ways to cook this rice are with a double-boiler and by steaming. Here is the double-boiler method. The steaming method is on page 29.

SERVES 4–6

Glutinous rice, measured to the
450 ml / 15 fl oz / 2 cup level
in a measuring jug

Wash the rice in several changes of water and drain. Put in a bowl, cover with plenty of water and leave to soak for 6 hours. Alternatively, you could soak it in boiling water for 2 hours. Drain. Heat water in the bottom of a double-boiler. When it starts to boil, fit in the top of the double-boiler and into it put the rice and enough water to come 1 cm / ½ inch above the rice. When the water with the rice begins to boil, cover the pot and cook on medium heat for 25 minutes.

All over the Far East
PLAIN CHINESE EGG (LO MEIN) NOODLES
•

This is the ideal recipe for cooking fresh, Chinese egg noodles. These can be found in the freezer or refrigerator of every major Chinese grocer. They generally come in 450 g / 1 lb bags. I tend to buy several bags at the same time. When I come home, I divide each bag into two ½ lb bags and then put them in the freezer. They last very well and do not need to be defrosted. They can be thrown directly into boiling water. (If you cannot get fresh egg noodles, use good-quality dried ones. Cook them like pasta: throw them into boiling water and cook until just done. If not using immediately, drain, rinse under cold water and drain again. Rub with a little sesame or other vegetable oil.)

SERVES 3–4

225 g / ½ lb fresh Chinese egg,
lo mein, noodles
1 tablespoon sesame or other vegetable oil

Bring about 2.25 litres / 4 pints / 10 cups water to a rolling boil in a large pan. Drop in the noodles and separate them with a fork or chopsticks. When the water comes to a boil again, put in 250 ml / 8 fl oz / 1 cup fresh water. The boiling will subside. Let it come to a boil again and put in a second 250 ml / 8 fl oz / 1 cup fresh water. The boiling will subside again. Let it come to yet another boil. Now drain the noodles in a colander. Run cold water over them and rinse out the starch. Let them drain for 5 minutes. Put in a bowl. Add the oil and toss. Cover and set aside until needed.

Hong Kong
CHINESE DIPPING SAUCE
ZHAN JIANG

This is an all-purpose dipping sauce that may be served with breads, pancakes, spring rolls and batter-fried foods.

SERVES 4

6 tablespoons Chinese light soy sauce
2 tablespoons distilled white vinegar
2 teaspoons sugar
2 teaspoons sesame oil
A few drops of Chilli Oil, see below
(optional)

Mix all the ingredients together. Divide among 4 small bowls – or as many bowls as there are diners.

Hong Kong
CHILLI OIL
LAJIAO YOU

Orange-coloured chilli oil is offered as a seasoning on the tables of most restaurants in Hong Kong. A few drops, or more liberal doses, are dribbled on to any foods that need extra 'heat'. It is also a common seasoning in Chinese kitchens serving Sichuan-style food. You can buy it ready-made from Chinese grocers, but it is easy enough to make at home. I find that it needs to be strained a couple of times if I want it to be really clear.

MAKES ABOUT 150 ML / 5 FL OZ / ½ CUP

10 tablespoons vegetable oil (preferably peanut oil)
1 tablespoon chilli powder (cayenne pepper), preferably of a bright red colour

Put the oil in a small pan and set it over medium-high heat. When the oil is hot, remove it from the heat and put in the chilli powder (cayenne pepper). Mix and leave to cool, then strain the oil through a clean cloth. It is now ready to be used. You may, however, let it sit for a few hours and strain it a second time. If you have an empty bottle or jar in your cruet set, you could use it for your chilli oil.

Thailand

FISH SAUCE SEASONED WITH LIME JUICE AND CHILLI
NAM PLA PRIK

You may put this sauce on the table when you are serving any Thai meal.

SERVES 4

1 fresh, hot green or red chilli
4 tablespoons fish sauce, nam pla
2 tablespoons lime or lemon juice

Cut the chilli crossways into very fine rounds. Put it in a small bowl. Add the fish sauce and the lime or lemon juice. Stir to mix.

Korea

HOT FERMENTED BEAN PASTE
KOCHU CHANG

Every household in Korea has a tall earthenware jar of Hot Fermented Bean Paste (kochu chang) sitting serenely in a courtyard, on a balcony or in some other convenient nook. It is an essential seasoning and is one of the several bean pastes used with great frequency throughout the nation. It serves as a cross between a chutney and a spice.

Its method of preparation is elaborate and long, calling for barley or glutinous rice powder to be mixed with malt, cooked slowly into a thick paste and then mixed with fermented soya bean powder, chilli powder and salt.

The resulting paste is red in colour (because of the chillies) and very thick. It is added to dipping sauces, to meats that are just about to be stir-fried, and to stews. Dollops of it are also served as a kind of salty sweet and hot chutney.

Kochu chang is available only in Korean shops. It can, however, be approximated at home with ingredients available to most of us. It is best to buy brown or reddish miso for this recipe. This when mixed with chilli powder (cayenne pepper), paprika and a little sugar, tastes and looks very much like real kochu chang.

MAKES 4–5 TABLESPOONS

4 tablespoons brown or red miso
1½ tablespoons paprika
1 teaspoon chilli powder (cayenne pepper)
1 tablespoon sugar

Combine all the ingredients and mix well.

Central Thailand

THAI CHILLI PASTE
NAM PRIK POW

Sometimes called 'chilli jam', this thick paste can also be bought, ready-made, from Thai grocers though it is hardly ever labelled in English. If you wish to buy it, you will have to ask for it by its Thai name. However, it is not difficult to make at home and is a wonderful paste to have sitting around in the refrigerator. You can add small amounts to soups and stews, even to Thai-style salads of lightly cooked squid or prawns (shrimp) to give them an extra kick. It is very hot, slightly sweet and sour.

In Thailand, instead of using an electric blender, the ingredients are pounded to a paste in a mortar. You may use a mortar if you so desire.

It is best to have good ventilation as you prepare this.

MAKES ABOUT 6 TABLESPOONS

1 tablespoon dried prawns (shrimp)
20 dried, hot red chillies
6–7 cloves garlic, peeled and coarsely chopped
7–8 good-sized shallots or 1 medium-sized onion (85 g / 3 oz), peeled and finely chopped
½ teaspoon shrimp paste, kapi (or anchovy paste)
3 tablespoons vegetable oil
1 tablespoon palm sugar or soft light brown sugar
1 tablespoon tamarind paste, see p. 218
¼ teaspoon salt

Put the prawns (shrimp) in a bowl and pour boiling water over to cover them well. Let them sit in the water for about 5 seconds then lift them out with a slotted spoon. (Discard the water.)

Put the prawns (shrimp), chillies, garlic and shallots into the small container of an electric blender. Add a little water only if you have to – about 1 tablespoon – and blend until you have a coarse paste. Add the shrimp paste and mix.

Heat the oil in a medium-sized, non-stick frying-pan over medium-high heat. Put in the chilli paste. Stir and fry for about 5 minutes or until the paste has browned and reduced. Turn off the heat. Add the palm sugar, tamarind paste and salt. Turn the heat to low. Stir and mix until the palm sugar has melted completely. This takes about a minute. Turn off the heat. Let the paste cool and then store it in a closed jar in the refrigerator.

Indonesia

CHILLI SAUCE WITH SHRIMP PASTE
SAMBAL TERASI

In Indonesia, long red chillies are pounded in a mortar or on a grinding stone and then fried with the other ingredients. If you cannot get fresh long red chillies, you can do what I have done. That is, use fresh red pepper mixed with some chilli powder (cayenne pepper). Instead of pounding by hand, I have used an electric blender.

This paste will keep for 1 week in the refrigerator. Store it in a tightly lidded jar. Serve it with all Indonesian meals. You could also serve it with Thai and Malaysian meals.

MAKES ABOUT 250 ML / 8 FL OZ / 1 CUP

2 small red peppers (225 g / 8 oz), de-seeded and coarsely chopped

2 teaspoons shrimp paste, *terasi* (or anchovy paste)

½ teaspoon salt

½–1 teaspoon chilli powder (cayenne pepper)

4 tablespoons vegetable oil

1 teaspoon dark brown sugar

2½ tablespoons lime or lemon juice

Combine the red pepper, shrimp paste, salt and chilli powder (cayenne pepper) in the container of an electric blender. Blend until smooth. Heat the oil in a medium-sized, non-stick frying pan over medium-high heat. When hot, put in the paste from the blender. Stir and fry for about 5 minutes, turning down the heat a little if necessary, until the paste turns dark and the oil separates from it. Add the sugar and stir to mix. Take the paste off the heat and put in a small bowl. Beat in the lemon or lime juice. Taste and adjust seasonings, if necessary.

Vietnam, Thailand, Malaysia, Indonesia

RED PEPPER SAUCE

•

In Vietnam, this sauce is made by pounding red chillies and salt in a mortar, cooking the mixture and then passing it through a sieve. Some countries do not bother with the cooking and straining. Others add a little sugar and vinegar. My method is very simple: I let an electric blender do all the work.

SERVES 4

2–3 dried, hot red chillies

About three-quarters of a large red pepper (100 g / 4 oz)

¼ teaspoon sugar

½ teaspoon distilled white vinegar

¼ teaspoon salt, or to taste

Put 3 tablespoons water in a small cup and crumble the dried red chillies into it. Soak for 30 minutes. Coarsely chop the red pepper, discarding all the seeds. Combine the chillies and their liquid with all the other ingredients in an electric blender. Blend until smooth.

All over South-East Asia

SEASONED VINEGAR

•

This seasoning is found in all Asian countries where the Chinese have lived or settled: Hong Kong, Indonesia, the Philippines, Malaysia, Thailand and Vietnam. Of course, the actual vinegar varies not only from country to country but often from village to village. Diners usually add just a few drops of the hot vinegar to their food. If they want to, they can also take a few chilli slices from the vinegar.

MAKES 4 TABLESPOONS

2 fresh, hot green or red chillies

4 tablespoons distilled white vinegar

Cut the chillies crossways into very thin rounds. Put the vinegar into a very small bowl. Add the chillies and let them steep for 30 minutes.

Much of South-East Asia

CRISPLY FRIED SHALLOT (OR ONION) FLAKES

•

A young lady in Padang, Indonesia, told me with great authority that shallot flakes turn much crisper if they are soaked in lightly salted water before being fried. Theories abound: this one makes sense, however, as salt draws out some of the moisture. I think starting the frying at a medium-hot, rather than a very hot, temperature also helps.

In much of South-East Asia shallots are cheap and used rather as onions are used in the West. Crisply Fried Shallot Flakes serve both as a garnish and as a seasoning. Often they are fried in bulk and kept in tightly

lidded jars to be used as needed. If you cannot obtain shallots, use onions. Cut them in half lengthways, and then crossways into very fine half-rings. Fry them just as you would the shallots. (Small amounts of shallots, intended for use the same day, may be fried without first being soaked in salted water.)

MAKES ENOUGH TO FILL A

350 ML / 12 FL OZ / 1½ CUP JAR

20 shallots (200 g / 7 oz), peeled, or 3 small onions, peeled and finely sliced

½ teaspoon salt

Vegetable oil for deep-frying (preferably peanut oil)

Cut the shallots lengthways into fine slivers. Put them in a bowl. Add the salt and toss lightly. Cover with 450 ml / 15 fl oz / 2 cups water and leave for 30 minutes. Drain the shallots well and pat them dry.

Put about 5 cm / 2 inches oil in a wok set over medium heat, or heat the recommended quantity of oil in a deep-fat fryer to 375°F / 190°C. When the oil is hot, put in the shallots. Stir and fry for 1 minute. Turn the heat down to medium low, or the deep-fat fryer to 325°F / 160°C. If you are using a wok, keep stirring and frying until the shallots are reddish-brown and crisp. Remove them with a slotted spoon and spread them out on paper towels to drain.

When they are cool and crisp, store them in a tightly lidded jar until needed.

All over East Asia

ROASTED PEANUTS

•

If you cannot buy roasted, unsalted peanuts, here is a simple method of roasting.

SERVES 4

150 g / 5 oz / about 1 cup raw, shelled peanuts (with their red skins)

Set a medium-sized, preferably cast-iron, frying-pan on medium heat. When hot, put in the peanuts. Stir and roast for 2–3 minutes or until the peanuts begin to show the first signs of taking on some colour. Turn the heat down to medium low. Continue to stir and cook for another 6–7 minutes or until the peanuts are roasted. Empty the peanuts on to a piece of paper towel and let them get cool enough to handle. Rub off their papery red skins and either blow them away or else pick out the peanuts and transfer them to a plate. Once the peanuts have cooled completely, they may be stored in a closed jar.

Most of South-East Asia
CRUSHED, ROASTED PEANUTS

·

Crushed, roasted peanuts are a common seasoning in most of South-East Asia. They add a nutty taste, a crunchy texture – and protein – to dishes in which they are used.

To roast the peanuts, just follow the recipe above or buy already roasted, shelled and skinned peanuts from the market. To crush them, lightly or finely as required, I whir them for a few seconds in a clean coffee-grinder or, if only a few tablespoons are needed, I chop them up with a large knife.

Much of South-East Asia
EGG STRIPS

·

These strips are a popular garnish for rice and noodles in many parts of South-East Asia. They are also used in salads and soups.

MAKES ENOUGH TO FILL A

350 ML / 12 FL OZ / 1½ CUP MEASURE

3 eggs

1 teaspoon sugar

⅛ teaspoon salt

About 2 teaspoons vegetable oil

Break the eggs into a bowl and add 1 tablespoon water. Beat, but not to a froth. Add the sugar and salt and beat lightly to mix. Brush a 18–20 cm / 7–8 inch non-stick frying-pan with about ½ teaspoon of the oil and set it on medium heat. When it is hot,

pour in a quarter of the egg mixture. Tilt the pan around so that the egg flows evenly to the edges. Let the mixture set, which it will do quite quickly. Turn the pancake over carefully and cook the second side until it is just firm (a matter of seconds). Remove the pancake to a plate and cover it with greaseproof (wax) paper. Make 3 more pancakes in this way, putting them on top of each other with a layer of greaseproof (wax) paper in between. Allow them to cool and remove the greaseproof (wax) paper. Roll them up one at a time and cut them crossways at 3 mm / ⅛ inch intervals. Put the resulting strips into a covered container and store in the refrigerator if you are not going to use them immediately.

Indonesia
PRAWN (SHRIMP) WAFERS
KRUPUK UDANG

Krupuk are wafers which, rather like the Indian poppadums, add a pleasing crunch to a meal. They nearly always appear at festive banquets, are amazingly good with drinks and may be eaten on their own as a snack. There are many, many varieties of *krupuk*. They may be flavoured with prawns (shrimp), made of cassava or of nuts.

One of my favourites, which is found only in the hills of western Sumatra, is made of cassava and comes thinly smeared with a sweet and hot red chilli jam.

Krupuk udang, made of prawns (shrimp) and starch, come in many sizes and colours, some rather startling. I have seen bright blue, pink, green and yellow *krupuk* gracing many a table. *Krupuk* need to be fried quickly – passed through hot oil, you might say – before they are served. To ensure crispness, the wafers must be bone dry before they hit the oil. Indonesian housewives routinely put *krupuk* in the sun for a brief period first. You could place them in a warm oven for 10 minutes. Once they are fried in the hot oil, they expand quite a bit and assume a lighter, airier texture. Ideally they should be cooked shortly

before they are eaten. If you cannot manage that, store them in an air-tight container after they have been cooked. Uncooked *krupuk* should also be stored in very tightly lidded jars.

Here is the general method for preparing these wafers. Put enough oil in a wok to have at least 4 cm / 1½ inches in the centre. In a frying-pan you will need about 2.5 cm / 1 inch oil. When it is a high temperature – about 365°F / 185°C – drop in 2 or 3 small *krupuk* (fewer if they are large). They will sink, rise almost immediately and greatly expand in size. Spoon oil over them during the few seconds that they take to cook. Do not let them brown. Adjust the heat if necessary. Remove the wafers with a slotted spoon and transfer them to a plate lined with paper towels.

Cook as many *krupuk* as you need this way.

Korea
CABBAGE PICKLE
KIMCHEE

It is not surprising that *kimchee* is used in Korean rituals and rites. After all, there is not a single meal, from breakfast until dinner, when it is not served. *Kimchee* is a pickle and there are, according to the *kimchee* museum in Seoul, at least 160 varieties.

It can be made from radish, cucumber, and even from fresh ginseng, but the most common *kimchee* remains the one that is made from cabbage.

Koreans use a long, fat cabbage which many call Chinese cabbage. It looks like a very large, overweight head of Chinese leaves (celery cabbage). A single head can weigh as much as 2 kg / 4½ lb.

This recipe calls for half a head of Chinese cabbage. It should be halved lengthways. The way the Koreans do it is to start cutting it at the bottom with a knife and then tearing the two halves apart with their hands.

It might be useful for you to know that ready-made *kimchee* is available from most Chinese grocers.

MAKES ENOUGH TO FILL A
2 LITRE / 3¼ PINT / 2 QUART JAR

Half a medium-sized head of Chinese cabbage
(450 g / 1 lb) or the same weight Chinese leaves
(celery cabbage)

Salt

For the 'stuffing':

450 g / 1 lb white radish (the very large variety
sold by oriental grocers)

5 cm / 2 inch piece of fresh ginger, peeled and
coarsely chopped

5–6 large cloves garlic, peeled and
coarsely chopped

4 spring onions (scallions), cut into fine rounds
all the way up their green sections

1½ tablespoons chilli powder (cayenne pepper)
– of a good, bright red colour, if available

1 teaspoon sugar

10 shelled oysters or tinned anchovy fillets

1 teaspoon plain (all purpose)
white flour

Halve the Chinese cabbage lengthways. Trim
the very bottom of the cabbage but keep the
leaves attached. If it is very thick, cut it into
half again, lengthways. (Chinese leaves /
celery cabbage should be cut into halves
only.) Wash the cabbage well, carefully
removing the dirt between each leaf.

In a large bowl, combine 1.5 litres / 2½
pints / 1½ quarts water with 3 tablespoons
salt. Put the cabbage into the solution. Weigh
it down with a clean, heavy plate so that it
does not float. Cover loosely and leave for 8
hours.

To prepare the 'stuffing', peel the radish
and cut it crossways into 5 cm / 2 inch
chunks. Now cut each chunk lengthways into
3 mm / ⅛ inch thick slabs. Cut each slab into
3 mm / ⅛ inch thick julienne strips. The easy
way to do this is to spread the slabs out in
front of you like a deck of overlapping
playing cards. Then start cutting lengthways
from one end and do not stop until you've
reached the other.

Put the ginger and garlic into the container
of an electric blender with 3 tablespoons
water. Blend until smooth.

In a large bowl, combine the radish,
ginger-garlic paste, spring onions (scallions),
chilli powder, sugar and oysters. If using
anchovy fillets, wipe off the oil and chop
them finely before adding them. Mix. Add 1
tablespoon salt. Mix.

Put the flour in a small pan and slowly add
250 ml / 8 fl oz / 1 cup water, mixing as you
go. Bring this water to a simmer. Simmer
gently until slightly thickened. Allow to cool.

Remove the cabbage from the salt water
and rinse thoroughly several times. Keep the
leaves attached. Drain.

Starting from the outside, put some stuffing
between each cabbage leaf. Put the largest
leaf on the top and tuck it under so that it
will hold the 'package' together. Do all of
your cabbage this way. If you have used fat,
Chinese cabbage, you will probably have two
such packets; if you have used Chinese leaves
(celery cabbage) you will probably have
more. Fit these packets tightly inside a clean,
wide-mouthed crock or jar of a 2 litre / 3¼
pint / 2 quart capacity. Pour the flour water
over the top. Make sure there is some room
on top for the fermenting pickle to expand.
Cover and set aside for 3–7 days, depending
upon the weather. Taste the pickle now and
then to see if it has turned sufficiently sour.
Once the pickle is ready, it should be
refrigerated.

To serve, remove just as much of the
cabbage as you need and put in a small bowl.
Leave the liquid behind.

In Korea, the liquid is used to flavour stews
and soups.

PLATE OF FRESH FRUIT
•

In much of Asia, meals end not with desserts
and puddings but with fresh, cleansing fruit.
Sometimes it is just one glorious seasonal
fruit, such as the durian whose sensuous
'fingers' are removed from its deadly looking
shell and arranged on plates, or it could be
bunches of mangosteens that diners cut open
for themselves, staining their hands all purple

into the bargain. It could also be a pile of
perfumed summer mangoes that have been
chilled in iced water. In Hong Kong, it could
be litchis, the choice fruit of the ancient
emperors. In Korea, meals often end with a
collection of several fruits, all pared and cut
into neat mouthfuls, sitting on a common
platter set in the centre of the table. Each
piece of fruit is pierced with a small, two-
pronged fork so that it can be picked up with
ease and nibbled at will. In Thailand, where a
whole school is devoted to the art, fruit
comes carved in the most elaborate floral and
geometric designs; you cannot even get a
simple papaya in your hotel room without
some slight hint of delicate fingers at work.
In Japan, where the fruit is not tropical,
dessert could be a single, perfect fruit, a ripe,
ripe persimmon, luminescently orange, its
skin cut open like the petals of a flower,
sitting in solitary splendour on a plate.

While I do not suggest that you spend all
day carving fruit – enough effort is required
to prepare the main meal – here are helpful
hints on fruits that you may be unfamiliar
with, and which are now often sold in many
Western shops and supermarkets.

Mango
Sweet, juicy and, at its best, smooth-textured,
a mango to me is the king of fruit. There are
hundreds of varieties, each with its own taste,
texture and colour. Most varieties in the
northern hemisphere ripen in the summer,
from late April to early July, so that would be
the best time to buy them. Mangoes sold by
most shops in the West are hard and under-
ripe. They are always picked under-ripe, even
in Asia and are meant to ripen off the tree.
In Asia, the shopkeepers often do the job
for you. In the West, we have to do the job
ourselves.

When buying mangoes, smell them at the
stem end, and if they seem to have the
potential of being sweet, make the purchase.
You will be taking a bit of a chance, but if it
works out once, look for the same variety
again. When you get home, wrap the hard

mango in newspaper and put it in a basket or an open cardboard box. Do not refrigerate it. You can ripen several mangoes together in this way, wrapping each one separately in newspaper first. In Thai villages, baskets of mangoes are left to ripen in straw under the bed. When the perfume becomes over-whelming, the household knows that the mangoes are ready to be eaten! Examine your mangoes every day. They should eventually yield very slightly to the touch, but should *not* have black spots on them. You may now chill the mangoes in the refrigerator, or put them to cool in a bucket of water to which you have added plenty of ice.

While there are people who believe that mangoes are best eaten with the hands, and in a bathtub, there is a neater approach for those who would like to use an implement – and stay at the table. The mango usually has two flatter sides. Cut a thick slice lengthways off each of these sides as close to the stone as you can. (Peel the remaining mango and devour it in the kitchen by yourself. This is your reward for the work you are putting in.) Put these two slices on a plate. This is one serving. The mango pulp may now be scooped decorously out of the skin with a spoon. Alternatively, you cut a cross-hatch pattern in the flesh, making rows at about 1 cm / ½ inch intervals with a sharp knife. Cut all the way down to the skin, but do not cut through it. Now put the fingers of both your hands under the skin and push upwards. The flesh of the mango will rise up in an arch and open in a most interesting pattern. Eat it with a spoon. Another alternative is to peel the mango, slice it and cut it into dice. Serve the stone only to those who do not mind using their fingers.

Litchis (also spelled lychees)

These, to my mind, must always be eaten in quantity. Eating one or two is like eating one or two peanuts. Litchis have a red or reddish-brown, papery, rough, crisp skin. As you peel the egg-sized fruit, a sweet, clear juice begins to drip from it. The inside is white,

translucent and glistening, not unlike the skin of a peeled squid. Pop the litchi into your mouth, but remember that there is a long stone in the centre.

Chill the litchis before serving.

You may put a whole bunch of litchis in a bowl in the centre of your table and let people break off their own, peel them and eat them. Or you can peel the litchis yourself and arrange them on a plate with other cut fruit. Do not remove the stone: that is the least people can do for themselves.

Rambutan

This is a large, red litchi with red hairlike spikes on the outside. It tastes a little like a litchi, but is much less juicy. The Thais often leave half-peeled rambutans on a fruit plate to show off their interesting skins. Rambutans also have stones in them.

Mangosteen

The fruit that has won most kudos among Western travellers is perhaps the mangosteen. One ancient traveller compared it to nectar and ambrosia, saying that it, 'surpassed the golden apples of the Hesperides and was, of all the fruit of the Indies, the most delicious.' I can remember sitting on a park bench in Malacca and greedily devouring about a dozen of them in one session, sticky juice dripping all over me.

In spite of its name, the mangosteen is in no way related to the mango. It is purplish or reddish-brown on the outside, the size of a tangerine and quite hard. There is a knack to cracking it open with a good twist, which I have now finally mastered, but I will suggest an easier method.

Take a sharp knife and make an equatorial cut all around the fruit. Do not cut all the way through: you do not want two equal halves. Now pull the top off like a cap. Sitting propped up inside a natural cup, like a scoop of ice-cream, will be 5–8 white, juicy, translucent segments. You may eat them with a spoon. They will be sweet with just a hint of sourness, and very good.

Passion fruit

From the outside, this looks like a large dented egg of purplish (or sometimes yellow) colour. Split the fruit open and you will find crunchy seeds covered with a clear, gelatinous flesh nestling in the hollow. At their best, passion fruit have a sweet and sour taste that seems to combine the flavour of limes and berries. If it is too sour, a little sugar should be sprinkled over the pulp before it is eaten.

The pulp may also be strained and then served over ice-cream.

Custard apple

This is a heart-shaped fruit that seems to be covered with a green alligator skin. It must be fully ripe when it is bought, which means that it should yield easily to the touch when pressed. Serve each person a whole custard apple. They can, themselves, split it open in half, lengthways, with their hands. The inside is filled with white, creamy, sugar-sweet buds that often harbour smooth, black seeds. Ease your spoon into the custard-like pulp. The art of eating this fruit lies in knowing how to dislodge the seeds from the pulp while the buds are still in your mouth and then delicately spitting out the seeds, while ret-aining the fruit – and your dignity. Custard apples are best served chilled.

Pineapple

By now I'm sure you all know how to serve this fruit. When buying it, smell it – it should smell sweet; look at its colour – the yellower it is, the riper it will be; feel its very top, near the leaves – it should have a little give. Peel it, remove its 'eyes', cut it into 6–8 parts lengthways, core it and then serve it in wedges as they do in South-East Asia. You could also cut the wedges crossways into slices if you want smaller pieces. In this part of the world, pineapples are generally not cut into round slices with a hole in the centre, the way we are used to seeing them come out of a can, but you may certainly cut them that way if you wish.

Pineapple is best when it is slightly chilled. If it is not too sweet, sugar may be added, but remember that this will make it syrupy, so it will not be suitable for a plate of mixed fruit.

Durian

Dare I mention it? This is the fruit that is banned from hotels and aeroplanes because of its lingering odour. Or it is made to travel firmly enclosed in an inner tube! South-East Asians are always surprised when a Westerner can allow himself to go near it, let alone eat it. I love it passionately and recommend it without hesitation.

It looks unprepossessing – large, green and full of murderous spikes, a football made by a dinosaur for a dinosaur. It needs to be cracked open with a hatchet wielded by a practised hand. Lying inside its five compartments are pale, off-white segments of the creamiest, smoothest texture imaginable. These segments are sweet, the most heavenly blend of cream, bananas and flowing ripe brie. Eat them out of the hand.

Note: In Indonesia, the durian is said to be an aphrodisiac and the saying goes, 'When the durian comes in, the sarongs go up.' Might that induce you to try it?

Papaya

This should be very ripe and sweet. It should yield slightly to the touch and have a nice yellowish colour on the outside. Chill it first, then cut it lengthways into half. Scoop out all the seeds.

You may now cut it into long slices, or you may serve a whole half with a wedge of lime, or you may peel the papaya halves and cut them into cubes.

Persimmon

The persimmon, which grows in China, Japan and Korea, is a delicious, sugar-sweet fruit that I happen to love. When people in the West are disappointed in its taste, it is often because they are biting into it while it is still unripe and still painfully astringent.

There are actually many varieties of persimmon, but the two most easily available in the West today are the hard, apple-type persimmons which may be peeled, cored and eaten, just like apples, while they are still hard, and the second variety that needs to be

Coconut husks are removed in Indonesia.

meltingly soft before it goes into the mouth or it will leave it puckered and unhappy. This second type must be left, unrefrigerated, until it is positively squishy. Then it should be quartered lengthways and its flesh eaten with a spoon. If you get confused between the two, it is best to ask your greengrocer whether the persimmon you are buying may be eaten as is or whether you should wait

205

until it is very soft. Persimmons have inedible seeds that need to be removed.

Bananas and watermelon

Sliced bananas and watermelon chunks may be added to any plate of tropical fruit that you wish to serve.

Thailand

MANGOES WITH GLUTINOUS RICE
MA MUANG KHAO NIAW

Mangoes herald the arrival of summer and there is almost no seasonal sweet that the Thais look forward to more than this – sliced mangoes served with glutinous rice that has been enriched with thick coconut cream.

Use any sweet, ripe mangoes. For more on the fruit, see p. 203. The Thais use the *ok rong* mango, which is very pale in colour. We have to use whatever we can find. Here, I cut the mangoes as the Thais do, so there are very few ridges to mar their smoothness.

If using fresh coconut milk, see p. 212 for directions for getting at the cream which rises to the top of the milk. If using canned coconut milk, just stir the can well and use the thick milk.

Even though this is a Thai speciality, it can also be served at the conclusion of Malaysian, Indonesian, Vietnamese and Filipino meals.

SERVES 4

Freshly cooked Glutinous Rice, see p. 198 or p. 199, measured to the 475 ml / 16 fl oz / 2 cup level in a measuring jug

120 ml / 4 fl oz / 1 cup fresh coconut cream, see p. 212, or well-stirred, canned coconut milk

½ teaspoon salt

4 tablespoons sugar

4 chilled mangoes

Combine the hot, freshly cooked rice with the coconut cream or milk, salt and sugar. Mix gently and set aside to come to room temperature. Divide the rice into 4 parts and put one part each in the centre of 4 plates.

Cut 2 slices off the flatter sides of each of the 4 mangoes. Now cut each of these slices crossways into 4–5 sections. Peel each section and put them back together in the shape of the original slice. Put 2 slices, flat side down, on either side of the rice on each plate.

Philippines

GINGER TEA
SALABAT

Nearly all of Asia drinks ginger tea in some form or other. It is meant to be very good for coughs and colds and is a digestive, to boot. In the Philippines, it is often offered at breakfast and with midday snacks or *merienda*. It is easy to make.

SERVES 4

Three 2.5 cm / 1 inch cubes of fresh ginger

4–5 teaspoons honey or light, soft brown sugar or demerara sugar (use according to taste)

Peel the ginger and chop it coarsely. Put it into a small pan along with 1 litre / 1¾ pints / 1⅓ cups water and the honey or sugar. Bring to a boil. Turn the heat to low and simmer gently for 15–20 minutes. Strain and serve. You may also serve this tea cold.

Japan

SERVING JAPANESE RICE WINE
SAKE

Even though Japanese habits are changing and it is considered chic to drink whisky with a meal, and quite common to have beer, *sake*, the indigenous rice wine, remains the national drink. Famed as the mythical drink of the gods in ancient times and consumed exclusively by nobles and priests through the Middle Ages, today *sake* is available to the masses even in cardboard cartons that are sold out of coin machines.

Sake is colourless, like vodka, though much less potent. Its alcoholic content can go from 15–17 per cent for the general market, and up to 20 per cent for some very special domestic varieties. At weddings and banquets it may be served cool, straight out of specially ordered cedar casks, rather like beer out of barrels. On such occasions, it is drunk from thick, squarish cedar cups, sometimes with a little salt placed on a corner.

These days, *sake* may also be served chilled. Chilled *sake* is being promoted quite a bit now in Japan to lure back the infidels who have been seduced by the fashionable white wines of France. The most common way to drink *sake*, however, is not cooled or chilled, but warmed. Warming releases its aromas and allows the alcohol to enter the bloodstream with a more pronounced sense of urgency. *Sake* that has been warmed once is not considered good for drinking any more as its aromas have been dispersed. (It is, however, good for cooking.) It is for this reason that only small quantities of *sake* are warmed at a time. Servings, too, are small as the entire amount – a few thimblefuls – is supposed to be drunk at one go, before it has a chance to cool off. It is considered polite to serve one's neighbours when their glasses are empty and to let them do the same for you. It is not quite the done thing to serve oneself when in company. *Sake* can be drunk through every course of a Japanese meal, though many purists do not drink it at the same time as they are eating anything with rice.

Once a bottle of *sake* has been opened, it behaves a bit like wine and it is best to drink it all up. You may, if you have to, keep it for 2–3 weeks in a cool place or a refrigerator but its life is basically limited.

To heat and serve *sake*: *Sake* bottles and cups are sold by many oriental shops. If you do not wish to buy a set, it is very easy to improvise. For drinking, use the smallest liqueur glasses in your possession. The size will probably be just right. For heating and serving, use any pretty glass or ceramic bottle of roughly 300 ml / 10 fl oz / 1¼ cup capacity. Fill it with *sake*. Half-fill a medium-sized pan with water and stand the bottle of *sake* in it. Heat the water gently. The *sake* should be very warm, not very hot. The temperature you should aim for is around 130°F / 54°C. Heat several batches, one after the other, as you need them.

TECHNIQUES

The general techniques used in Far Eastern cookery are not very different from those used in the West. A few pointers, however, may be helpful.

Cutting and boning meats and vegetables

Meats and vegetables are frequently cut into strips or dice before they are cooked, so that the pieces cook evenly. This is particularly important for quick stir-frying and for the general appearance of the food. Aesthetics play a very special role in this region, reaching a pinnacle in Japan where restaurants are judged on the look of their food as much as on its taste.

To slice meat into thin slices and strips
It frequently helps (though it is not essential) to partially freeze, say, a beef steak, before you cut it against the grain into thin slices. If strips are called for, stack a few slices together at a time to make the cutting quicker, and then cut into strips.

To bone a chicken leg
The chicken recipes in this book often call for boneless dark leg meat as it stays much more moist than white meat and has a better flavour. Boning a chicken leg is actually quite easy. (a) Using a sharp knife, make a deep slit along the length of the thigh bone and drumstick. (b) Free the meat at both ends, cutting at right angles to the bones. (c) Now cut – almost scrape – the meat off the thigh bone and the drumstick, freeing the meat from the middle joint as you do so. (d) The chicken meat may now be cut into pieces of the desired size.

To bone a whole chicken
Lay the chicken, breast-side down, on a flat surface. Use a boning knife or a thin, pointed knife, and begin at the tail end. Do not cut off the tail. Start scraping the meat off as close to the bones as you can. Work the blade down the chicken, staying close to the bones and turning the chicken whenever you need to. Do not pierce the skin. Flip the meaty section over, turning it inside out, almost as if it were a glove, as you go along. Sever the thigh bones from the back, scraping the meat away from the bones until the drumstick joint is reached. Sever the drumstick joint, leaving the drumstick intact. Remove the thigh bones. Continue to scrape the meat away from the back and rib cage until the wing joints are reached. Sever the wing joints from the back, leaving the wings intact. Continue to scrape the meat from the back and rib cage until the central bone structure has been removed. Turn the skin-side out. The only bones you should be left with are those in the drumsticks and wings.

To cut a whole cooked chicken or duck and reassemble it in the Chinese manner
(a) Snap back the wings to expose the connecting joint. Slice through this joint to separate the wings from the body. (b) With a heavy cleaver, cut the wings into 3 pieces each, preserving all the 'S'-shaped curves and cutting through the middle of bones rather than at their ends. (c) Do somewhat the same with the legs, first removing them from the main body and then (d) cutting them into 5 pieces. (e) Turn the main body of the bird on its side and, with a well-aimed, hard hit, separate the breast from the back. You may have to hit a second time to get through. Sometimes it helps to hit the top of the cleaver with a heavy mallet to get through thick bones. (f) Cut the back crossways into 3 pieces and lay them, in their correct order, on a serving plate. (g) Place the breast, cavity-side down, in front of you and position the cleaver so that it runs lengthways along the centre of the breast, a little to one side of the ridge. Hit the top of the cleaver with a mallet and cut the breast in two. (h) Cut each breast section crossways into 4–5 pieces. Lay the breast pieces, in their correct order, on top of the back pieces.

Now reassemble the legs and wings and put them in their correct places on the plate.

To cut vegetables into julienne strips, dice and slivers
Each vegetable demands its own cutting technique. Generally speaking, you should first cut the vegetable into slices of the required width. Then cut them lengthways into strips. These strips can be cut crossways if small dice are required.

To cut a carrot into julienne strips 5 cm / 2 inches long, cut off the top and tip and then cut the carrot crossways into 5 cm / 2 inch chunks. (a) Cut each chunk lengthways into slices of the desired thickness. (b) Cut each slice lengthways again, to make the strips. (c) Cut each strip into dice, if required.

To cut a shallot or garlic clove into fine strips or slivers, lie it down flat on your work surface. Then, holding the knife parallel to the work surface, cut the shallot or garlic clove horizontally into half or into thirds, depending on its width. Now cut it lengthways into fine slivers.

To peel, devein and clean prawns (shrimp)

In the United Kingdom, these instructions and illustrations apply to the large uncooked prawns known as Pacific or king prawns. These are usually sold frozen and in the shell, but with the heads already removed, but in the rest of the world, they apply to the common prawns (shrimp) that are sold, fresh or frozen, with the heads often removed in the West. If frozen, defrost. (a) First, peel off the shell and, with it, the tiny legs. (b) Pull off the tail. (c) Make a shallow cut down the back of the prawn. (d) Remove the fine digestive cord which runs along the length of it.

It is always a good idea to wash off prawns (shrimp) before cooking them. I think this makes them taste sweeter. To do this, put the peeled and de-veined prawns (shrimp) into a bowl. Add about 1 tablespoon coarse or kosher salt for every 450 g / 1 lb of prawns (shrimp) (unpeeled weight). Rub the prawns (shrimp) with the salt. Wash off the salt. Repeat this one more time. Drain the prawns (shrimp) well and pat them dry. They may now be covered and refrigerated and are ready for cooking.

To clean squid

Twist off the head (with the tentacles). The inner body sac will probably come away with it. If it does not, pull it out. Discard the sac and the hard eye area, which you may have to cut off with a knife. Retain the tentacles. If possible, pull off some of the brownish skin on the tentacles. (You may safely leave this on, if you wish.) Peel the brownish skin from the tube-like body. Discard this skin and pull out the smooth inner cartilage (or pen). The squid can now be washed and used.

Marinating

Meats are often cut up and put into marinades before they are cooked. A marinade tenderises meat and injects it with all the flavours and aromas of its myriad ingredients. The meat can then be grilled or quickly stir-fried while retaining the tastes of all its seasonings.

Basting sauces

As meat, fish or poultry is grilling, it is often basted. Sometimes, as in Japan, the basting sauce has sugar in it so it not only provides flavour but a final glaze as well. In Malaysia, basting sauces may contain coconut milk which provides the lubrication needed to keep the meat, poultry or fish from drying out. In Indonesia and Malaysia, a most practical (and aromatic) brush is made from a stick of lemon grass which is lightly pounded at the end!

Spice pastes

Most curry-style dishes require that a spice paste be prepared first. To this end, fresh and dried spices are pounded in a mortar and then fried in oil to get rid of their raw taste. Freshly pounded spice pastes of good quality are sold in most Thai and Malaysian markets. We in the West have to prepare our own, but we have electric blenders and coffee-grinders to make our lives easier.

Fresh, hot red chillies, pounded to a paste, are a major ingredient in Thai, Indonesian and Malaysian dishes. While many people pound their own chillies at home in a mortar, others are content to buy them, already pounded, in small plastic bags. When I cannot get fresh, hot red chillies, I blend together sweet red peppers and chilli powder (cayenne pepper); this mixture gives just the right colour to the dishes where it is needed.

Cooking coconut milk

When cooking fresh coconut milk, care must be taken that it does not curdle. Stir it constantly as it cooks. Canned coconut milk does not behave in quite the same way as fresh coconut milk as it often has thickeners in it. I often add it only towards the end of the cooking period and then just bring it to a simmer and leave it at that.

If I wish to simmer canned coconut milk for longer periods, I thin it out first with water or stock.

Garnishes which are flavourings

A garnish in the West often means a sprig of parsley, a radish or a tomato cut into a flower. This sits on the edge of the plate, to be admired and perhaps even nibbled upon. It frequently has no real connection with the food it enhances. In the East, what might look like a garnish is often an integral part of a dish. For example, crisply fried shallots and crushed, roasted peanuts may be sprinkled over a dish at the last minute. They are there because without their flavour and texture the dish would be incomplete.

Grilling

Grilling is very popular throughout the Far East. *Satays* (tiny pieces of meat, skewered on bamboo sticks and freshly grilled on charcoal) are sold in the bazaars of Indonesia, Malaysia, Vietnam and Thailand, as everyone loves to eat out. The Koreans cut their meat into strips, marinate it and grill it on their dining-tables. Each home is equipped with special portable burners and grills just for this purpose. The Japanese pierce a fillet of fish with several skewers, then grill it with frequent bastings of sweetish sauces. The skewers are very helpful when it comes to turning the fillets over. As they are inserted against the grain, the fish does not fall apart.

Bamboo skewers should be soaked in water for 30 minutes before use so that they do not burn. Exposed parts can be wrapped in foil.

For fish, I like to use the hinged, double racks that enclose the fish entirely and make turning a totally fearless joy.

Although most of the grilled dishes in this book can be cooked under an indoor kitchen grill (broiler), the taste will be more authentic if you are able to use a barbecue instead. When grilling on charcoal, it is important to get the coals white-hot before you start.

Also, I find that the kettle-shaped grills with lids tend to char the foods much less and tend to cook meats like chicken all the way through rather than leaving them charred on the outside and half-cooked on the inside.

Steaming

Steaming is used for cooking anything from rice to complete dishes. Just as every home in the West has a roasting pan, so every home in the Far East tends to have a steamer. Steaming cooks gently and preserves flavour.

One of the most satisfactory utensils for steaming is a wok because its width easily accommodates a whole fish, a casserole or a large plate of food. Use a wok with a flat base or set a round-based wok on a wire stand. Put a metal or wooden rack or a perforated tray into the wok. (You could use a small inverted tin can instead.)

Now pour in some water. Bring it to a gentle boil and lower in the food so it sits on the rack, tray or can. The water should stay about 2 cm / ¾ inch below the level of the food that is being steamed. Extra boiling water should be kept at hand just in case it is needed to top up the level.

Cover the whole wok, including the food, with a domed wok lid or a large sheet of aluminium foil. The domed lids are preferable as condensed steam rolls down the sides instead of dripping on to the food itself.

If you like, you can also invest in the many-tiered bamboo or aluminium steamers sold in Chinese markets.

Stir-frying

This is fast cooking over high heat in a small amount of oil. A wok is best for this. The oil is heated and flavourings such as garlic and ginger are often tossed around in it before cut meats and vegetables are added. These too, are tossed around quickly until cooked.

Deep-frying

You need several centimetres / inches of oil in a wok or frying-pan and a good deal more in a deep-fat fryer in order to deep-fry. The oil must be heated to the required temperature before you drop in a single morsel of food. Properly deep-fried foods are not at all greasy; the outside is beautifully crisp while the inside is completely cooked.

Oil that has been used for deep-frying may be re-used. Let it cool completely and then strain it. Store it in a bottle. When you cook again, use

half old oil and half fresh oil. Oil that has been used for frying fish should be re-used only for fish.

Dry-roasting

Spices are often dry-roasted before use. It is best to do this in a heavy cast-iron frying-pan which has first been heated. No oil is used: the spices are just stirred around until they brown lightly. Roasted spices develop a heightened, nutty aroma.

They can be stored for several months in an air-tight jar but are best when freshly roasted.

Blanching and refreshing

In order to keep vegetables crisp and their colour bright, they may, after preparation, be plunged very briefly into a large pan of water that is at a rolling boil – boiling furiously. The reason for using a lot of boiling water is that you do not want the temperature of the water to drop when the vegetables are put into it: this would slow their cooking time and therefore affect both their colour and crispness. The vegetables should be cooked in the water until barely tender (but still crisp), drained quickly and then either plunged into a large quantity of iced water or rinsed under cold running water. This helps to set their colour and stop the cooking process. A similar process is used for cooking the dried, flat rice noodles known as *banh pho*. They are dropped into boiling water for about a minute and then drained. After this they are rinsed under cold water, not just to cool them but to wash off the sticky starch.

Poaching

Many recipes require that chicken breasts be poached in water to just cover. Breast meat is fairly dry and it toughens easily. To poach properly, it is important that the water be barely simmering. If it boils too rapidly, it will toughen the meat.

Braising

This also involves cooking foods slowly in liquid but over a long period. Whole birds and fish can be cooked this way. The liquid is always flavoured.

EQUIPMENT

A wok

This is an all-purpose utensil that may be used for steaming, simmering, stir-frying or deep-frying.

A wok is traditionally a round-bottomed pan. Because of its shape, flames can encircle it and allow it to heat quickly and efficiently. It is most economical for deep-frying as it will hold a good depth of oil without needing the quantity a straight-sided pan would require. It is ideal for stir-frying as foods can be vigorously tossed around in it. As they hit nothing but well-heated surfaces, they cook fast and retain their moisture at the same time.

Choosing a wok: What kind of wok should you buy? Advances are being made all the time and every year seems to bring new woks on to the market. Traditional woks of good quality are made either of thin tempered iron or carbon steel. The ideal wok is 35 cm / 14 inches in diameter and fairly deep. (Saucer-shaped shallow woks are quite useless.) A round-bottomed wok works well on a gas hob (burner). A new, somewhat flat-bottomed wok has been invented for people who have electric hobs (burners). I cannot say I love it. Instead I have opted for a yet newer invention in my country house in the USA which has an all-electric kitchen.

This is an electric wok – but a very special one. It is the only electric wok I know which heats very quickly, becomes *very* hot and allows foods to be both stir-fried and simmered, though I must add that it is better for stir-frying than it is for simmering.

Seasoning a wok: The iron and carbon steel woks leave the factory coated with oil. This needs to be scrubbed off with a cream cleanser. Then a wok needs to be seasoned. Rinse it in water and set it over low heat. Now brush it all over with about 2 tablespoons vegetable oil. Let it heat for 10–15 minutes. Wipe the oil off with a paper towel. Brush the wok with more oil and repeat the process 3–4 times. The wok is now seasoned. Do not scrub it again; just wash it with hot water and then wipe it dry. It will *not* have a scrubbed look. It will, however, become more and more 'non-stick' as it is used.

Wok accessories: For use on a gas hob (burner), a wok needs a stand that not only stabilises it but allows air to circulate underneath. The perfect stand is made of wire. The collar variety with punched holes seems to kill free circulation of air heat and should not be used on gas hobs (burners).

When you buy a wok, it is also a good idea to invest in a curved spatula, a steaming tray and a lid.

Cast-iron frying-pans

I find a 13 cm / 5 inch cast-iron frying-pan ideal for roasting spices and a large one perfect for pan-grilling thin slices of meat. All cast-iron frying-pans can be heated without any liquid and they retain an even temperature.

Once properly seasoned, they should never be scrubbed with abrasive cleaners.

Electric blender and coffee-grinder, mortar and pestle

In the Far East, mortars, pestles and grinding stones of varying shapes, sizes and materials are used to pulverise everything from sesame seeds to fresh, hot red chillies. I find it much easier to use an electric blender for wet ingredients and a clean electric coffee-grinder for dry ones. For small quantities, you may still want to use a heavy mortar and pestle.

Grater

The Japanese make a special grater for ginger and Japanese horseradish which produces a fine pulp. It has tiny hair-like spikes that are perfect for their purpose. It you ever find one, do buy it. Otherwise use the finest part of an ordinary grater for grating fresh ginger.

Double-boiler

This is simply one pan balanced over another. The lower pan holds boiling water and allows the ingredients in the other pan to cook very gently. Double-boilers are available from good kitchen-ware shops but they can be easily improvised.

Electric rice-cooker

Many households in the Far East seem to have one of these gadgets. Its main use is to free all burners on the hob (burner) for other purposes and make the cooking of rice an easy, almost mindless task. I do have one and use it only for plain rice.

Deep-fat fryer

For those who are afraid of deep-frying, this is a godsend. Because it has a lid that closes over all splattering foods, this piece of equipment also helps to make deep-frying a painless, safe and clean task.

Racks for grilling fish

In Indonesia and Malaysia, hinged double racks are used for grilling fish over charcoal. The fish lies sandwiched between the two racks and can be easily turned and basted. Many types of hinged, double fish racks are available in the West, some even shaped like a fish. Most of them are sold by kitchen equipment stores. I find them exceedingly useful.

The kitchen of a house in Penang's China Town in Malaysia.

INGREDIENTS

anchovy paste The best substitute I can think of for the varying types of shrimp paste used in South-East Asia. Most of the better supermarkets and certainly all speciality food shops sell it.

bainiku See plum paste, sour.

bamboo shoots Unfortunately, we cannot get fresh bamboo shoots in the West and must make do with tinned ones. Good quality ones are crisp, creamy white with a clean refreshing taste. Among the better brands is Companion. Their winter bamboo shoots in water are generally of excellent quality. So are those labelled Green Bamboo Shoots. You can buy bamboo shoots in rather large hunks which can then be cut up into cubes of the desired size or you can buy the cone-shaped and very tender bamboo shoot tips which are usually cut into comb-like wedges.

All bamboo shoots that come out of a tin have a faintly tinny taste. They should be washed in fresh water and drained before being used. Any bamboo shoots that are unused may be covered with clean water and stored in a closed jar in the refrigerator. In order to keep the bamboo shoots fresh, the water should be changed every day.

banh pho See noodles.

barley, roasted This is used to make tea in both Korea and Japan. In Korea, this tea may well be considered the national drink. The roasted grains are sold as *mugi cha* in Japanese shops and *bori cha* in Korean shops. Store as you would any tea, in a closed cannister.

basil Many different types of fresh basil are used in South-East Asia. Each country – sometimes states within the same country – has different names for the basils such as *daun kemangi* and *ruku ruku* in Indonesia. There is sweet basil *ocinum basilicum* (*bai horappa* in Thailand), holy basil *ocinum sanctum* (*bai kaprow* in Thailand), lemon basil *ocinum canum* (*bai manglak* in Thailand). Ordinary basil and fresh mint are the best substitutes for the very aromatic South-East Asian basils.

bean curd White, milky, custard-like squares made out of soaked, mashed and strained soy beans. Bean curd is sold by all oriental grocers and health food shops. It is generally labelled soft, medium or hard. For the purposes of this book, use soft bean curd for soups, hard bean curd when it needs to be fried and medium bean curd for everything else. Bean curd squares are sold packed in water. When you bring them home, if you're not using them immediately, put them in a bowl, cover with fresh water and refrigerate. Change the water every day. Bean curd tends to turn very satiny if it is simmered very gently for 2 minutes.

bean sauce, black Commercially prepared sauces made out of fermented soy beans are used throughout Malaysia and other parts of South-East Asia. They can be very thick, filled with crumbled beans, or they can be smooth and somewhat thinner. Use any black bean sauce that is available. Once you have opened a bottle you should keep it tightly closed in the refrigerator.

bean sauce, yellow Like the sauce above, this is a commercially prepared sauce of fermented soy beans, only it has a very pale brown, almost yellowish colour. It can be smooth but I like to use the kind that has whole or halved beans in it.

Bean Sauce with Chilli, Chinese Sometimes called Bean Paste with Chilli, this reddish-brown paste is sold bottled at Chinese grocers. It is quite hot.

bean paste, fermented See *kochu chang*, *miso* and *toen chang*.

bean paste, sweet, red See Red bean paste, sweet.

bean sprouts, mung These are crisp sprouts grown from the same mung beans that are sold in Indian stores as whole *moong*. They can now be bought in supermarkets and health food shops as well as all Eastern grocers. They are good when they are crisp and white. As they are usually kept in water, they tend to get soggier and soggier as they get older. When you buy bean sprouts and bring them home you should rinse them off first and then put them into a bowl of fresh water. The bowl should be covered and then refrigerated. If the beans are not used by the next day, you should change the water again.

It is considered proper to 'top' and 'tail' bean sprouts before using them. This means pinching off the remains of the whole bean at the top as well as the thread-like tail at the bottom. This requires a lot of patience. The sprouts do indeed look better when they have been pinched this way but I have to admit that I very rarely do it. Bean sprouts are also sold in tins. I never use them as they do not have the crunch that makes the sprouts worthwhile in the first place.

black beans, salted These are salted, spiced and fermented soy beans. In their dry form they are often sold in plastic bags. They need to be rinsed slightly to remove excess salt and then chopped before being used. They are also available in tins as 'Black Beans in Salted Sauce'. These are whole black beans that tend to float in liquid. Lift them out of their liquid, chop them and use them as the recipe suggests.

black fungus See fungus, black.

bonito stock See *dashi*.

bonito, dried Known as *katsuo-bushi* in Japan, this fish of the tuna family is filleted and dried until it resembles petrified wood. It is then shaved with a plane to make *hana-katsuo*. It is these pinkish, paper-thin shavings that are used to make the basic Japanese stock, *dashi*. The best *hana-katsuo* is freshly shaved. It does, however, come already shaved, packed in plastic bags or in cornflakes-like boxes. Once *hana-katsuo* packets have been opened, store the flakes in air-tight containers as moisture spoils them.

bori cha See barley, roasted.

cakalang Pronounced 'chaa-kaa-laang', this is fresh bonito (see above) that has been smoked. It is used in many parts of Indonesia such as North Sulawesi and the Moluccas. Smoked mackerel makes a very good substitute.

candle nuts Called *kemiri* in Indonesia and *buah keras* in Malaysia, these nuts are used in curry pastes to give thickness and texture. As they are not easily available in the West, a reasonable substitute would be raw cashew nuts or raw macadamia nuts, both of which are available from health food shops.

cardamom, whole pods These small, green-coloured pods have the most aromatic black seeds inside them. The pods are used to flavour curries, rice dishes and Indian-style desserts. In the West, bleached, whitish pods can be found in most supermarkets. They are less aromatic but they may be used as a substitute for the green variety.

cardamom seeds, ground The seeds of the cardamom pods are sold by themselves in both their whole and ground forms. The powder can be put into rice dishes, desserts and Indian-style meat dishes.

cashew nuts These nuts travelled from the Americas via Africa and India all the way to China. In this book they are used in their raw form as a substitute for candle nuts. It might be useful for you to know that all so-called 'raw' cashews have been processed to remove the prussic acid they contain in their natural state.

cassia bark This is Chinese cinnamon, sometimes known as 'false cinnamon'. It is thicker, coarser and generally cheaper than true cinnamon but with a stronger flavour.

chilli bean sauce A reddish-brown, very hot and spicy sauce made of soy beans, red chillies and other seasonings. It is used in the cooking of western China and is sold in bottles by oriental grocers.

chilli oil This is an orange-coloured oil that gets its heat and its colour from red chillies. Small amounts of it can be put into dishes as they are being cooked to add a bit of pep to them. Many Chinese restaurants have small bottles of oil on the table for those who wish to season their own foods further. Chilli oil can be bought from any oriental grocer, or see the recipe on p. 199.

chilli paste, Thai The Thai chilli paste, *nam prik pow*, is made by frying pounded shallots, garlic, dried shrimp and chillies together and then combining them with palm sugar and tamarind until the seasonings have the consistency of a thick jam. My recipe appears on p. 200. *Nam prik pow* is sold by Thai grocers. Unfortunately, the bottles are not always labelled as such in English. It is best to ask for help and tell the shop assistant whether you want it hot, medium or mild as it comes in all three strengths. It lasts for a long time and should be kept tightly covered and refrigerated. It may be added to soups, stews and stir-fries. If you cannot find it, you can add a certain amount of similar seasoning to your food by combining one part each of chilli powder and sugar with two parts vegetable oil. Even simpler alternatives are suggested in some recipes.

Chilli Paste with Garlic, Chinese This reddish paste is available in bottles at Chinese grocers. Dollops of it make an excellent, spicy addition to dipping sauces.

chilli powder A powder made by grinding dried, hot red chillies, not the Mexican-style chilli powder that is mixed with cumin. Since people prefer different degrees of hotness, you should add as much or as little of the chilli powder as you like. Be warned that chilli powders vary in their heat. Coarse, Korean powder is made by pounding dried red chilli skins. It is hot but not excruciatingly so and has an exquisite carmine colour. I tend to stock up on it whenever I visit Korean supermarkets. They seem to be the only ones that sell it. It is this powder that gives many Korean foods their rich red colour. It is a good chilli powder to know about.

Chilli Sauce This ready-made, sweet, sour and hot sauce is sold bottled by Chinese grocers.

chillies, fresh, green and red Chillies originated in the Americas and then travelled via Africa and India all the way to China and Korea. The East has adopted them with a passion almost unmatched in the countries of their origin. Red chillies are just ripe green chillies. However, their flavour is slightly different, though their intensity can be exactly the same.

Red chillies are used in hundreds of South-East Asian curry pastes not only for their heat but for the beautiful colour and thickening they give to the sauce. The ideal chillies for South-East Asian sauces are the slim red ones that can be a good 13 cm / 5 inches in length. They are usually of medium heat. If you cannot find them use a combination of our more common red pepper combined with paprika and chilli powder as a substitute. Hot chillies must be handled carefully. When you are cutting them, be careful not to touch your eyes or your lips with your fingers or they will burn.

Tiny 'bird's eye' chillies, both red and green (called *prik-khi-nu* in Thailand), are ferociously hot. They are often thrown in whole or cut into thin rounds over curries, partly as a colourful garnish and partly for flavour.

Chillies are a very rich source of iron and Vitamins A and C. As they vary tremendously in size, shape and heat, it might take a little experimenting to find the ones you like most. To store fresh red or green chillies wrap them first in newspaper, then in plastic, and store in the refrigerator. They should last several weeks. Any that begin to soften and rot should be removed as they tend to infect the whole batch.

To remove seeds from dried chillies, break off the stem end and shake the seeds out. Rotating a chilli between the fingers can help. Sometimes it is necessary to break the chilli in order to get all the seeds out.

Chillies are also used to provide a decorative element. Sometimes they are sliced into rings, at other times into slivers, and often they are cut to resemble flowers.

To make chilli flowers: Just cut off a little bit of the very tip. Leave the stem attached. Now make 4 cuts lengthways, starting from a little above the stem and going all the way to the tip. You should now have 4 sections that are attached at the bottom.

Remove all the seeds and then put the chillies to soak in cold water until they open up into flowers.

Chinese cabbage There is great confusion about what Chinese cabbage is. To me, Chinese cabbage is the very chunky, pale green, slightly elongated, wide-ribbed cabbage that is generally about 13 cm / 5 inches or more in diameter. Its leaves resemble the leaves of the vegetable that is sold as Chinese leaves (celery cabbage). They rise upwards in the same way. They are, however, much wider and have greater flavour. In the United States it is sometimes called Napa cabbage. This is the vegetable that is used to make the Korean cabbage pickle called *kimchee*. If you cannot get it, use Chinese leaves (celery cabbage) as a substitute.

Chinese celery This resembles Italian flat-leaved parsley. It is larger and coarser and its thin stalks have a decided celery flavour. Celery sticks, diced fine, and celery leaves can be used as substitutes. Follow directions in individual recipes.

Chinese rice wine Several rice wines are used in Chinese cookery, the most common being Shao-Hsing. This is whisky-coloured and has a rich sweetish taste.

A reasonable substitute is dry sherry. I find that La Ina comes the closest in flavour. This sherry has a far better taste than the produce labelled 'Chinese cooking wine'.

Chinese egg noodles See noodles.

Chinese ham Salted, smoked and dried, whole Chinese hams are a common sight in China and Hong Kong. The best ones come from Yunnan and Jinhua (Zhejiang province). Smaller, cut portions are sold by grocers and are used both as flavourings and accents as well as in dishes such as the Hunan speciality of ham slices with a sweet sauce served with thin slices of steamed bread. Before being used, they need to be scraped clean of mould, soaked thoroughly – a 1 cm / ½ inch thick slice should be soaked for at least 30 minutes – and then steamed for 30 minutes to 1 hour.

The only worthy substitute is American, Smithfield-type ham.

Chinese leaves Also called celery cabbage. This is an exceedingly slim version of Chinese cabbage. See Chinese cabbage.

Chinese mushrooms See mushrooms

chives, Chinese The leaves of Chinese chives are flat and have a pronounced garlic-like flavour. During the season in which the plant is budding, buds, still attached to their stalks, are also sold. They add a wonderful touch to stir-fried dishes. Ordinary chives can be used as a substitute (use their young buds as well).

Chinese sausages Available only in Chinese markets, they can usually be found hanging in the open. Lightly sweet and salty, they need to be cooked before being eaten. The most common method is to steam them for about 20 minutes. The Chinese often lay them on top of rice during the last 20 minutes of its cooking time. This steams the sausages and flavours the rice. The sausages are sliced before being served. They can also be minced and added to vegetables as they are being stir-fried. The most commonly available sausages are the reddish ones, which are pork, and the darker ones, which are duck's liver.

coconut, fresh When buying a coconut, look for one that shows no signs of mould and is free of cracks. Shake the coconut. If it has a lot of water in it, it has a better chance of being good. People generally weigh a coconut in each hand and pick the heavier of the two. In the West it is always safer to buy an extra coconut just in case one turns out to be bad.

To break open a coconut, use the unsharpened side of a cleaver and hit the coconut hard all around its equator. You can hold the coconut in one hand over a large bowl while you hit with the other, or you can rest the coconut on a stone while you hit it and then rush it to a bowl as soon as the first crack appears. The bowl is there to catch the coconut water. Some people like to drink it. I do. This coconut water, by the way, is generally not

used in cooking. But it is a good indication of the sweetness and freshness of the coconut.

You should now have two halves. Before proceeding any further, cut off a small bit of the meat and taste it. The dreaded word here is 'rancid'! Your coconut should taste sweet. If it is lacking in sweetness, it can be endured. But it must never be rancid or mouldy inside. Now remove the tough outer shell by slipping a knife between it and the meat and then prising the meat out. Sometimes it helps to crack the halves into smaller pieces to do this.

This meat now has a thin brown skin. If your recipe calls for fresh grated coconut, peel the skin off with a vegetable peeler or a knife, cut the meat into small cubes and throw the cubes into the container of a food processor or electric blender. When you blend you will not get a paste. What you will get is something resembling grated coconut. You can freeze what you don't use.

Grated coconut freezes very well and it is a good idea to keep some at hand.

As a substitute for freshly grated coconut, you can use desiccated, unsweetened coconut which is sold in most health food shops. Here is how you do this: To get the equivalent of 60 g / 2 oz / 8 tablespoons of freshly grated coconut, take 30 g / 1 oz / 5 tablespoons unsweetened, desiccated coconut and soak it in 4 tablespoons water for about 1 hour.

coconut milk This is best made from fresh coconuts but is also available canned, or it can be made by using powdered milk, unsweetened desiccated coconut or blocks of creamed coconut. No prepared coconut milk keeps well – this includes canned coconut milk after the can has been opened. Its life in a refrigerator is no longer than 2 days.

Using fresh coconut: First you prise off the flesh as suggested above. Whether you peel the brown skin or not depends on the dish. If it needs to look pale and pristine, remove the skin. If not, leave it on and grate the meat in a food processor or electric blender (see above). To make about 350 ml /

12 fl oz / 1½ cups coconut milk, fill a glass measuring jug to the 450 ml / ¾ pint / 2 cup mark with grated coconut. Empty it into an electric blender or food processor. Add 300 ml / ½ pint / 1¼ cups very hot water. Blend for a few seconds. Line a sieve with a piece of muslin or cheesecloth and place it over a bowl. Empty the contents of the blender into the sieve. Gather the ends of the cloth together and squeeze out all the liquid. For most of my recipes, this is the coconut milk that is needed. It is sometimes referred to as 'thick coconut milk'. If a recipe calls for thin coconut milk, the entire process needs to be repeated using the squeezed-out coconut and the same amount of water. If you let the thick coconut milk sit for a while, cream will rise to the top. That is why I suggest that you always stir the coconut milk before using it.

If just the cream is required, then spoon it off the top.

Canned coconut milk: This is available from most Asian grocers but the quality varies. There is a brand which I like very much and use frequently. It is Chaokoh and is a product of Thailand. It is white and creamy and quite delicious. As the cream tends to rise to the top in a can as it does with fresh coconut milk, always stir it well before using it. Sometimes, because of the fat it contains, canned coconut milk tends to get very grainy. You can either whir it for a second in an electric blender or else beat it well. I find that whereas you can cook a fish, for example, in fresh coconut milk for a long time, canned coconut milk, which behaves differently, is best added toward the end. Canned coconut is very thick, partly because it has thickeners in it. As a result, many of my recipes require that canned coconut milk be thinned before use.

Powdered coconut milk: You can now buy packets of powdered coconut milk from oriental grocers and supermarkets. Their quality varies from good to poor, the poor ones containing hard-to-dissolve globules of fat. Emma brand from Malaysia is acceptable. Directions for making the milk are always on the packets. The process usually involves

mixing an equal volume of powder and hot water and stirring well. Unwanted lumps should be strained away. This milk is best added to recipes towards the end of the cooking time.

Using unsweetened, desiccated coconut: Put 115 g / 4 oz / 2 cups of unsweetened desiccated coconut into a pan. Add 600 ml / 1 pint / 2½ cups water and bring to a simmer. Now pour the contents into the container of an electric blender or food processor and blend for 1 minute. Strain the resulting mixture through a double thickness of cheesecloth, pushing out as much liquid as you can. You should get about 350 ml / 12 fl oz / 1½ cups of thick coconut milk. If you repeat the process with the same amount of water, using the leftover coconut, you can get another 450 ml / ¾ pint / 2 cups of thin coconut milk.

Using creamed coconut: Available in block form, this can also be turned into coconut milk. I do not advise that you do this if you need large quantities of milk. However, if just a few table-spoons are required, you can, for example, take 2 tablespoons of creamed coconut and mix them with 2 tablespoons hot water. The thick coconut milk that will result should only be put into dishes at the last moment.

coriander seeds, whole and ground These are the round, beige seeds of the coriander plant. They are sold either whole or ground. You can grind them yourself in a coffee-grinder and then put them through a fine sieve. If roasted and ground coriander seeds are called for, put a few tablespoons of seeds in a small, cast-iron frying-pan over medium-high heat. Stir and roast for a few minutes or until the seeds are a few shades darker and smell roasted. Then grind in a clean coffee-grinder or other spice-grinder. If they are very coarse, put them through a fine sieve. What is not needed immediately may be stored in a tightly lidded jar and saved for later use.

coriander, green, leaves, roots and stem This is the parsley of the eastern and southern half of Asia. Generally, just the delicate, fragrant, green leaves are used. In Thai curries, however, the equally fragrant white root is ground or chopped in as well. It should be very well washed first. Some recipes also call for the stems, which are generally cut crossways into minute dice. When you buy fresh coriander, the best way to keep it is to stand it in a glass of water, cover it with a plastic bag and refrigerate. Break off the leaves, stems and roots as you need them and keep the rest refrigerated. The water should be changed daily and dead leaves removed.

cumin seeds, whole and ground This spice came into South-East Asia with Arab and Indian traders. Sometimes it is used whole, though in this region it is generally ground with the spice paste for curries. If roasted and ground cumin seeds are called for, put a few tablespoons of seeds in a small, cast-iron frying-pan over medium-high heat. Stir and roast for a few minutes or until the seeds are a few shades darker and smell roasted. Then grind in a clean coffee-grinder or other spice-grinder. What is not needed immediately may be stored in a tightly lidded jar and saved for later use.

curry leaves, fresh and dried These highly aromatic leaves are used in much of South-East Asian cookery. In Indonesia, they are known as *daun salaam* and are a slightly larger variety. They are always used in their fresh form. They are now increasingly available in the West. You could use the dried leaf if the fresh is unavailable. Its aroma is very limited. Indian grocers sell both fresh and dried curry leaves. They come attached to stalks. They can be pulled off their stalks in one swoop. Keep curry leaves in a flat, plastic bag. They last for several days in the refrigerator. They may also be frozen, so when you do see them in the market, buy them and store them in your freezer.

daikon See radish, white.

dashi Dashi is Japanese soup stock. The most common kind is made with a

combination of shavings from dried bonito fillets (*hana-katsuo*) and a dried kelp called *konbu*. A recipe for *dashi* can be found on p. 198.

dashi-no-moto This is instant *dashi*. It comes in the form of granules and is generally salted. It is sold under many brand names. The kind I use requires 2 teaspoons of the granules to be mixed with 450 ml / ¾ pint / 2 cups hot water to become a basic Japanese stock. Sometimes I add to it 1 teaspoon *mirin*, 1 tablespoon Japanese light soy sauce and a good pinch of salt if I want extra flavour.

daun salaam See curry leaves.

dried mandarin peel See mandarin peel, dried.

evaporated milk Available in cans, this is milk which has been condensed but not sweetened. It is used quite a lot in the cooking of Malaysia and the Philippines.

fennel seeds These seeds look and taste like anise seeds, only they are larger and plumper. To grind fennel seeds, just put 2–3 tablespoons into the container of a clean coffee-grinder or other spice-grinder and grind as finely as possible. Store in an air-tight container.

fish sauce Known as *nam pla* in Thailand, *nuoc mam* in Vietnam, and *patis* in the Philippines, it is used in these countries much as soy sauce is used in China. It must be noted, however, that it exists, in some form, in *all* Far Eastern countries. It is a thin, salty, brown liquid made from salted shrimp or fish. It has a very special flavour of its own. You can either use salt as a substitute or else improvise a sauce by combining 1 tablespoon water with ½ teaspoon salt, ¼ teaspoon soy sauce and ¼ teaspoon sugar. In odd recipes, I have suggested simpler alternatives. A Japanese version of this sauce is called *shotsuru*.

Five-spice powder A Chinese spice mixture, it contains star anise, fennel,

cloves, cinnamon and Sichuan peppercorns. It is sold already ground by Chinese grocers. To make it yourself, combine 2 whole star anise, 1 teaspoon whole fennel seeds, 1 teaspoon whole cloves, a 5 cm / 2 inch stick of cinnamon or cassia bark and 1 tablespoon Sichuan peppercorns. Grind as finely as possible and store in a tightly lidded jar.

fruit, fresh See pages 203–206.

fungus, black Also known as *mo-er* mushrooms and cloud ears, this tree fungus is a speciality of the Sichuan province. It is sold in the form of little, dried, curled-up black chips. Once they have been soaked, they enlarge quite a bit. At this stage, you should feel with your fingers for their little hard 'eyes' and snip them off. Rinse them well as they tend to be very gritty. They have no particular flavour of their own but add a very nice crunchy texture. Of late, it has been rumoured that they are very good for the heart as well. Black fungus comes in two sizes, small and large. Unless otherwise stated, use only the smaller, more delicate ones.

galangal Known as *laos* and *lengkuas* in Indonesia, *langkuas* in Malaysia and *kha* in Thailand, this ginger-like rhizome has a very distinct earthy aroma of its own. It is now sold, both fresh and frozen, by South-East Asian grocers. In the curry-type recipes which require it, fresh or frozen galangal is best. You could use the sliced, dried variety but it would need to be soaked before it is ground.

garlic This is used in large quantities in South-East Asia. Very often it is sliced, fried into crisp chips and either scattered over foods as a garnish or mixed in with them to give them an added, delicious flavour.

ghee This is butter that has been so thoroughly clarified that it can even be used for deep-frying. As it no longer contains milk solids, refrigeration is not necessary. It has a nutty, buttery taste. All Indian grocers sell it and I find it more convenient to buy it. If, however,

you need to make it, take 450 g / 1 lb of unsalted butter, put it in a pan over low heat and let it simmer very gently until the milky solids turn brownish and cling to the sides of the pan or fall to the bottom. The time this takes will depend on the amount of water in the butter. Watch carefully towards the end and do not let it burn. Strain the *ghee* through a triple layer of cheese-cloth. Home-made *ghee* is best stored in the refrigerator.

ginger, fresh You almost cannot cook without ginger in the Far East. This rhizome has a sharp, pungent, cleansing taste and is a digestive to boot. Its brown skin is generally peeled, though in Chinese cookery the skin is often left on.

When finely grated ginger is required, it should first be peeled and then grated on the finest part of a grater so it turns into pulp. When a recipe requires that 2.5 cm / 1 inch of ginger be grated, it is best to keep that piece attached to the large knob. The knob acts as a handle and saves you from grating your fingers.

Ginger should be stored in a dry, cool place. Many people like to bury it in dryish, sandy soil. This way they can break off and retrieve small portions as they need them while the rest of the knob keeps growing.

glutinous rice See rice.

glutinous rice powder This powder, made of glutinous rice (also called sweet rice) is used mainly for desserts. It is sold by all East Asian grocers. Store as you would any flour.

groundnut oil See oils.

hana-katsuo See bonito, dried.

Hoisin Sauce This is a thick, slightly sweet, smooth Chinese bean sauce with a light garlic flavour. It may be used in cooking or as a dip. It is sold by Chinese grocers. If you buy it in a can, store the unused portion in a tightly lidded jar which you should refrigerate.

holy basil (*bai kaprow*) See basil.

jaggery A form of raw, lump, cane sugar. It is sold in pieces cut off from larger blocks. You should look for the kind that crumbles easily and is not rock-hard. It can be found in Indian grocers. This is the best substitute for the palm sugar that is used in South-East Asia.

kaffir lime rind, fresh and dried See kaffir lime.

kaffir lime, leaves and rind A dark-green, knobbly lime. Its peel and leaves are used in South-East Asian cookery. They are all highly aromatic and there is no real substitute for their flavour. If you are lucky enough to get fresh leaves, you should tear them in half and pull off their coarse centre veins before using them in a dish. If a recipe requires that the leaves be cut into fine, hair-thin shreds, first remove the centre vein and then use a pair of kitchen scissors to cut the shreds. Left-over leaves can be made to last by freezing them in a flat plastic packet. Whole limes may be frozen as well. The peel and leaves are sometimes available dried. You should use them in whatever form you can find them. The leaves, dried rind and lime itself are sold by Far Eastern and some Chinese grocers. The rind is sometimes labelled as *piwma grood*. The dried rind needs to be soaked in water first. When soft, discard the soaking water (it is bitter) and then scrape off any pith that may be clinging to the rind.

kailan This is the Cantonese name for a wonderful green of the cabbage family. Deep green in colour, it is close in taste to broccoli but does not have this vegetable's head. It is basically all leaves with tasty stems and small flowering heads. It is usually available from Chinese grocers.

katsuo-bushi See bonito, dried.

kecap manis See soy sauce.

kenari **nuts** These almond-like nuts grow profusely in the Moluccas, the Spice Islands of Indonesia, on tall trees that provide shade for the more delicate nutmeg trees. The nuts are put into everything from ginger tea and cakes to salad dressings. Almonds make the best substitute.

kochu chang A spicy paste made with fermented soy beans and red chillies, this is a very common seasoning in Korea and can be bought in the West only from Korean supermarkets. A recipe to improvise your own is on p. 200.

kokum Various souring agents are used in Indonesian cookery. *Asem candis* is very popular in western Sumatra. This is the dried skin of a mangosteen-like fruit. As it is hard to find in the West, I use the Indian *kokum* which is very similar.

konbu Green, calcium-rich, dried kelp used for making stock (*dashi*) in Japan. It is sometimes sold as *dashi-konbu*. It resembles long, large leaves and comes either folded up or cut into small pieces. *Konbu* (sometimes spelled *kombu*) should never be washed as its flavour resides near the surface. It should be wiped with a damp cloth just before use. *Konbu* may be allowed to simmer gently but should never boil vigorously. When buying it, the price is generally a good indication of the quality.

krupuk These are Indonesian wafers somewhat similar to Indian poppadum and can be served with most meals. They come in different flavours. The base, however, is frequently tapioca. When uncooked, *krupuks* are hard and brittle. When fried, they expand and turn very crisp.

krupuk udang See prawn (shrimp) wafers.

lemon grass, fresh and dried Known as *seré* in Indonesia, *serai* in Malaysia, *takrai* in Thailand, and *tangiad* in the Philippines, lemon grass is a tall, hard greyish-green grass used for its aroma and flavour in much of South-East Asian cookery. Usually, only the bottom 15 cm / 6 inches are used. The very bottom can be bruised (hitting it with a hammer will do that) and then thrown into a pan, or the lemon grass can be sliced first.

Lemon grass is fairly hard. To slice, first cut off the hard knot at the very end and then slice crossways into paper-thin slices. Even when lemon grass is to be ground to a pulp in an electric blender, it needs to be sliced thinly first or else it does not grind properly. Lemon grass is best stored with its bottom end in a little water. This prevents it from drying out. You can also freeze the stalks. To defrost, just run under hot water briefly.

In South-East Asia, lemon grass is always used fresh. We are beginning to see it more and more in the West. Unfortunately, many of us in the West still have to make do with the dried variety. I buy the dried, sliced lemon grass and then soak it before I use it. Lemon grass, as its name suggests, has a citrus flavour and aroma though it is not at all sour. The best (though nowhere as good) equivalent is lemon peel. The peel of quarter of a lemon may be used instead of a stick of lemon grass. A few of my recipes call for powdered lemon grass. This is sold by South-East Asian grocers.

lime, lime juice Limes of various sorts are plentiful in East Asia and are used with some abandon. The Philippines has the very small *kalamansi* lime which is squeezed over many foods and makes excellent limeade. There is the kaffir lime of Indochina with its unmatched aroma, and then there is the lime that we know in the West, though here it is generally found in a smaller size. If you cannot get limes, use lemons as a substitute.

long beans Also known as asparagus beans and yard-long beans, these can indeed be very long. In East Asia they come in two colours, pale and dark green, the darker one being the crisper of the two. In the West, we have to take what we can get. They are generally cut into smaller lengths and then used just like green beans. The best substitute is, indeed, green beans.

mandarin peel, dried This is the dried peel of a mandarin orange, used in cooking. It should not be confused with preserved mandarin peel, which is seasoned and generally eaten out of the hand.

matsutake **mushrooms** See mushrooms.

minari A Korean herb found in the West only in Korean supermarkets. It is somewhat like a tall, elongated version of parsley but has its own, special aroma. Generally, only the long stems are used in cooking. I have used the stems of flat-leaved Italian parsley as a substitute.

mint Mints of various sorts fill the vegetable shops of South-East Asia. They are used in cooking and are also nibbled at on the side or, as in Vietnam, added to morsels of food just as they are about to be eaten. Nothing but fresh mint can be used for this purpose.

Remember that you can always grow mint indoors in a pot.

mirin Sweetened *sake* used in cooking, available from Japanese grocers. It is sometimes labelled as *aji-mirin*, or has some other prefix. If you cannot find *mirin*, make an approximation by combining equal parts of *sake* and sugar and then cooking them gently until the sugar dissolves and the liquid is reduced to half.

miso A Japanese paste made from fermented soy beans, also containing other fermented grains. Among the *miso* easily available in the West is *aka-miso*, a reddish-brown variety. This is the one used most commonly in this book. *Miso* can always be found in health food shops. Sometimes it is labelled according to its colour, such as red *miso*, brown *miso*, yellow *miso* and white *miso*.

In Japan, *miso* is available in almost every shade and texture. It can be used for soups and stews, it can be lathered on to vegetables such as aubergines (eggplants) before they are grilled and it can also be used in the preparation of pickles and dressings.

To make soup, *miso* needs to be dissolved in water and then strained. In

Japan, it is never allowed to boil vigorously. The Koreans, who use a similar paste called *toen chang*, do allow it to boil, with no disastrous results.

mitsuba A Japanese herb of the parsley family, it has its own, rather unusual taste. Italian, flat-leaved parsley makes the best substitute.

mung beans, whole Yellow beans with green skins. These beans are sold both in East Asian and Indian markets. It is these beans that are sprouted and sold as bean sprouts.

mung beans, hulled and split These yellow split beans are sold by almost every East Asian grocer/market. If you have access to an Indian grocer, buy *moong dal*. It is the same thing. Before cooking you should look through it for sticks and stones and then wash it in a few changes of water.

mushroom soy sauce This soy sauce flavoured with mushrooms can be found only in Chinese supermarkets. If you cannot find it, use Chinese light soy sauce as a substitute.

mushrooms Hundreds of varieties are sold in East Asia, from tiny pinheads to large meaty ones. In the West, we can only get some of them and then mostly in their dried or canned versions. Of late, a few expensive speciality stores have begun to sell fresh, oriental mushrooms.

Chinese dried mushrooms: These are available in most oriental shops. The Japanese *shiitake* is the same mushroom. Price is generally an indication of quality. The thicker the caps, the meatier the texture. They need to be soaked in plenty of warm water before they are used. Once the mushrooms are soft, lift them out of their soaking liquid – this leaves the grit behind. The texture of the stalks remains hard, even after soaking, so they need to be cut off and discarded. The water in which the mushrooms have soaked should be strained and saved. It can be added to stocks or used to cook vegetables.

Straw mushrooms: Smooth and meaty at the same time, there is nothing quite as delicious as a fresh straw mushroom. I eagerly await the day when they will be as commonly available in the West as they are in the East. We have to make do with the tinned variety. Drain them first, rinse off, and then use as the recipe suggests.

Among the fresh oriental mushrooms now increasingly available in speciality shops are oyster mushrooms (delicate, excellent in stir-fries); *shiitake* (the Japanese name for the mushroom commonly used, both fresh and dried, in China, Korea and Japan, they have meaty caps but woody stems, and can be used in soups, stews and stir-fries); and *matsutake* (woodsy, and much celebrated, wild pine mushrooms available only in the autumn, which may be grilled/broiled or used in a soup or *chawanmushi* where they are featured).

mustard seeds, black and yellow Black mustard seeds are used in curry pastes in some parts of South-East Asia. The seeds are tiny, round and of a blackish or reddish-brown colour. They can be bought from Indian grocers. Yellow mustard seeds may be substituted for the black ones.

nam prik pow See chilli paste, Thai.

noodles Noodles were thought to have originated in this area, though many now believe that they were born in the Middle East and travelled both East and West from there. They are sold dried and fresh, made out of wheat, rice or even beans and there are, literally, hundreds to choose from.

Fresh Chinese egg noodles: Ask for *lo mein* noodles in a Chinese grocery. They are usually sold in the refrigerated section in plastic bags. 450 g/1 lb usually serves 4–6 people. If you intend using smaller portions, it is a good idea to divide the noodles while they are still fresh, wrap the portions separately and freeze what you are not going to use that day. The rest can be refrigerated until you are ready to cook them. Frozen egg noodles defrost quickly and easily when dropped into boiling water. Just stir them about in the beginning. The best way to cook these noodles is to drop them into a large pan of boiling water. As soon as the water comes to a boil again, throw in a teacup of fresh water. Repeat this about three times or until the noodles are just tender. The noodles can now be drained and used as the recipe suggests.

Dried Chinese egg noodles: When fresh noodles are not available, use the dried ones. Drop them into a large pan of boiling water and cook them as you would cook fresh noodles. Some varieties tend to cook very fast, so test them frequently.

Fresh rice noodles: These are white, slithery and absolutely delicious. In South-East Asia, they are available in all sorts of sizes and shapes. Their freshness generally lasts for just a day. Many do not need to be cooked at all. Others are heated through very briefly. Unfortunately, these noodles are very hard to find in the West except in areas where there are large concentrations of East Asians.

Dried rice noodles: We have to make do with dried rice noodles in the West. For most of the recipes in this book, buy *banh pho* or any other flat rice noodle, soak it in warm water for about 30 minutes or until it is soft (or in tap water for 2 hours) and then cook it very briefly in a large pan of boiling water. Drain it and rinse it in cold water before using it as the recipe suggests. This gets rid of the extra starch. If you wish to hold the noodles for a while, rub a little oil on them, cover and set aside. The noodles may be re-heated by dropping them into boiling water for a second or two. You may also use the microwave oven for this. *Banh pho* is the noodle to use for making the Vietnamese noodle soup called *pho*.

Cellophane noodles: Also called bean thread or transparent noodles, they are made from ground mung beans and are sold dried at Chinese grocers. They are very fine and white in colour and should be soaked for 10–15 minutes before use.

Somen: These are fine Japanese wheat noodles that generally come in 450 g/1 lb packets with the noodles tied up with ribbons into five portions.

Drop them into boiling water and cook for 1–2 minutes or until just done. Drain and rinse under cold water to remove some of the starch. These noodles are often used as a substitute for fresh rice noodles in South-East Asian recipes.

Udon: These are slightly rounded or flat Japanese wheat noodles. They can be bought most easily in the West in their dried form. Cook them as you would Chinese fresh egg noodles, but then rinse them out under cold water to remove some of their starchiness.

nori A special seaweed (often referred to as 'laver'), brimming with vitamins, that is dried and roasted so it has a papery texture. The blacker it is, the better its quality seems to be. It was first cultivated in what is now called Tokyo Bay in the seventeenth century and then processed in the town's Asakusa district. Today's pollution does not allow that but the seaweed is still frequently referred to as Asakusa *nori*. It is generally sold in sheets that are about 18 x 20 cm/7 x 8 inches. In order to bring out the flavour, one side should be passed over a lowish flame several times until the sheet becomes crisp. It may then be eaten as is, crumbled over rice and noodles or used to make *sushi*. Store in an air-tight container.

oils For most of the recipes in this book, I would recommend using peanut or corn oil. If oil is used for deep-frying, it can be re-used. Skim off all extraneous matter with a skimmer and then drop a chunk of ginger or potato into it and let it fry. This chunk will absorb a lot of the unwanted flavours. Strain the oil when it is cool enough to handle through a triple thickness of cheesecloth or a large handkerchief. Let it cool completely and then store it in a bottle. When re-using, mix half old oil with half fresh oil.

Olive oil: This is used mainly in the Philippines because of that nation's Spanish heritage, and sometimes in Indonesia because of that country's ancient Portuguese connection.

orange peel, dried See mandarin peel.

oyster sauce Now often called Oyster-Flavoured Sauce, this thick, brown, Cantonese-style sauce is made with oysters and is salty and slightly sweet at the same time. It is used to flavour all sorts of dishes from vegetables to noodles. Once opened, a bottle of oyster sauce should be stored in the refrigerator. It keeps indefinitely.

palm sugar This is a delicious, raw, honey-coloured sugar used in much of South-East Asia. It is sold by South-East Asian grocers both in cans and in plain plastic containers. It comes in lump or fairly flowing forms. The best substitute for it is either Indian jaggery (make sure it is not rock-hard) or brown sugar. It keeps well if tightly covered. Refrigeration is not needed.

paprika Not generally used in South-East Asian food. I use it frequently in place of red chillies in order to give the dishes their traditional colour. Paprika tends to darken as it sits in glass bottles.

Since I use it only for the colour, it is important that you use good-quality paprika that is bright red.

peanuts For roasting and crushing peanuts, see pages 201 and 202.

peppers, red and green A lot of the time cooked foods in South-East Asia are garnished with strips of fresh, hot red and green chillies. Since this tends to make the dishes even hotter than they already are, I frequently garnish with strips of red and green peppers. Curry pastes in this region often require a pounded paste made from fresh red chillies. It is very hard in the West to find these chillies. The best substitute is a combination of red peppers blended with chilli powder (cayenne pepper) and paprika.

pho Fresh Vietnamese rice noodle (pronounced 'fa'). See noodles.

pine nuts These are sold in Far Eastern, Middle Eastern and South Asian shops. To roast them, put them in a heated, cast-iron frying-pan and stir them around until they turn golden-brown.

plums, pickled, Chinese Known as *suanmei*, this sour fruit is actually a variety of apricot. It is pickled in brine and often crushed before being used. Chinese grocers sell it as Pickled Plums. Japanese *umeboshi* (see next entry) may be substituted.

plum paste, sour (*umeboshi*) Unripe Japanese plums (actually a variety of apricot that is somehow always referred to as 'plum') pickled in brine with the aromatic red *shiso* leaf which both colours and flavours them. Considered to be digestives, they are also very high in Vitamin C and are often eaten at breakfast. *Bainiku* is the paste made from seeded *umeboshi*. It is used as a seasoning and souring agent. Bottled paste is sold by Japanese grocers. You can also make it yourself by mashing the plums after removing their seeds. Once bottles are opened or pastes made, they should be kept in the refrigerator.

plum sauce This sweet and sour Chinese sauce is sold by all Chinese grocers in bottles and cans. Once opened, it should be stored in the refrigerator.

potato flour (potato starch) There is really no adequate substitute for this, though at times cornflour (cornstarch) may be used. When the substitution is possible, I have suggested it. Potato flour (potato starch) can sometimes be found in the kosher sections of supermarkets. Chinese supermarkets also carry it in their Japanese sections. That is where I find it, labelled *katakuri-ko* and potato flour (potato starch).

prawn (shrimp) wafers (*krupuk udang*) These Indonesian prawn-flavoured wafers look like translucent discs when they are bought. Sometimes they are tinted in rather shocking shades of red, green, blue and yellow. Once they are fried, they expand and turn very light and crisp. They are ever-present at the Indonesian table. They can be bought from oriental grocers. Once the packet has been opened, the remaining wafers should be transferred to a tightly closed jar or tin.

prawns (shrimp) Only raw prawns (shrimp) should be used for most of the dishes in this book. The kind I have used are sold without heads but in their skins. See p. 207 for instructions on peeling and deveining prawns (shrimp).

prawns (shrimp), dried These are sold in plastic packets at Chinese and all South-East Asian grocers and are best when pinkish in colour. Price is often an indication of quality. They should be rinsed off and then soaked for 5–10 minutes in hot water before being lifted out of the water and ground. They add a tremendous amount of concentrated flavour to the dishes in which they are used. They last well if kept in a well-closed plastic container in the refrigerator.

Even though I have made their use optional in this book, dried prawns (shrimp) is one seasoning that you should get to know.

radish, preserved Even though these long, white radishes are preserved with both salt and sugar, they are not brined and appear quite dry when you buy them. They tend to be yellowish-brown in appearance. Possibly Chinese in origin, they are used throughout this region of Asia. When chopped up and added to foods, they add a great deal of flavour.

Preserved radishes are sold by Chinese and other oriental grocers. There is really no substitute for them so if you cannot find them, it is best to do without.

radish, white The oriental radish, the one used in this book, is large, thick and mild. It can be 5 cm / 3 inches in diameter. It should be peeled in thick strips before it is used. Use a knife: peelers tend to remove only one layer of the skin so I find them inadequate. In Japan, this radish is called *daikon*. In the United Kingdom it is often called by the Indian name, *mooli*.

It is sold by all oriental and South Asian grocers.

red bean paste, sweet This is to the Far East what chocolate is to the West. It is made from red aduki beans and

sugar. It is not hard to make, only time-consuming. Luckily, it is sold in cans at Chinese grocers and is used in hundreds of Eastern sweets, especially as a filling for pastries.

rice This is the staple food in most of East Asia. Each country, sometimes provinces within each country, favours its special rice. Use long-grain rice for all the dishes from Indonesia, Malaysia, Vietnam, Thailand, the Philippines and Hong Kong. Use Japanese short-grained rice for dishes that come from Japan and Korea.

Rice is generally washed before it is used, though suppliers in more and more countries are beginning to clean and package rice in such a way that less, or no, washing is seemingly required. Directions for cooking both types of rice can be found on p. 198.

In some regions of Indochina, such as northern Thailand, glutinous rice is the staple. The grains are short and opaque. Cooking directions are given on p. 199. Glutinous rice is often labelled 'sweet rice'. Another rice to know about is Thai jasmine rice. It is a long-grain variety, highly aromatic, and a great favourite of mine. Every oriental grocer carries it. Use it whenever long-grain rice is called for, cooking it according to the recipe on p. 29. As its texture is somewhere in between long-grain and Japanese rice, you could, at a pinch, use it to accompany Korean and Japanese dishes as well.

rice flour This is made from ground rice and is sold by most East Asian, South-East Asian, Indian and Pakistani grocers. For details on glutinous rice powder, see that entry.

rice papers, Vietnamese These are the translucent and thin wrappers that are used to make Vietnamese spring rolls. They generally come with the markings of the mats on which they were dried still imprinted on them. They need to be dampened slightly in order to become soft. The best way is to pass them, one at a time through warm water and then let them rest briefly on the edge of a sink or large

216

bowl. Rice papers come in various sizes and are sold by just a few select oriental grocers.

rice, roasted and ground In many parts of South-East Asia such as Thailand, Laos and Vietnam, rice is roasted in a dry wok and then ground to a powder. This nutty powder is then used both as a flavouring and as a thickener. Generally, glutinous rice is used for this purpose though you may use plain long-grain rice as well.

To roast and grind rice: Put a small, cast-iron frying-pan on medium-low heat. Allow it to get very hot. Now put in about 4 tablespoons rice. Stir and roast it until it turns a medium-brown. Some of the grains may even pop. Empty the rice on to a plate and let it cool a bit. Then put it into the container of a clean coffee-grinder or other spice-grinder and grind to a powder.

Store what is not immediately needed in a tightly lidded jar.

rice sticks These are very fine, dried, rice vermicelli which may be fried until golden and crisp – it takes but a few seconds – or soaked in warm water for a couple of hours, drained and then soaked in boiling water for 2 minutes. They are used in much of East Asia. (To make matters confusing, wider, flat rice noodles are sometimes also labelled 'rice sticks' though they tend to say *banh pho* underneath that.)

rice wine, Chinese See Chinese cooking wine.

sake This is the Japanese rice wine used for both cooking and drinking. For more on *sake* see p. 206.

sansho **pepper** Also known as 'Japan pepper'. It is of the prickly ash family, as is Chinese Sichuan pepper, but has an entirely different flavour and aroma. It is sold, already ground, by Japanese grocers.

satay **sauce** A bottled sauce. An equivalent is suggested on p. 132.

sesame oil Oriental sesame oil is made from roasted sesame seeds. It therefore has a deliciously nutty taste and aroma. It is not used for cooking as such. Small amounts are added to dressings and foods just to give them a sesame flavour and, sometimes, a sheen. Store sesame oil in a cool place away from light, but not in the refrigerator as it turns cloudy there.

sesame paste Chinese and Japanese sesame pastes are made from roasted sesame seeds and have a darker colour than Middle Eastern sesame paste, *tahini*. If you cannot get the former, then use the latter. All sesame paste has oil floating on the top. You need to mix the contents of the jar or can thoroughly before using it. It can be very hard initially but mixing will soften it up.

Always store sesame seed paste in the refrigerator.

sesame seeds You may use white sesame seeds or beige ones for all the recipes in this book.

To roast sesame seeds: Set a small, cast-iron frying-pan over medium-low heat. When it is hot, put in 1–3 tablespoons of sesame seeds. Stir them around until they turn a shade darker and give out a wonderful roasted aroma. Sesame seeds do tend to fly around as they are roasted. You could turn down the heat slightly when they do this or cover the pan loosely. Remove the seeds from the pan as soon as they are done. You may roast sesame seeds ahead of time. Cool them and store them in a tightly lidded jar.

They can last several weeks this way though I must add that they are best when freshly roasted.

To roast and lightly crush sesame seeds: Roast the seeds as suggested above. Now put them into the container of a spice-grinder or clean coffee-grinder and whir them for just a second or two. The seeds should *not* turn to a powder. You may also crush them lightly in a mortar.

shallots For Westerners who tend to use shallots in small quantities, it is always a bit startling to see South-East Asians use shallots in massive amounts. The shallot is the onion of this region.

It is ground into curry pastes, sliced into salads and fried into crisp flakes to be used both as a garnish and as a wonderful flavouring.

Shao-Hsing See Chinese rice wine.

shichimi Japanese seven-spice seasoning. It is also sold as Seven-Spice Red Pepper (*Shichimi Togarashi*). Available only from Japanese grocers, it contains a coarsely crushed mixture of red pepper, a special Japanese pepper called *sansho*, roasted sesame seeds, roasted white poppy or hemp seeds, white pepper and tiny bits of orange peel and seaweed. Use my easy mixture, which I call 'Sesame Seed Seasoning', as a substitute.

To make Sesame Seed Seasoning: Set a small cast-iron frying-pan over medium-low heat. When it is hot, put in 1 tablespoon sesame seeds, 1 tablespoon Sichuan peppercorns and 1 small, dried, hot red chilli. Stir these around until the sesame seeds turn golden-brown. Allow the mixture to cool, then grind it together with ¼ teaspoon salt in a clean coffee-grinder or other spice-grinder or mortar until you have a fairly smooth powder.

shirataki **'noodles'** Sold only by Japanese grocers, these 'noodles' are made from a starchy root. Rather like bean curd, they are packed in water and that is how they should be stored in the refrigerator. Change the water frequently. They should last a couple of weeks this way. Drain before using.

shiso **leaves** The serrated, green and very aromatic heart-shaped leaves are used in this book for the Japanese rice canapés known as *sushi*. They must be fresh and are sold only by Japanese grocers. If you cannot find them, use fresh basil leaves. The flavour will be very different but still interesting.

shiitake **mushrooms** See mushrooms.

shrimp, dried See prawns (shrimp), dried.

shrimp paste This paste, made out of fermented shrimp, is used as a

seasoning throughout South-East Asia. It comes in many forms ranging from a grey, watery paste to crumbly, brown blocks. Only South-East Asian grocers sell an array of shrimp pastes.

In this book, I have mainly used shrimp paste in the block form. There is really no substitute for the blocks, which are known variously as *blachan*, *kapi* and *terasi*. I have used anchovy paste in desperation. When *blachan*, *kapi* or *terasi* is used in uncooked dishes, such as condiments, it needs to be roasted first. To do this, break off the amount you need, or slice off a chunk, and either hold it over a low flame with a pair of tongs and turn it about until it is roasted or spread it out on a piece of foil and grill (broil) it. You can also wrap it in foil, lay it over a low flame and toast it lightly on two sides. You could, if you like, fry it in a tiny amount of oil instead. It will release strong odours as it roasts. Try doing this outdoors, if at all possible, or else open a window first and close the door leading to the inside of the house.

Sichuan peppercorns Reddish-brown, highly aromatic pods of the prickly ash family, slightly larger than peppercorns. They are available from Chinese grocers. They should be stored in a tightly lidded jar. They are ground to make the Sichuan pepper that is used in Chinese foods.

To roast Sichuan peppercorns: Set a small cast-iron frying-pan over medium-low heat. When it is hot, put in the peppercorns. Stir and fry them until they release their fragrance. They may smoke a bit, but the smoke will be highly aromatic.

soy sauce Many different soy sauces are used in East Asia. Not only do countries have their own brands, but regions, towns and even villages within these countries sometimes proudly boast of producing their very own. All soy sauces are made from fermented and salted soy beans. They range from salty to sweet, from light to dark, from thick to thin, and have many different textures. Dark soy sauces tend to be thicker than the light ones and

217

generally add a dark colour to the dish they are put in. Light soy sauce tends to be thinner and saltier. Several thick, textured, slightly sweet sauces, many of which are unavailable in most Western markets, are used in parts of South-East Asia. Very often, black bean sauce is the best substitute. Since soy sauces vary so much in their saltiness, it is always advisable to start by using slightly less than the amount required in the recipe as more can be added later.

Kecap manis is a thick, very sweet – indeed syrupy – soy sauce used in Indonesia. If you cannot find it you can make an approximation of it yourself by combining 250 ml / 8 fl oz / 1 cup dark soy sauce with 6 tablespoons treacle (or molasses) and 3 tablespoons brown sugar and simmering gently until the sugar has dissolved.

Japanese and Chinese soy sauces have very different flavours. Hence, it is best to use Japanese soy sauces when called for and Chinese soy sauces as required. A good brand of Chinese soy sauce is Pearl River which is sold by Chinese grocers. It is most confusingly labelled: 'Soy Superior Sauce' is dark and 'Superior Soy' is light. The best-known Japanese brand is Kikkoman though Hi-Maru is also good. The Japanese, too, make dark and light soy sauces. These are sold by all Japanese grocers.

star anise A flower-shaped collection of pods. Brownish-black in colour, this spice has a decided anise flavour. It is used in Chinese-style braised dishes and in some rice pilafs. Store in a tightly lidded jar. If a pod of star anise is called for, think of a pod as a petal of the flower and break off one section.

straw mushrooms See mushrooms.

swamp morning glory Also known as swamp cabbage and water spinach, it is sold in many Asian markets as *kang kung*. It is a vine with an edible stem and tendrils. The leaves are like very elongated hearts. It is all exceedingly nutritious and cooks rather like spinach. The stems are coarser and need to be slit in half. Many people

cook them for 1 minute before putting in the more tender leaves.

sweet basil (*bai horabba*) See basil.

tamarind This is a bean-like fruit of a tall tree. When ripe, the beans are peeled, seeded and packed in lumps or bricks. It is sold by South-East Asian and Indian grocers.

To make your own tamarind paste: Break off 225 g / 8 oz from a brick of tamarind and tear into small pieces. Put into a small non-metallic pot and cover with 450 ml / 15 fl oz / 2 cups very hot water, then set aside for 3 hours or overnight. (You could achieve the same result by simmering the tamarind for 10 minutes or by putting it in a microwave oven for 3–5 minutes.) Set a sieve over a non-metallic bowl and empty the tamarind and its soaking liquid into it. Push down on the tamarind with your fingers or the back of a wooden spoon to extract as much pulp as you can. Put whatever tamarind remains in the sieve back into the soaking bowl. Add 125 ml / 4 fl oz / ½ cup hot water to it and mash a bit more. Return it to the sieve and extract as much more pulp as you can. Some of this pulp will be clinging to the underside of the sieve. Do not fail to retrieve it.

The quantity above will make about 350 ml / 12 fl oz / 1½ cups of thick paste. All the calculations for my recipes have been done with this thick, chutney-like paste, so do not water it down too much.

Whatever paste is left over may either be put into the refrigerator, where it will keep for 2–3 weeks, or frozen. It freezes well.

tapioca pearls The tapioca pearls used in this book are, as the name suggests, the size of medium-sized pearls. Sago pearls can be used just as easily. They need to be soaked (see individual recipes) and then boiled until they are tender.

taro root A tuber with blackish, hairy skin, not unlike the potato but with a more glutinous texture. In West Indian shops it is sold as *eddoes*.

toen chang A medium-brown Korean paste made out of fermented soy beans. It is diluted, strained and used as a base for stews. In the West, it is sold only in Korean supermarkets. The best substitute is Japanese, medium-brown *miso*, sold in all health food shops.

turmeric Much of South-East Asia uses fresh turmeric. This is a rhizome not unlike ginger, only smaller in size and more delicate in appearance. Many Indian shops sell it. Even though ground turmeric available in most supermarkets is adequate, you should try using fresh turmeric whenever possible. A 2.5 cm / 1 inch piece of fresh turmeric is equal to about ½ teaspoon of ground turmeric. Just like ginger, it needs to be peeled and ground. This grinding is best done with the help of a little water in an electric blender.

turmeric leaves, fresh These long, highly aromatic leaves are often thrown into soups and curries in South-East Asia. They are hard to get in the West. You could plant the turmeric rhizome in a pot, keep it well watered and then use the leaves when they grow.

udon See noodles.

vinegar There are probably as many vinegars in East Asia as there are soy sauces, with every district in every country producing its very own brand. China, for example, has Red vinegar and Black vinegar, both of which are sold by Chinese grocers. The red is the milder and paler of the two and tastes a bit like Italian balsamic vinegar. Both are excellent. The Philippines have a pale, slightly milky vinegar made from palm toddy or coconut water, and Japan is proud of its very mild rice vinegars. To make matters easy, you could use cider vinegar for most of the recipes in this book. When Japanese rice vinegar is called for and you cannot find it, make your own version by combining 3 parts of distilled white vinegar, 1 part water and ¼ part sugar.

wasabi A pungent, green Japanese horseradish that is grated finely and

made into *wasabi* paste. It is used as mustard might be in the West and goes particularly well with raw fish dishes such as *sashimi* and *sushi*.

As it is not often available in its fresh form in the West, Japanese grocers here sell *wasabi* paste, ready to be used, in tubes. Remember that this nose-tinglingly sharp paste should be used in minute quantities. A little goes a long way.

You can also buy dry *wasabi* powder in cans. Mix small quantities with a little tepid water to make a paste, in the same way as you would make a paste with powdered mustard. Allow it to stand for about 10 minutes before using.

water chestnuts Dark-skinned and chestnut-sized, they grow in water and are sold fresh only by Chinese grocers. The inside flesh is deliciously crisp and white. Canned water chestnuts do not compare but may be used in cooked dishes.

wonton skins These are very thin sheets of pastry, about 7.5 cm / 3 inches square, that are sold all wrapped up in stacks of 30 or 36 or more by Chinese grocers and Chinese supermarkets. In cities with large Chinese districts, it is well worth looking for a source that prepares them fresh every day. Such places often make noodles and bean curd products as well. Wonton skins last several days in the refrigerator and may easily be frozen. Defrost the skins thoroughly before using. They dry out easily so keep them well wrapped, even as you work.

yellow bean sauce See bean sauce.

INDEX